PAUL McCARTNEY CHORD SONGBOOK COLLECTION

Published by:
Wise Publications,
8/9 Frith Street, London W1D 3JB, England.

Exclusive Distributors:
Music Sales Limited,
Distribution Centre, Newmarket Road, Bury St Edmunds, Suffolk IP33 3YB, England.
Music Sales Pty Limited,
120 Rothschild Avenue, Rosebery, NSW 2018, Australia.

Order No. AM979011
ISBN 0-7119-8282-1

Cover design by Roger Huggett/Sinc.
Music arranged by Arthur Dick.
Music engraved by Paul Ewers Music Design.
Complied by Nick Crispin.
Printed in the United Kingdom.

WISE PUBLICATIONS
part of The Music Sales Group

LONDON · NEW YORK · PARIS · SYDNEY · COPENHAGEN · BERLIN · MADRID · TOKYO

Takamine

Relative Tuning

The guitar can be tuned with the aid of pitch pipes or dedicated electronic guitar tuners which are available through your local music dealer. If you do not have a tuning device, you can use relative tuning. Estimate the pitch of the 6th string as near as possible to E or at least a comfortable pitch (not too high, as you might break other strings in tuning up). Then, while checking the various positions on the diagram, place a finger from your left hand on the:

5th fret of the E or 6th string and **tune the open A** (or 5th string) to the note (A)

5th fret of the A or 5th string and **tune the open D** (or 4th string) to the note (D)

5th fret of the D or 4th string and **tune the open G** (or 3rd string) to the note (G)

4th fret of the G or 3rd string and **tune the open B** (or 2nd string) to the note (B)

5th fret of the B or 2nd string and **tune the open E** (or 1st string) to the note (E)

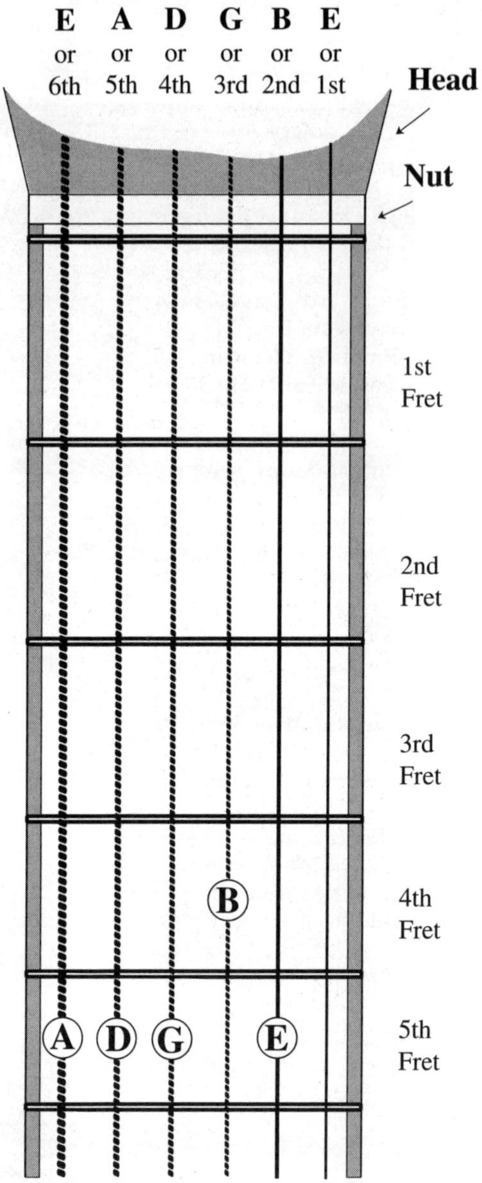

Reading Chord Boxes

Chord boxes are diagrams of the guitar neck viewed head upwards, face on as illustrated. The top horizontal line is the nut, unless a higher fret number is indicated, the others are the frets.

The vertical lines are the strings, starting from E (or 6th) on the left to E (or 1st) on the right.

The black dots indicate where to place your fingers.

Strings marked with an O are played open, not fretted. Strings marked with an X should not be played.

The curved bracket indicates a 'barre' - hold down the strings under the bracket with your first finger, using your other fingers to fret the remaining notes.

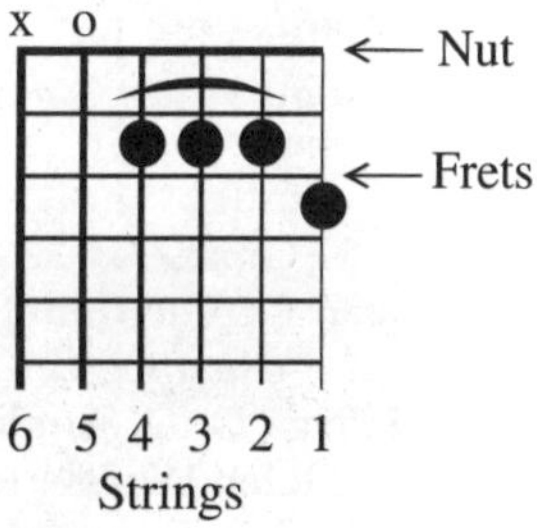

About You

Words & Music by
Paul McCartney

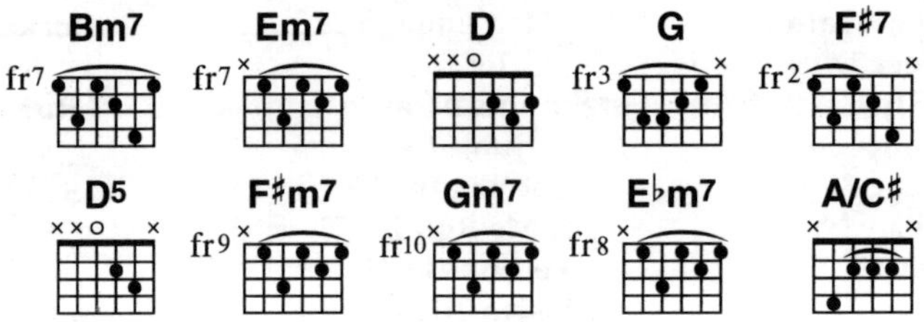

Intro

N.C.
One, two, three...

Verse 1

Bm7 Em7
You give me power to get out of bed
Bm7 Em7
When in the morning I'm feelin' dead
D G F#7
Livin' and loving is a lot to accept, it's true
D5 A/C# N.C. Bm7 Em7
Gonna say it a - bout you
D5 A/C# Bm7 Em7
Say it a - bout you.——

Verse 2

Bm7 Em7
Out of the darkness and into the light
Bm7 Em7
Straight to the centre of everything right
D G F#7
Darlin', don't worry, the sky will be bright and blue
D5 A/C# N.C. (Bm7)
When I say it a - bout you.

Chorus 1

```
Bm7  Em7         D5        A/C#      (Bm7)
          Gonna say it a - bout you
Bm7   Em7       D5       A/C#      Bm7
  Oh, yeah I'll say it a - bout you.
```

Bridge

```
                                      1.               2.
|: F#m7  | F#m7  Gm7  | Em7  | Em7  Ebm7 :| Em7  ||
```

Verse 3

```
Bm7  N.C.                                  Em7
          When did you teach me, to fly thru the air?
Bm7                          Em7
  Ah, sooner or later all will be there
D                           G                         F#7
  I read the headlines, now I can swear it's true
                D5        A/C#  N.C.  Bm7
And they said it a - bout  you.——
```

Chorus 2

```
Bm7  Em7         D5        A/C#
          Gonna say it a - bout you
Bm7  Em7         D5        A/C#
          Gonna say it a - bout you
Bm7  Em7         D5        A/C#
          Gonna say it a - bout you
Bm7  Em7         D5        A/C#
          Gonna say it a - bout...
Bm7  Em7
You.
```

Outro

```
|: Bm7  | Em7  :|  Play 4 times

| Bm7 (fermata) ||
```

After The Ball/Million Miles

Words & Music by
Paul McCartney

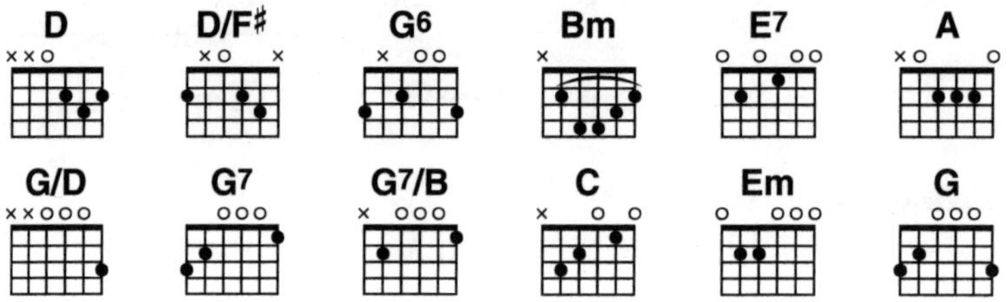


```
                   D               D/F♯              G6              Bm
Chorus 1    After the ball, after the ball, you were the one out in the hall
                                                   E7   A           D    G/D  D
            You were the one, the one who would love me after the ball
                                   D/F♯              G6              Bm
            After the ball, after the ball, you were the one out in the hall
                                                   E7   A           D    G/D  D
            You were the one, the one who would love me after the ball.

                   (D)                  D/F♯           G6              D
Verse 1     Well, I arrived, looked a - round but the room was full of strangers
                                                 A
            Nowhere was a friendly face to be found
                     D        D/F♯          G6          D
            Later on I a - woke but the party it was over
                                          A        D
            There you were waiting to bring me 'round.
```

Chorus 2 As Chorus 1

Solo

| G7 | G7/B | C | Em | Em | A D |
| G | G | G | G | G | G (fermata) ||

Outro

```
D    G    G7    C    D    G   D  G
How many million miles, day - oh?
D    G    G7    C    D    G   D  G
How many million miles, day - oh?
D            G       G7        C                    D       G     D  G
When I get up, up, up in the morning, whoa! Lord I know.
D              G       G7       C                   D      G
When I look up, up, up in the evening, whoa! Lord I know.
D    G    G7    C    D    G   D  G
How many million miles, day - oh?
D    G    G7    C    D    G   D  G
How many million miles, day - oh?
D    G    G7    C    D    G
How many million miles, day - oh?
```

Angry

Words & Music by
Paul McCartney & Eric Stewart

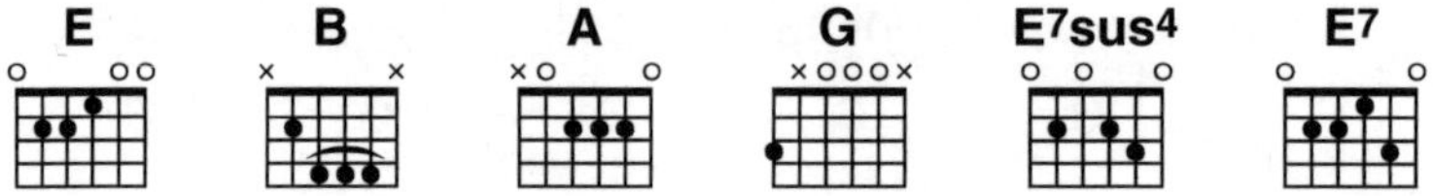

Intro | N.C. (E) | (E) | (E) | (E) |

| E B A G | E | E B A G | E ||

Chorus 1
E N.C. E
What the hell gives you the right to tell me what to do with my life?
Especially when you made a mess of every chance you had of success
Look at you, just look at you
I said I'm angry just looking at you
E7sus4 | E | E7sus4 | E |
Ah, come on.

Verse 1
(E)
I'm sick and tired of sitting back listening to all of your clap-trap
If you could get me to take the rap I guarantee
You'd leave me with a backslap
Push me to the left, push me to the right try to take me out of the way
Even if you kick me off the edge of the world
E7
You're still going to hear me say...

Chorus 2

```
E7     N.C.                                                        E
What the hell gives you the right to tell me what to do with my life?

Especially when you made a mess of every chance you have of success

Look at you, oh look at you

I said I'm angry just looking at you.
E7sus4            E
Shouting down a - gain mahama
E7sus4            E
Shouting down a - gain
Esus4             E            E7sus4         E
Shouting down a - gain mahama, shouting down a - gain.
```

Solo

```
| A     | A     | A     | A     | A     | A     ||

| N.C. (E) | (E)    | (E)    | (E)    |

| E B A G | E      | E B A G | E      ||
```

Verse 2

```
E
I can't begin to tell you all the reasons why you're making me crazy

I've got so many answers like you're stupid, like you're crooked,

Like you're lazy

Hit me with your left, hit me with your right

Hit me from the top to the toe

Even when you chew me up and spit me out

I'm still going to want to know.
```

Chorus 3 As Chorus 2

Play 4 times w/ad lib. vocals

Outro

```
||: E7sus4 | E       | E7sus4 | E                    :||
                               Can't begin to tell you.
  (fermata)
| A      ||
```

Another Day

Words & Music by
Paul & Linda McCartney

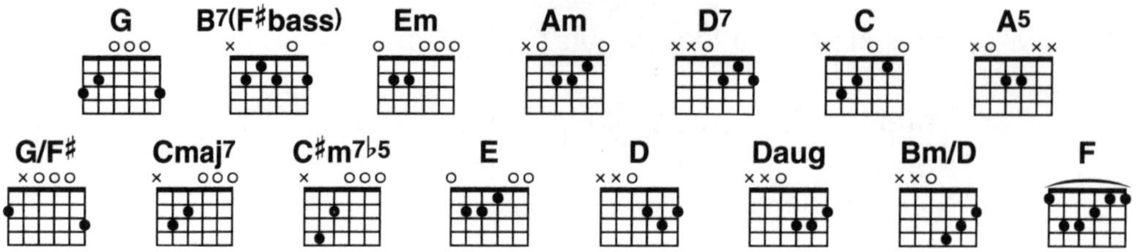

Verse 1

G B7
Every day she takes a morning bath she wets her hair
Em Am
Wraps a towel around her, as she's heading for the bedroom chair
D7 G
It's just another day
C G
Slipping into stockings
C G
Stepping into shoes
C G A5
Dipping in the pocket of her raincoat
D7 G N.C.
It's just another day.

Verse 2

(N.C.) G B7
At the office where the papers grow she takes a break
Em Am
Drinks another coffee and she finds it hard to stay awake
D7 G
It's just another day.

Chorus 1

C Am
Du du du du du
D7 G
It's just another day.
E7 Am
Du du du du du
D7 G
It's just another day.

Bridge 1

Em Cmaj7
So sad, so sad
C♯m7♭5 Cmaj7 Em
Sometimes she feels so sad
Cmaj7
Alone in her apartment she'd dwell
C♯m7♭5 Cmaj7 Em
Till the man of her dreams comes to break the spell.
E Am D
Ah,— stay, don't stand a - round
Daug Bm/D
And he comes and he stays
B7 Em C
But he leaves the next day, so sad.
C♯m7♭5 Cmaj7 Em N.C.
Sometimes she feels so sad.

Verse 3

G B7
As she posts another letter to the sound of five
Em Am
People gather 'round her, and she finds it hard to stay alive
D7 G
It's just another day.

Chorus 2 As Chorus 1

Bridge 2 As Bridge 1

Verse 4 As Verse 1

Chorus 3

C Am
Du du du du du
D7 G
It's just another day.
E7 Am
Du du du du du
D7 G F C G
It's just another day._________

Baby's Request

Words & Music by
Paul McCartney

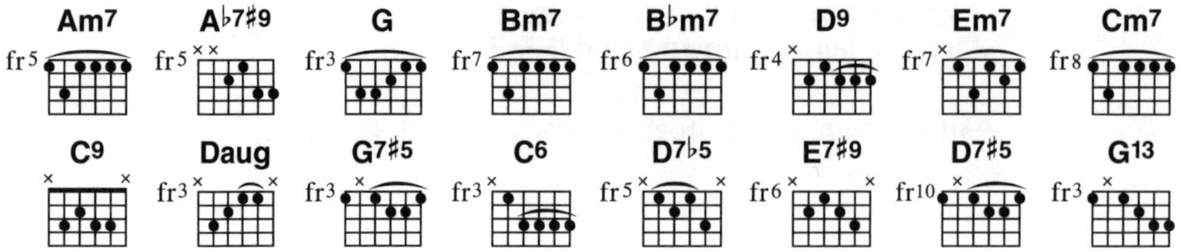


```
Intro       | Am7 (pause) | A♭7♯9 (pause) | G  Bm7  B♭m7 | Am7  D9 ||

                      G                Bm7  B♭m7  Am7    D9
Verse 1     When the moon lays his head on a   pillow
                    G           Bm7   Em7  Cm7
            And the stars settle down for a rest
            Am7           D9          G           Em7
              Just do me one small favour, I beg you
                    Am7         C9          G       Daug
            Please play me my baby's re - quest.

                   G              Bm7   B♭m7       Am7    D9
Verse 2     It's the song that we heard when we started
                    G               Bm7   Em7     Cm7
            Now the birds have all flown from our nest
            Am7                 D9            G                Em7
              But you could bring back mem'ries de - parted
               Am7          C9          G
            By playing my baby's re - quest.
```

Bridge 1

G7♯5 C6 D7♭5 G E7♯9 Am7 D9
My ba - by said that she knows how it goes
G G7♯5
But you're the one who really knows
C6 Am7 D7♭5 G E7♯9 Am7
So go a - head, just one more time
D9 G D7♯5
And then we'll go to bed.

Solo

| G Bm7 B♭m7 | Am7 D9 | G Bm7 Em7 | Cm7 ||

Am7 D9 G Em7
But you could bring back mem'ries de - parted
Am7 C9 G
By playing my baby's re - quest.

Bridge 2

G7♯5 C6 D7♭5 G E7♯9 Am7 D9
My ba - by said that she knows how it goes
G G7♯5
But you're the one who really knows
C6 Am7 D7♭5 G E7♯9 Am7
So go a - head, just one more time
D9 G D7♯5
And then we'll go to bed.

Verse 3

G Bm7 B♭m7 Am7 D9
When the moon lays his head on a pillow
G Bm7 Em7 Cm7 Bm7 B♭m7 Am7
And the star settles down for a rest
(Am7) D9 G Em7
Just do me one small favour, I beg you
Am7 C9 G
Please play me baby's re - quest
Am7 C9 G
Mh-hm, play me baby's re - quest
Em7 Am7 C9 G Daug G G13
Please! play me my baby's re - quest, one more time.

Back In The Sunshine Again

Words & Music by
Paul McCartney & James McCartney

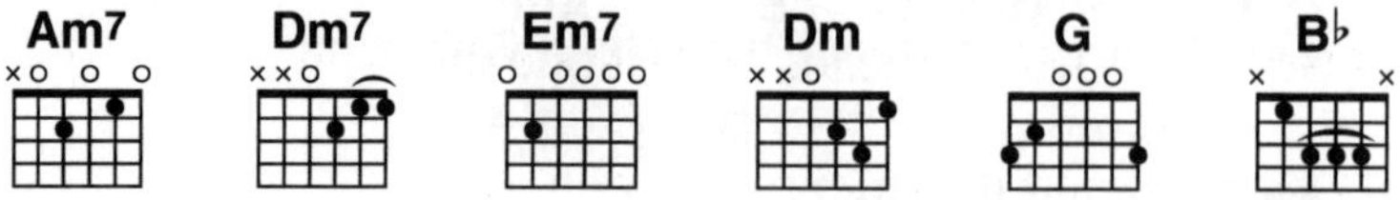

Verse 1

Am7 Dm7 Am7 Em7
Here we are
Am7 Dm7 Am7 Em7
Back in the sunshine again
Am7 Dm7 Am7 Em7
No more worries
Am7 Dm7 Am7 Em7
And no more pain
Am7 Dm7 Am7 Em7
Well we're leaving behind
Am7 Dm7 Am7 Em7
All our trouble and strife
Am7 Dm7 Am7
That's the way it's gonna be
(Am7) Em7 Am7 Dm7 Am7 Em7
Oh,— for the rest of my life.

Chorus 1

Am7 Dm7 Am7
Well here we are, here we are
Em7 Am7 Dm7 Am7 Em7
Back in the sunshine again
Am7 Dm7 Am7 Em7
No more worries, no more wor - ries
Am7 Dm7 Am7
And no more pain, no more pain.

Bridge 1

Dm
Life's to short to spend it lonely
G
You only throw it a - way
B♭ Dm
Listen to your voice of reason
G Em7
Yeah call it a day, ay, ay, ay.

Verse 3

```
Am7               Dm7  Am7        Em7
   Take a ride,        take a ride
               Am7              Dm7  Am7  Em7
Out to the land of the free,     ooh——
Am7                     Dm7                     Am7  Em7
Don't hurry, take your time, take your time
      Am7                 Dm7  Am7  Em7
Come spend it with me,       ooh.——
```

Play 3 times w/vocal ad lib.

Interlude

```
|: Am7      | Dm7      | Am7      | Em7              :|
 (- shine.)                         Back in the sun -
```

Chorus

```
Am7               Dm7  Am7  Em7
  Here we are,         ooh
                 Am7              Dm7  Am7  Em7
We're back in the sunshine again
(Em7)     Am7                Dm7                Am7      Em7
No more worries, no more worries, no more worries
Am7                  Dm7  Am7  Em7
And no more pain.
```

Bridge 2

As Bridge 1

Outro

```
Am7                Dm7  Am7
Here we are
      Em7          Am7              Dm7  Am7  Em7
We're back in the sunshine again
          Am7      Dm7              Am7
No more worries, no more worries
Em7             Am7  Dm7  Am7  Em7
And no more pain
         Am7             Dm7  Am7
Here we are, here we are
     Em7                    Am7                Dm7  Am7  Em7
Yeah,      we're back in the sunshine again
          Am7      Dm7  Am7
No more worries, oh     no
    Em7         Am7  Dm7
And no more pain
      Am7           Em7                        Am7  Dm7
Why, why, we're back in the sunshine a - gain
          Am7           Em7
No more worry or pain
             Am7
Yeah, we're back in the sunshine again.
```

Back On My Feet

Words & Music by
Paul McCartney & Declan MacManus

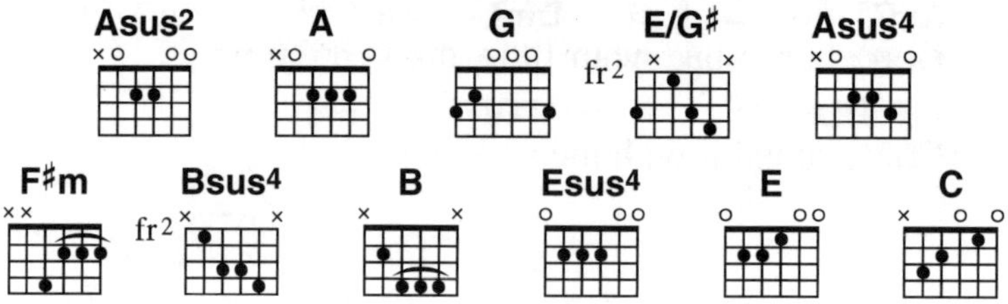

Intro | Asus2 | A | Asus2 | A ||

Verse 1

Asus2
How many days will the wet weather last?
G E/G♯
I want to know will the clouds when they roll back
Asus4 A F♯m
Reveal a man in an old mac
Bsus4 B
Living on a park bench
Esus4 E | Asus2 | Asus2 |
Sitting on his own?

Verse 2

(Asus2)
Cut to the rain as it runs down the glass
G E/G♯
Eventually through the lightning and thun - der
Asus4 A F♯m
We see a man going un - der
Bsus4 B
This is how it happens
Esus4 E
This is what he said.

Chorus 1

E A
I don't need love
E A
Though temp - tation is sweet
E F♯m
Give me your hand

Bridge 1

G7♯5 C6 D7♭5 G E7♯9 Am7 D9
My ba - by said that she knows how it goes
G G7♯5
But you're the one who really knows
C6 Am7 D7♭5 G E7♯9 Am7
So go a - head, just one more time
D9 G D7♯5
And then we'll go to bed.

Solo

| G Bm7 B♭m7 | Am7 D9 | G Bm7 Em7 | Cm7 ||

Am7 D9 G Em7
But you could bring back mem'ries de - parted
Am7 C9 G
By playing my baby's re - quest.

Bridge 2

G7♯5 C6 D7♭5 G E7♯9 Am7 D9
My ba - by said that she knows how it goes
G G7♯5
But you're the one who really knows
C6 Am7 D7♭5 G E7♯9 Am7
So go a - head, just one more time
D9 G D7♯5
And then we'll go to bed.

Verse 3

G Bm7 B♭m7 Am7 D9
When the moon lays his head on a pillow
G Bm7 Em7 Cm7 Bm7 B♭m7 Am7
And the star settles down for a rest
(Am7) D9 G Em7
Just do me one small favour, I beg you
Am7 C9 G
Please play me baby's re - quest
Am7 C9 G
Mh-hm, play me baby's re - quest
Em7 Am7 C9 G Daug G G13
Please! play me my baby's re - quest, one more time.

Bridge 2

C
I'll stand up again
A
Kick up a fuss again too
C
I'll be right again
A
Be upright without you

(We see a life through the eyes of a man

As he live and he dies by a simple tattoo)
C
I'll be back again
A
When I land on my feet
C
I'll stand up again
A
Kick up a fuss again, wouldn't you?

(Well there you go, though we tried hard to know him

It's there on his face

He's a case where there's clearly no hope)
C
Give me your hand again

'Til I land again
A
(His face starts to fade

As we pull down the shade

And the picture we made
C
Is in glorious cinema - scope.)

Outro

𝄆 (C) | C | A | A 𝄇
I'll be back... I'll be back... *Repeat to fade*

The Back Seat Of My Car

Words & Music by
Paul McCartney

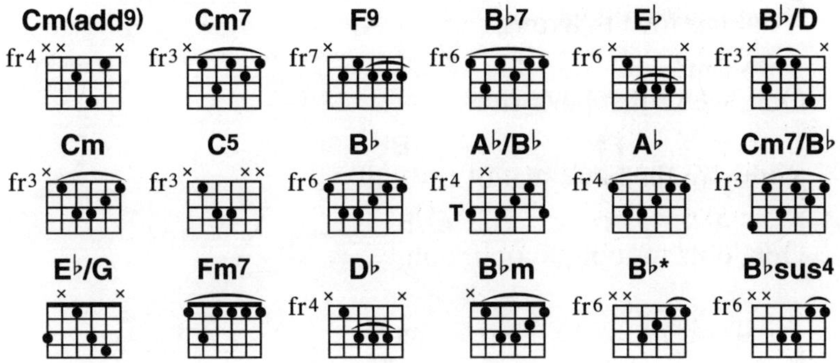

Intro ‖ Cm(add9) | Cm(add9) ‖

Verse 1

Cm7   **F9**
Speed along the highway
Cm7   **F9**
Honey, I want it my way
      B♭7   **E♭**
But listen to her daddy's song
B♭/D   **Cm**   **C5**
   "Don't stay out too long."
         Cm7   **F9**
Ooh, we're just busy hiding
Cm7   **F9**   **B♭**
Sitting in the back seat of my   car.
         A♭/B♭   **B♭**   **A♭/B♭**
Ooh, ooh,— ooh,— ooh, ooh.——

Verse 2

Cm7 F9
The lazy lights are pretty

Cm7 F9
We may end up in Mexico City

B♭7 E♭
But listen to her daddy's song

B♭/D Cm C5
"Making love is wrong."

Cm7 F9
Ooh, we're just busy riding

Cm7 F9 B♭
Sitting in the back seat of my car

A♭/B♭ B♭ A♭/B♭
Ooh, ooh,— ooh,— ooh, ooh.——

Interlude 1

‖: Cm7 F9 | Cm7 F9 :‖
Ooh,— ooh,— | ooh,— ooh.—

| B♭7 | E♭ B♭/D | Cm ‖

Cm7 F9
Oh, we was only hiding

Cm7 F9 B♭
Sitting in the back seat of my car

A♭/B♭ B♭ A♭/B♭
Ooh, ooh,— ooh,— ooh, ooh.——

Verse 3

Cm7 F9
And when we've finished driving

Cm7 F9
We can say we were late in ar - riving

B♭7 E♭
And listen to her daddy's song

B♭/D Cm C5
We believe that we can't be wrong. Hey!

```
             E♭   B♭/D                 Cm
Chorus 1     Oh, oh, we believe that we can't be wrong
             E♭   B♭/D                 Cm
             Oh, oh, we believe that we can't be wrong
                        Cm7                 F9
             We can make it to Mexico City
             Cm7           F9          B♭
             Sitting in the back seat of my car.

                                        Play 3 times
             ‖:(B♭)     | A♭/B♭   | B♭      | A♭/B♭    :‖
Interlude 2       Ooh,  ooh,—     ooh,—     ooh.—
             | Cm7    F9     | Cm7    F9  | B♭    ‖
               Ooh,— ooh,—     ooh,— ooh.

             E♭   B♭/D                 Cm
Chorus 2     Oh, oh, we believe that we can't be wrong
             E♭   B♭/D                 Cm
             Oh, oh, we believe that we can't be wrong
             E♭   B♭/D                 Cm
             Oh, oh, we believe that we can't be wrong
             E♭   B♭/D                 Cm
             Oh, oh, we believe that we can't be wrong
             E♭   B♭/D                 Cm
             Oh, oh, we believe that we can't be wrong
             E♭   B♭/D                 Cm            Cm7/B♭ A♭  E♭/G  Fm7  A♭/B♭
             Oh, oh, we believe that we can't be wrong,      no, no,     no.
             E♭     B♭/D                  Cm          Cm/B♭
             Wah, ah, we believe that we can't be wrong,———
                                  A♭  E♭/G  | Fm7  N.C.(E♭) |
                     yeah, yeah, yeah.———
                                                  𝄐
             D♭     Cm | B♭m  A♭  | E♭/G  Fm7 | E♭      ‖
             Oh,— oh,— oh,— oh,— oh,— oh,— oh.


Outro        ‖: B♭*     | B♭sus4  :‖  Repeat to fade w/vocal ad lib.
```

Backwards Traveller

Words & Music by
Paul McCartney

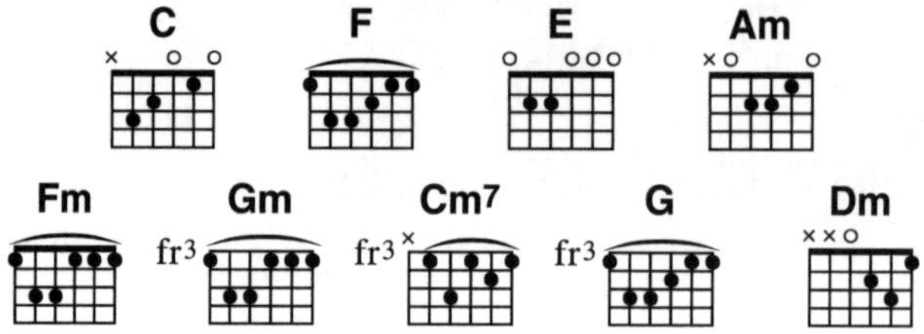

Verse 1

C   F   Em
Hey, did you know that I'm
Am   Em
Always going back in time
F   Em   Am
Rhyming slang, Auld Lang Syne my dears
F   Fm
Through the years.——

Chorus 1

C
I am the backwards traveller
Gm
Ancient wool unraveller
F   Cm7   Gm
Sailing songs,   wailing on the moon.

Chorus 2

C
I am the backwards traveller
Gm
Ancient wool unraveller
F   Cm7   Gm
Sailing songs,   wailing on the moon
                                   C
Ah, hey, wailing on the moon
              G   Dm   Am
And we were sailing songs,   wailing on the moon
                                   Dm
We were wailing on the moon.

Ballroom Dancing

Words & Music by
Paul McCartney

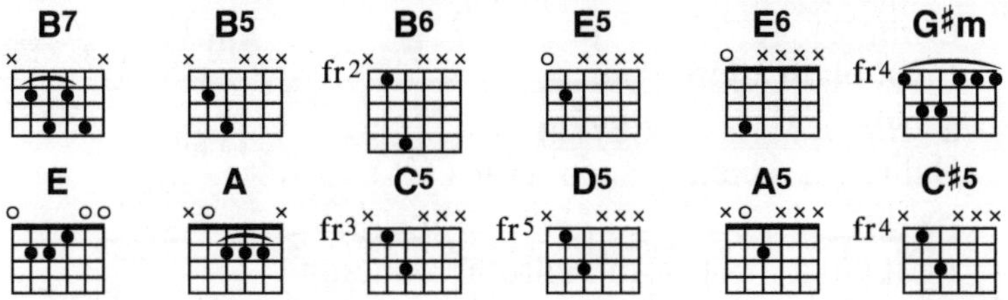

B5 riff
Intro | B7 | B7 | B5 B5 B6 B5 B5 B6 | B5 B5 B6 B5 B5 B6 ||

Verse 1
B5 riff
Well I used to smile when I was a pup

Sailing down the nile in china cup
E5 riff
With the recipe for a lovely day
B5 riff
Sticking out my back pocket.

E5 riff
| E5 E5 E6 E5 E5 E6 |

Pre-chorus 1
E5 riff
But it wasn't always such a pretty sight
G♯m
'Cause we used to fight like cats and dogs
E5 riff B5 riff
Till me made it up in the ballroom.

Chorus 1

B5 E B5 E5 riff
Ball - room dancing made a man of me
B5 riff
One, two, three, four
E5 riff
I just plain adore your
B5 riff E5 riff
Ballroom dancing, seen it on TV
B5 riff E5 riff
I got what I got from ballroom dancing
A B5
Big B.D.

Verse 2

B5 riff
Well I used to fly when I was a kid

And I didn't cry if it hurt a bit
E5 riff
On a carpet ride to a foreign land
B5 riff
At the time of Davy Crockett.

Pre-chorus 2 As Pre-chorus 1

Chorus 2 As Chorus 1

Instrumental

‖: B5 | B5 | E5 | E5 | B5 | B5 | [1.] E5 | E5 :‖
[2.] | C5 | D5 | B5 | B5 | B5 | B5 ‖

‖: A5 B5 N.C. | C♯5 B5 N.C. | A5 B5 N.C. | N.C. :‖ *Play 4 times*

‖: B5 | B5 | E5 | E5 :‖ B5 | B5 | B5 | B5 ‖

Verse 3

B5 riff
Well it went so fast and we all grew up

Now the days that passed in the China cup

E5 riff
Are the memories of another day

B5 riff
And I wouldn't want to knock it.

Pre-chorus 3 As Pre-chorus 1

Chorus 3

B5 E B5 E5 riff
Ball - room dancing made a man of me

B5 riff
One, two, three, four

E5 riff
I just plain adore your

B5 riff E5 riff
Ballroom dancing, seen it on TV

B5 riff E5 riff
I got quite a lot from ballroom dancing

A B5
Big B.D.

C5 D5 E5 N.C.
Oh!——

Band On The Run

Words & Music by
Paul McCartney & Linda McCartney

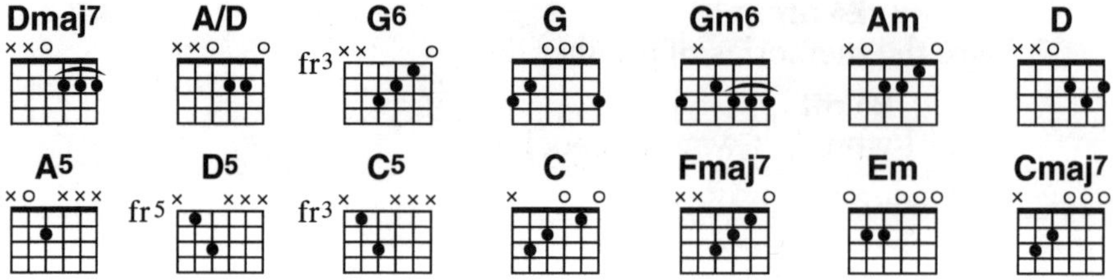

Intro

N.C. ‖: Dmaj7 | A/D | G6 | G :‖

| Dmaj7 | Gm6 | Dmaj7 | Gm6 ‖

Verse 1

```
Dmaj7                        A/D
Stuck inside these four walls
G6                  G
Sent inside forever
Dmaj7                 A/D
Never seeing no one
G6           G       Dmaj7
Nice again    like you
Gm6     Dmaj7   Gm6     Dmaj7  Gm6
Mama, you,      Mama, you.
```

Instr. 1

‖: Am | D | Am | D | Am :‖

Verse 2

```
(Am)
   If I ever get out of here
D
   Thought of giving it all away
Am
   To a registered charity
D
   All I need is a pint a day
    Am
If I ever get out of here. (If we ever get outta here)
```

Interlude | N.C.(A5) | D5 D5 C5 | N.C.(A5) | D5 D5 C5 |

| N.C.(C5) |: C | Fmaj7 :|

Verse 3

C Fmaj7
Well, the rain exploded with a mighty crash

C
As we fell into the sun

Fmaj7
And the first one said to the second one there

Em
I hope you're having fun.

Chorus 1

G C Em C Am
Band on the run, band on the run

Fmaj7 C Fmaj7
And the jailer man and sailor Sam were searching every one

C Fmaj7 C Fmaj7
For the band on the run

C Fmaj7 C Fmaj7
Band on the run

C Fmaj7 C Fmaj7
Band on the run

C Fmaj7 C Fmaj7
Band on the run.

Verse 4

C Fmaj7
Well, the undertaker drew a heavy sigh

C
Seeing no one else had come

Fmaj7
And a bell was ringing in the village square

Em
For the rabbits on the run.——

Chorus 2

G C Em Am
Band on the run, band on the run

Fmaj7 C Fmaj7
And the jailer man and sailor Sam were searching every one

C Fmaj7 C Fmaj7
For the band on the run

C Fmaj7 C Fmaj7
Band on the run.

Instr. 2 | Em G | C | Em C | Am |

| Fmaj7 | C | Fmaj7 | Fmaj7 ||

Chorus 3

C Fmaj7 C Fmaj7
Yeah the band on the run

C Fmaj7 C Fmaj7
The band on the run

C Fmaj7 C Fmaj7
Band on the run

C Fmaj7 C Fmaj7
Band on the run.

Verse 5

C Fmaj7
Well, the night was falling as the desert world

C
Began to settle down

Fmaj7
In the town they're searching for us everywhere

Em
But we never will be found.

Chorus 4

G C Em C Am
Band on the run, band on the run

Fmaj7 Cmaj7
And the county judge who held a grudge

Fmaj7
Will search for evermore

C Fmaj7 C Fmaj7
For the band on the run

C Fmaj7 C Fmaj7
The band on the run

C Fmaj7 C Fmaj7
Band on the run

C Fmaj7 C Fmaj7 Em G C (fermata)
The band on the run.

Beautiful Night

Words & Music by
Paul McCartney

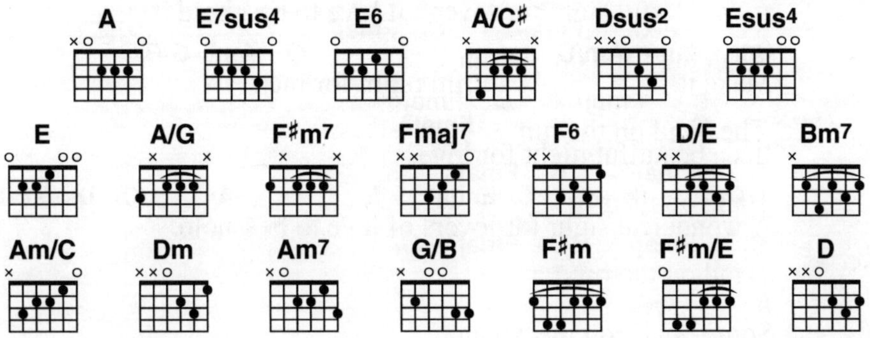

Verse 1

A
Someone's gone out fishing
E7sus4 E6
Someone's high and dry
A A/C# Dsus2 Esus4 E
Someone's on a mission to the lonely Lore - lei
A A/G F#m7 Fmaj7 F6
Some folk's got a vision of a castle in the sky
A D/E A A/C# Dsus2 Esus4 E
And I'm left stranded, wondering why.

Verse 2

A
You and me together
E7sus4 E6
Nothing feels so good
A A/C# Dsus2 Esus4 E
Even if I get a medal from my local neighbour - hood
A A/G F#m7 Fmaj7 F6
I won't need a castle, they've got castles in Ver - sailles
A D/E A
And I'm still stranded, wondering why.

Chorus 1

(A)   Bm7 Am/C Dm   G   Am7 G/B
Make it   a   beautiful night for me

C   Fmaj7
It's a beautiful night for love

Dm   Esus4   E   A
A wonderful sight for lovers of love to be - hold

(A)   Bm7 Am/C Dm   G   Am7 G/B
Make it   a   beautiful night for me

C   Fmaj7
It's a beautiful night for love

Dm   Esus4   E   A   A/C♯ Dsus2 Esus4 E
A wonderful sight for lovers of love to be - hold.

Verse 3

A
Some boat's on the ocean

E7sus4   E6
We're here in this room

A   A/C♯   Dsus2   Esus4 E
Seems to me the perfect way to spend an after - noon

A   A/G   F♯m7   Fmaj7 F6
We can look for castles, pretty castles in the sky

A   D/E   A
No more wondering,   wondering why.

Bridge

F♯m   A
Things can go wrong, things can go right

F♯m   F♯m/E D   A
Things can go bump, in the   dead of the night

F♯m   A
So let me be there, let me be there

F♯m   F♯m/E D   A
Let me be there with   you in the dead of the night.

Chorus 2

(A) Bm7 Am/C Dm G Am7 G/B
Make it a beautiful night for me
C Fmaj7
It's a beautiful night for love
Dm Esus4 E A
A wonderful sight for lovers of love to be - hold
(A) Bm7 Am/C Dm G Am7 G/B
Make it a beautiful night for me
C Fmaj7
It's a beautiful night for love
Dm Esus4 E A A/C♯ Dsus2 Esus4 E
A wonderful sight for lovers of love to be - hold
A A/C♯ Dsus2
Yeah, it's a beautiful night
Esus4 E A
Yeah, it's a beautiful night. Ah...

Outro

F♯m D A
Yeah, beautiful night, beautiful night
F♯m D A
Yeah, it's such a beautiful night, beautiful, beautiful night, yeah.
F♯m D A
𝄆 Beautiful night, beautiful night, beautiful night. 𝄇 *Repeat to fade*

Beware My Love

Words & Music by
Paul McCartney & Linda McCartney

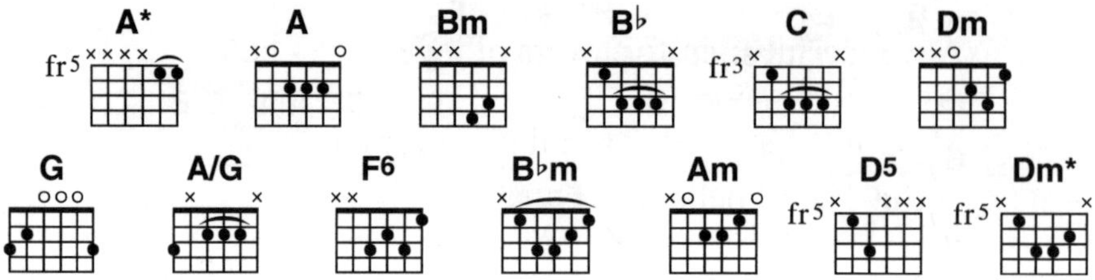

Intro

| (C) | (G7) | (C) (G/B) | (Am) ||

Organ cue

Play 4 times

||: A* A Bm A | Bm :|| A* A Bm A ||

Fade in

Verse 1

A B♭
Can't say I've found out
C Dm
I can't tell you what's all about
A B♭
Don't know who does
A
I tell you to.

Chorus 1

Dm
Be - ware, my love
G
Beware, my love
Dm
Be - ware, my love
G
Beware, my love
Dm
Be - ware, my love
G
Beware, my love.

Link 1

B♭
Wow wow
Dm
No, no, no
A A/G F6
I must be wrong, baby, yeah.

Verse 2

B♭
But I don't believe
Dm
That he's the one
A
But if you insist
A/G F6
I must be wrong, I must be wrong
B♭m
I have to leave
Am
And when I'm gone
A
I'll leave my message in my song
D5 N.C.
That's right.

Chorus 2

Dm*
Beware, my love
C
He'll bowl you over
B♭
Beware, my love
A
Be - fore you're much older
Dm*
He'll sweep you up
C
Under his carpet
B♭
You'd be in luck
A
If you could stop it. (Come on, now.)

Interlude | B♭ | B♭ | Dm | Dm |

| A | A/G | F6 | F6 |
Beware my love

| B♭m | B♭m | Am | Am |

| A | A/G | F6 | D5 N.C ||
(Let me tell ya)

Verse 3

Dm*
Well, he'll wear you out
C
And in a miniute
B♭
You'll hear a shout
A
And then you'll be in it
Dm
So, so beware my love
C
'Cause he'll take you under
B♭
Beware, my love
A
The sound of his thunder yeah.

Verse 4

B♭
But I don't believe
Dm
That he's the one
A
But if you insist
A/G F6
I must be wrong, I must be wrong
B♭m
I have to leave
Am
And when I'm gone
A
I'll leave my message in my song
D5 N.C.
That's where I'm gonna leave it baby.

Chorus 3

Dm*
Beware, my love
C
Don't you know he'll bowl you over
B♭
Beware, my love
A
Be - fore you're much older. He's gonna....

Verse 5

Dm*
Yes, he's gonna wear you out
C
When in a miniute
B♭
You'll hear a shout
A
And then you'll be in it.

(Baby gonna be there.)

Outro

Dm
𝄆 Ah, beware, ah be
C
There, ah baby beware,
B♭
Be - ware, beware my love, yeah
A
And any minute. 𝄇 *w/ad lib. vocal*

A **B♭**
Can't say I've found out
C
I tell you to...
Dm
𝄆 Be - ware, my love
G
Beware, my love. 𝄇 *Play 7 times*

𝄐
| **G** ‖

Big Barn Bed

Words & Music by
Paul McCartney & Linda McCartney

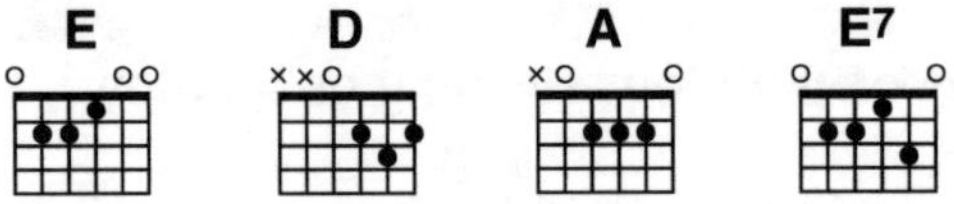

Capo first fret

Intro | E | D A | E | D | E | D | E ||

Verse 1

```
D                          E
  Who's that coming round    that corner
D                                E
  Who's that coming round that bend
D                          E
  Who's that coming round    that corner, will it
D       A     E
  Will it be my friend?
```

Chorus 1

```
          D    A   E
||: Keep on___ sleeping in a big barn bed
       D   A  E
Keep on___ sleeping in a big barn bed :||
```

Interlude 1

```
                A E                A E
||: A-dan da,     yeah, a-dan da.      :||
```

Verse 2

D
Who you gonna weep on, who you gonna sleep on
E A E
Who you gonna creep on next?
D
Weeping on a willow, sleeping on a pillow
E A E
Leaping armadillo, yes.

Chorus 2 As Chorus 1

Solo | D | E | D | E |

| D | E D A E
Will it, will it be my friend?

Chorus 3 As Chorus 2

Interlude 2 As Interlude 1

Verse 3 As Verse 2

Outro
D A E
‖: Keep on___ sleeping in a big barn bed
D A E
Keep on___ sleeping in a big barn bed. :‖ *Play 5 times*

| E7 (fermata) ‖

Biker Like An Icon

Words & Music by
Paul McCartney

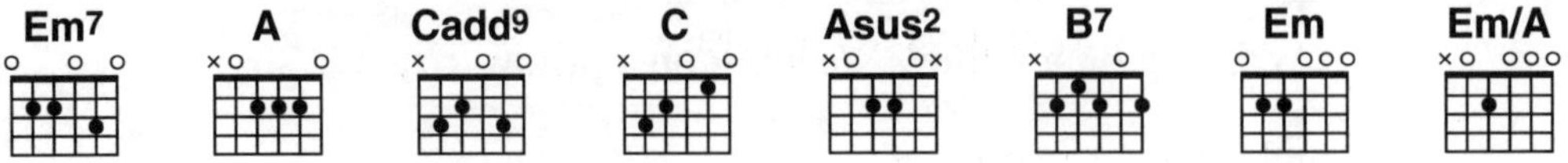

Intro |: Em7 | A | Em7 | A :|

Verse 1

Em7 A
There was a girl who loved a biker
Em7 A
She used to follow him across America
Em7 A Em7 A
But the biker didn't like her.

Verse 2

Em7 A
She didn't care, she still persisted
Em7 A
Though her brother said she was twisted
Em7 A
And the family said they wouldn't miss her
Em7
Anyway.

Chorus 1

Cadd9 C
She loved the biker like an icon
Asus2 B7 Em Em/A Em
Gazing at his picture everyday
Cadd9 C
She loved the biker like an icon
Asus2 B7 Em Em/A Em
Slowly watching precious water drip away.

Verse 3

(Em7) A
She did her best to fix a meeting
Em7 A
She pulled it off one night in Hollywood
Em7 A
When he met her he couldn't let her
Em7
Get away.

Verse 4

(Em7) A
He didn't ask for her permission

Em7 A
He took advantage of her position

Em7 A
But he was always her ambitiion

Em7
Anyway.

Chorus 2

As Chorus 1

Solo

‖: Em7 | A | Em7 | A :‖ *Play 4 times*

(A) Cadd9 C
She loved the biker like an icon

Asus2 B7 Em Em/A Em
Slowly watching precious water drip away.

Verse 5

Em7 A
The family tried so hard to find her

Em7 A
They showed her picture across America.

Em7 A
But no trace of her sweet face

Em7
Was ever found.

Chorus 3

Cadd9 C
She loved the biker like an icon

Asus2 B7 Em Em/A Em
Gazing at his picture everyday

Cadd9 C
She loved the biker like an icon

Asus2 B7 Em Em/A Em
Slowly watching precious water drip away, hey, hey.

Outro

Cadd9 C
‖: She loved a biker like an icon

Asus2 B7 Em Em/A Em
Slowly watching precious water drip away, yeah, yeah. :‖

Cadd9 C
She loved a biker like an icon... | Asus2 B7 | Em ‖

Bip Bop

Words & Music by
Paul McCartney & Linda McCartney

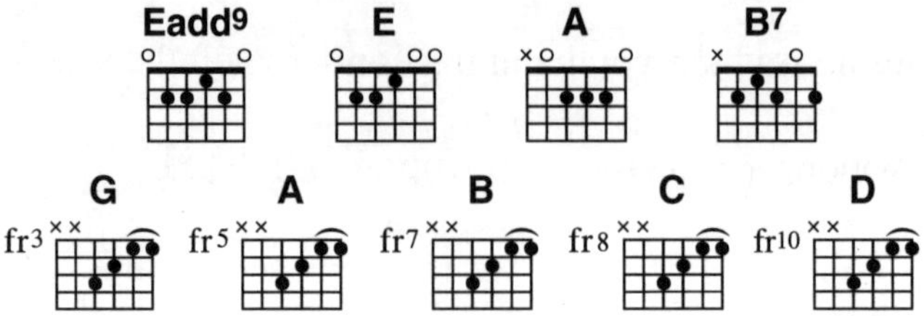

E riff

Intro | Eadd9 E Eadd9 E | Eadd9 E | Eadd9 E Eadd9 E | Eadd9 E |

| A | A | Eadd9 E Eadd9 E | Eadd9 E |

| B7 | A | Eadd9 E Eadd9 E | Eadd9 E |

| G | A B | C D ||

Chorus 1

E riff
Bip bop, bip 'n bop, bip bop, bip bop band

Bip bop, bip 'n bop, bip bop, bip bop band
A
Dig your bottom dollar, put it in your hand
E riff
Bip bop, bip 'n bop, bip bop, bip bop band
B7 A
Why d'you hide you hand bag underneath the stand?
E riff | G | A B | C D ||
Bip bop, bip 'n bop, bip bop, bip bop band.

Chorus 2

E riff
Wip wop, wip 'n wop, wip wop, wip 'n band

Wip wop, wip 'n wop, wip wop, wip 'n band

A
Why d'you hide you hand bag, underneath the stand?

Wip wop, wip'n wop, wip wop, wip 'n band

B7 A
Put your hair in curlers, we're gonna see a band

E riff
Bip bop, bip 'n bop, big bop big bop band.

| G | A B | C D ||

Chorus 3

E riff
Bip bop, bip 'n bop, bip bop, bip bop band

Bip bop, bip 'n bop, bip bop, bip bop band

A
Dig your bottom dollar, put it in your hand

E riff
Bip bop, bip 'n bop, bip bop, bip bop band

B7 A
Treat me like a good boy, treat me like a man

E riff | G | A B | C D ||
Bip bop, bip 'n bop, bip bop, bip bop band.

Chorus 4 As Chorus 2

Chorus 5

E riff
Bip bop, bip 'n bop, bip bop, bip bop band

Bip bop, bip 'n bop, bip bop, bip bop band

A
Dig your bottom dollar, put it in your hand

E riff
Bip bop, bip 'n bop, bip bop, bip bop band

B7 A
Take me hair and curlers, but treat me like a man

E riff
Bip bop, bip 'n bop, bip bop, bip bop band.

Bluebird

Words & Music by
Paul McCartney & Linda McCartney

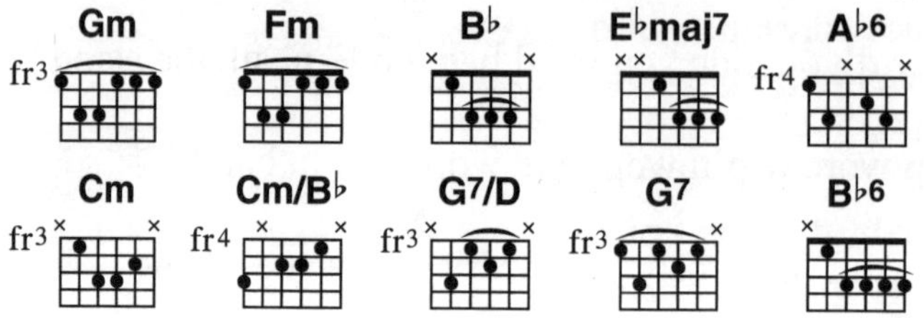

Verse 1

Gm
Late at night when the wind is still
Fm B♭
I'll come flying through your door
Fm B♭
And you'll know what love is for

I'm a bluebird.

Chorus 1

E♭maj7
I'm a bluebird, I'm a bluebird
A♭6
I'm a bluebird, yeah ,yeah ,yeah.
E♭maj7
I'm a bluebird, I'm a bluebird,
A♭6
I'm a bluebird, yeah ,yeah ,yeah.

Verse 2

Gm
Touch your lips with a magic kiss
Fm B♭
And you'll be a bluebird too
Fm B♭
And you'll know what love can do

I'm a bluebird.

Chorus 2 As Chorus 1

Bridge 1

```
Cm                Cm/B♭
Bluebird, (blue - bird)
   G7/D  G7
Ah ha
Cm                Cm/B♭
Bluebird, (blue - bird)
   G7/D  G7
Ah ha
A♭6       E♭maj7
Bluebird.——
```

Verse 3

```
Gm
Fly away through the midnight air
      Fm                  B♭
As we head across the sea,
       Fm                  B♭
And at last we will be free.

You're a bluebird.
```

Chorus 3

```
         E♭maj7
You're a bluebird, you're a bluebird
                  A♭6
You're a bluebird,    yeah, yeah, yeah
         E♭maj7
You're a bluebird, you're a bluebird
                  A♭6
You're a bluebird,    yeah, yeah, yeah.
```

Bridge 2 As Bridge 1

Interlude | Gm | Gm | Fm | B♭6 ||

Fm **B♭6**
At last we will be free

E♭maj7 **A♭6**
Bluebird, you and me

E♭maj7 **A♭6**
At last we will be free.

Bridge 3 As Bridge 2

Verse 4

Gm
All alone on a desert island

Fm **B♭**
We're living in the trees

Fm **B♭**
And we're flying in the breeze

We're the bluebirds.

Chorus 4

E♭maj7
We're the bluebirds, we're the bluebirds

Cm A♭6 N.C.
We're the bluebirds.

Outro

Cm **Cm/B♭**
Singin' bluebird, (blue - bird)

G7/D G7
Ah ha

Cm **Cm/B♭**
Bluebird, (blue - bird)

G7/D G7
Ah ha

A♭6 **E♭maj7**
Bluebird.——

C'mon People

Words & Music by
Paul McCartney

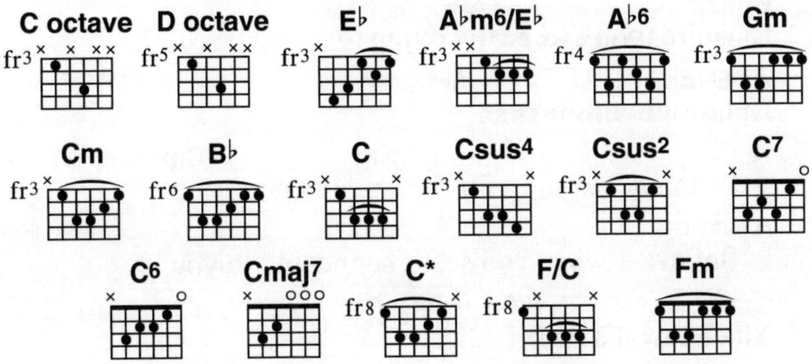

Intro (C octave Doctave)

Verse 1

E♭
Well we're going to, yeah we're going to
A♭m6/E♭
Get it right this time,
E♭
We're going to, really going to
A♭m6/E♭
Raise it to the sky.
A♭6 Gm Cm
People are ready to for - give a few mis - takes
A♭6 B♭
But let's get started, form a party
C Csus4 Csus2 C
Don't you know how long it takes!

Chorus 1

C7 C6 Cmaj7 C
C'mon people let the fun be - gin
C7 C6 Cmaj7 C
We've got a future and it's rushing in,
C7 C6 Cmaj7 C
Call all the minstrels from the ancient shrine
C7 C6 Cmaj7 C (C octave Doctave)
Pass down the message that it's right this time.

Verse 2

```
E♭
   Well I'm trying to, yeah I'm crying to
A♭m6/E♭
   Lay it on the line,
E♭
   We're trying to, really dying to
A♭m6/E♭
Get it right this time.
A♭6                                   Gm          Cm
   So many yearning for the way it's gonna be
A♭6                                    B♭
   Believe it when you see it happening to you
                  C*  F/C  | F/C  C*  |
You know it's real.
```

Chorus 2

```
C7          C6              Cmaj7      C
   C'mon people let the world be - gin
C7              C6              Cmaj7     C
   We've got a future and it's charging in
C7                  C6              Cmaj7      C
   We'll make the best of all we have, and more
C7                 C6               Cmaj7      C     N.C.
   We'll do what never has been done be - fore.
```

Bridge 1

```
‖: Fm             | Gm  Cm  | Fm                      |
      Oh yeah.                  Oh yeah, oh yeah.
| Gm  Cm  :‖ (C octave   D octave) ‖
```

Verse 3

```
Eb
   Well I'm going to, yeah I'm going to
Abm6/Eb
   Get it right this time
Eb
   I'm going to, really going to
Abm6/Eb
Raise it to the sky.
Ab6                              Gm                 Cm
   I must admit I may have made a few mis - takes,
Ab6                               Bb
   But let's get started, form a party
                                 C*    F/C  F/C  C
Don't you know how long it takes!——
```

Chorus 3

```
C7             C6               Cmaj7   C
   So c'mon people let the fun be - gin
C7                C6               Cmaj7   C
   We've got a future and it's rushing in,
C7                C6                   Cmaj7   C
   Call all the minstrels from the ancient shrine
C7                C6                  Cmaj7   C
Pass down the message that it's right this time.
```

Bridge 2

```
|: Fm            | Gm  Cm  | Fm                     | Gm  Cm :|
      Oh yeah.                   Oh yeah, oh yeah.
```

Outro

```
C7            C6                Cmaj7      C
   C'mon people let the world be - gin
C7                C6               Cmaj7   C
   We've got a future and it's char  -  -

C7              | C6        | Cmaj7  | C                 |
   - ging in.——                          Now c'mon
                                    1 - 8.       9.
|: C7      | C6        | Cmaj7   | C        :| C (fermata) ||
   people.                 w/vocal ad.lib.
```

Café On The Left Bank

Words & Music by
Paul McCartney

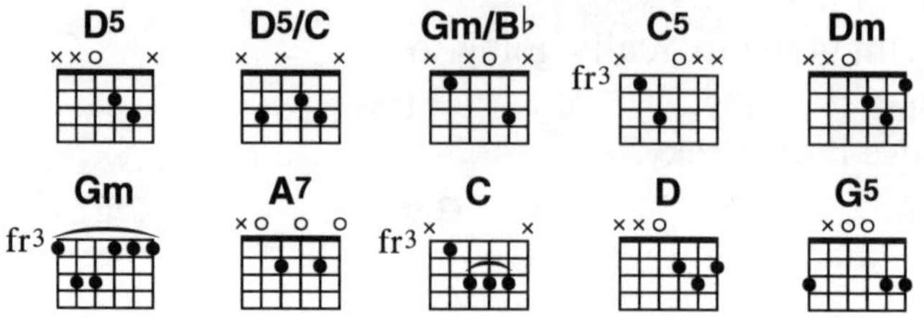

Intro

| D5 D5/C | Gm/B♭ | Gm/B♭ | C5 |

|: Dm | Gm | Dm | Gm :|

Verse 1

```
Dm                        Gm        C  Gm
Café on the left bank, ordina - ry wine
Dm                   A7                D
Touching all the girls with your eyes
```

Verse 2

```
Dm                              Gm        C  Gm
Tiny crowd of Frenchmen round a T.V. shop
Dm                       A7                D
Watching Charles De Gaulle make a speech.
```

Bridge 1

```
Gm                          Dm
Dancing after midnight, sprawling to the car
Gm                               Dm   A7
Continental breakfast in the bar.___
```

Verse 3

```
Dm                                 Gm               C    Gm
English-speaking people drinking Ger - man beer
Dm                     A7               D
Talking far too loud for their ears.
```

Solo

```
| Gm    | Gm    | Dm    | Dm    |
| Gm    | Gm    | Dm    | A7    ||
```

Verse 4 As Verse 1

Solo

```
||: Dm   | Gm    | Dm    | Gm    :||
```

Bridge 2

```
Gm                                  Dm
Dancing after midnight, crawling to the car
Gm                                         Dm   A7
Cocktail waitress waiting in the bar.___
```

Verse 5

```
Dm                                 Gm               C    Gm
English-speaking people drinking Ger - man beer
Dm                         A7              D5        D5/C  Gm/B♭  G5  C5
Talking way too loud for their ears.
```

Outro

```
||: Dm            Gm          Dm                      Gm
    Café on the left bank, café on the left bank. :||  Repeat to fade
    Vocal tacet 1°
```

Calico Skies

Words & Music by
Paul McCartney

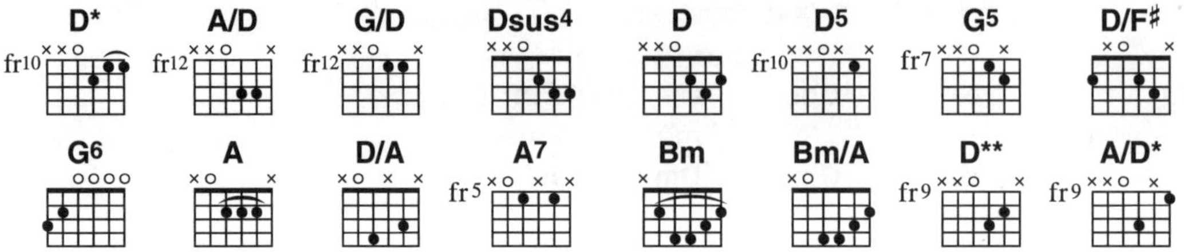

Tune guitar down a semitone

(count in 3)

Intro
| D* | A/D G/D | D* | Dsus4 D/ (slide) |
|/D* | A/D G/D | D5 G/D G5 | D ||

Verse 1
D* A/D G/D D* Dsus4 D
It was writ - ten that I would love you
D* A/D G/D D5 G/D G5 D
From the mo - ment I o - pened my eyes
D* A/D G/D D* Dsus4 D
And the morn - ing when I first saw you
D* A/D G/D D5 G/D G5 D
Gave me life under ca - li - co skies.

Chorus 1
D/F♯ G6 A D/A A7 D/A A Bm
I will hold you for as long as you like
Bm/A G6 A D/A A7 D/A A D
I'll hold you for the rest of my life.

Link 1
| D* | A/D G/D | D* | Dsus4 D/ (slide) |
|/D* | A/D G/D | D5 G/D G5 | D ||

```
           D*        A/D    G/D      D*          Dsus4  D
Verse 2      Always look - ing for ways to love      you
           D*          A/D  G/D      D5   G/D G5    D
             Never fail - ing to fight at    your side
           D*              A/D G/D     D*           Dsus4  D
             While the an - gels of love pro - tect      us
           D*             A/D  G/D        D5  G/D  G5  D
             From the in  -  nermost se - crets we hide.

Chorus 2   As Chorus 1

                                                      slide
Link 2     ||: D*     | A/D  G/D | D*       | Dsus4  D/ |

           | /D*      | A/D  G/D | D5 G/D G5 | D      :||

           D*              A/D  G/D    D*     Dsus4  D
Verse 3      Long live all    of us crazy sol  -  diers
           D*               A/D  G/D     D5  G/D G5 D
             Who were born under ca - li  -  co  skies
           D*            A/D    G/D  D*       Dsus4  D
             May we nev - er be called to han  -  dle
           D*         A/D    G/D      D5  G/D  G5    D
             All the wea - pons of war we   des - pise.

           D/F#  G6          A   D/A  A7   D/A  A    Bm
Chorus 3   I'll    hold you for as    long as    you like
           Bm/A  G6          A   D/A  A7  D/A  A    D
           I'll    hold you for the   rest of    my life
           Bm/A  G6          A   D/A  A7   D/A  A    Bm
           I'll    hold you for as    long as    you like
           Bm/A  G6          A   D/A  A7   D/A  A
           I'll    love you for the   rest  of    my...
           A   D/A  A7  D/A  A   D*
           For the   rest of    my life.

                                                      slide
Outro      | (D*)     | A/D  G/D | D*        | Dsus4  D/ |

                                               𝄐
           | /D*      | A/D  G/D | D**  A/D* | D*        ||
```

Call Me Back Again

Words & Music by
Paul McCartney & Linda McCartney

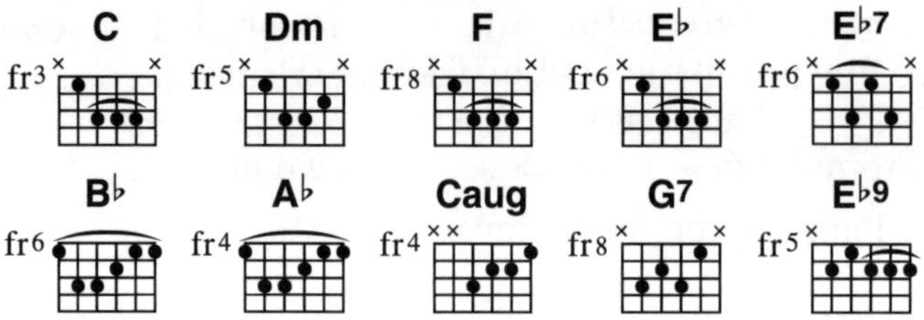

Intro

C Dm ‖ F | Dm | E♭ | F C Dm | F N.C. ‖

Verse 1

```
(N.C.)            F  Dm
Well when I,——— when I was
E♭                F
  Just a little baby boy
     (F)   Dm
Every night——— I would call
E♭7                       F
  Your number brought me joy
B♭        A♭
I called your house
F    E♭        C      Caug
Every night since then.
```

Chorus 1

```
          F
But I ain't never, no no never
G7
Heard you calling me
E♭9                           F
  Come on and call me back a - gain
                E♭9            F    C   Dm
Come on and call me back a - gain.
```

```
Solo        | F      | Dm     | E♭     | F  C  |

            | F      | Dm     | E♭     | F     |

                Bb                 Ab    F                 C      Caug
            Oh, I've heard your name every night since then.


                    F
Chorus 2    But I ain't never, no no never
            G7
            Heard you calling me
            Eb9                         F
              Come on and call me back again
                  Eb9           F      C  Dm  F  N.C.
            Yeah,    call me back a - gain.


            (N.C.)      F  Dm
Verse 2     Well when I,___ when I was
            Eb            F
              Just a little   baby boy

            Every night, every night
            Dm            Eb7
              I would call   because your number
            F
            Brought me joy.
               Bb              Ab
            Oh, I've called your name
            F    Eb        C     Caug
            Every night since then.


                    F
Chorus 3    But I ain't never, no no no no never
            G7
            Heard you calling me
            Eb9                         F
              Come on and call me back a - gain
                           Eb9          F
            ||: Come on and call me back a - gain. :||  Repeat to fade w/vocal ad lib.
```

Country Dreamer

Words & Music by
Paul McCartney & Linda McCartney

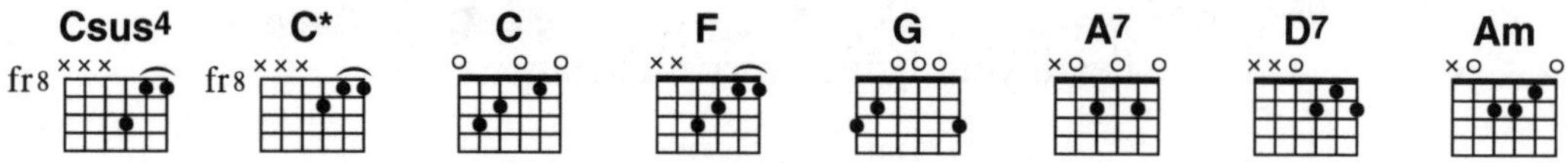

Intro ‖: Csus4 | Csus4 | C* | C* :‖ *Play 4 times*

| Csus4 | Csus4 | C* | C* N.C. ‖

Verse 1

```
C            F          C
 I'd like to walk in a field with you
G                         C        G
 Take my hat and my boots off too
C            F      C          A7
 I'd like to lie in a field with you
D7              G                C   A7
 Would you like to do it too, May?
D7              G                C
 Would you like to do it too?
```

Verse 2

```
C            F          C
 I'd like to stand in a stream with you
G                              C         G
 Roll my trousers up and    not feel blue
C            F          C              A7
 I'd like to wash in a stream with you
D7              G                C
 Would you like to do it too?
```

Chorus 1

```
Am                  G
  You and I, country dreamer
F                                   C
  When there's nothing else to do
Am                  G
  Me oh my, country dreamer
F                                   G
  Make a country dream come true.
```

Verse 3

```
C          F          C
  I'd like to climb up a hill with you
G                   C         G
  Stand on top and ad - mire the view
C          F          C       A7
  I'd like to roll down a hill with you
D7          G               C    A7
  Would you like to do it too, May?
D7                  G           C
  Now would you like to do it too?
```

Chorus 2 As Chorus 1

Verse 4

```
C          F          C
  I'd like to climb up a hill with you
G                       C         G
  Take my hat and my boots off too
C          F           C          A7
  I'd like to lie in a field with you
D7          G               C    A7
  Would you like to do it too, May?
D7          G               C    A7
  Would you like to do it too, May?
D7          G               C
  Would you like to do it too?
```

Coming Up

Words & Music by
Paul McCartney

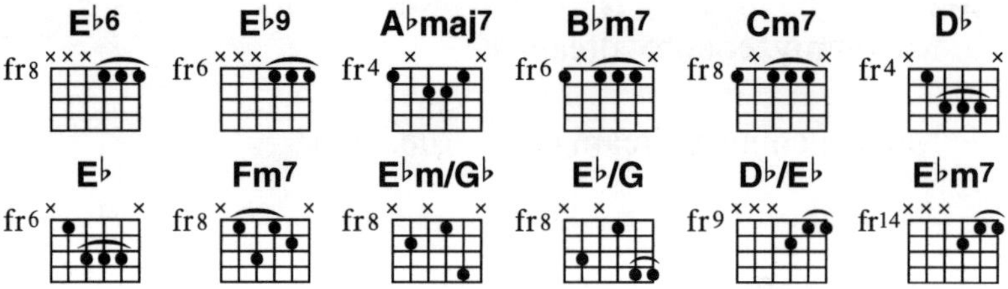

Intro ‖: E♭6 | E♭6 E♭9 | E♭6 | E♭6 E♭9 :‖

Verse 1

E♭6 E♭9
You want a love to last forever
E♭6 E♭9
One that will never fade away
E♭6 E♭9
I want to help you with your problem
E♭6 E♭9
Stick around, I say.

Chorus 1

A♭maj7 B♭m7 | Cm7 D♭ |
Coming up
E♭ Fm7 | Cm7 D♭ |
Coming up, yeah
A♭maj7 B♭m7 | Cm7 D♭ |
Coming up like a flower
E♭ Fm7 | E♭m/G♭ E♭/G ‖
Coming up, I say.
| E♭6 | E♭6 E♭9 ‖

Verse 2

E♭6 E♭9
You want a friend you can rely on
E♭6 E♭9
One who will never fade away
E♭6 E♭9
And if you're searching for an answer
E♭6 D♭/E♭
Stick around, I say.

Chorus 2

A♭maj7 B♭m7 | Cm7 D♭ |
It's coming up
E♭ Fm7 | E♭m E♭/G |
It's coming up, yeah
A♭maj7 B♭m7 | Cm7 D♭ |
It's coming up like a flower
E♭ Fm7 | E♭m/G♭ E♭/G ‖
Coming up, yeah.
| E♭6 | E♭6 E♭9 ‖

Link 1

| A♭ | A♭ | A♭ | A♭ |

| E♭6 | E♭6 E♭9 | E♭6 | E♭6 E♭9 ‖

Verse 3

E♭6 E♭9
You want some peace and understand - ing
E♭6 E♭9
So everybody can be free
E♭6 E♭9
I know that we can get together
E♭6
We can make it, stick with me.

Chorus 3

A♭maj7 B♭m7 | Cm7 D♭ |
It's coming up
E♭ Fm7 | E♭m E♭/G |
It's coming up, yeah
A♭maj7 B♭m7 | Cm7 D♭ |
It's coming up like a flower
E♭ Fm7 | E♭m/G♭ E♭/G ‖
Coming up, for you and me.
‖: E♭6 | E♭6 E♭9 ‖:

Link 2

| A♭ | A♭ | E♭6 | E♭6 E♭9 |

| E♭6 | E♭6 E♭9 | E♭6 | E♭6 E♭9 |
Coming
| E♭6 | E♭6 E♭9 | E♭6 | E♭6 E♭9 | E♭9 ‖
up. Coming up.

```
                   A♭maj7  B♭m7 | Cm7  D♭ |
Chorus 4   It's coming up
                   E♭  Fm7     | E♭m/G♭  E♭/G |
           It's coming up,     I   say
                   A♭maj7  B♭m7    | Cm7  D♭ |
           It's coming up         like a   flower
                E♭  Fm7        | E♭m/G♭  E♭/G         |
           Coming up,                  I feel it in my
           | E♭6     | E♭6   E♭9  | E♭6     | E♭6  E♭9 | E♭6     ||
           Bones.     Yeah  yeah   yeah.

              E♭6                            E♭9
Verse 4    You want a better kind of future
           E♭6                          E♭9
           One that everyone can share
           E♭6                                   E♭9
           You're not alone, we all could use it
           E♭6                            E♭9
           Stick around we're nearly there.

                   A♭maj7  B♭m7 | Cm7  D♭ |
Chorus 5   It's coming up              ooh
                   E♭  Fm7       | E♭m/G♭  E♭/G |
           It's coming up,     ev'ry - where
                   A♭maj7  B♭m7    | Cm7  D♭ |
           It's coming up         like a   flower
                E♭    Fm7       | E♭m/G♭  E♭/G |
           Coming up,  for all to  share.
                   A♭maj7  B♭m7 | Cm7  D♭ |
           It's coming up              yeah
                   E♭  Fm7       | E♭m/G♭  E♭/G |
           It's coming up,     any  -  way
                   A♭maj7  B♭m7    | Cm7    D♭        |
           It's coming up         like a   flower coming
            𝄐
            E♭    ||
            Up.
```

Daytime Nightime Suffering

Words & Music by
Paul McCartney

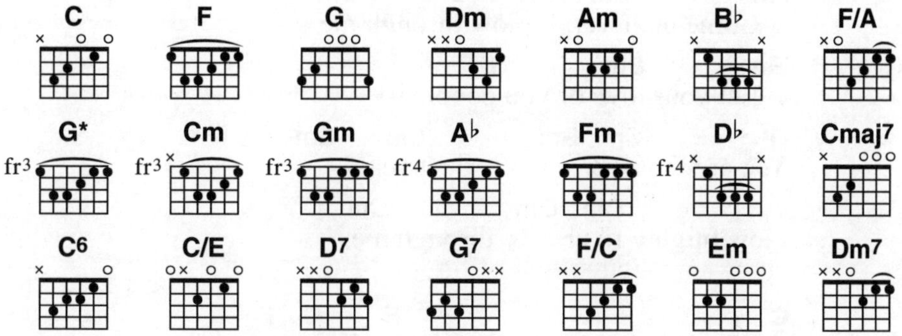

Verse 1

```
C                                    F   G   F   G
   What does she get for all the love she gave you
C                                  F
   There on the ladder of re - grets?
Dm             Am              B♭            N.C.    | B♭ F/A B♭ F ||
   Mighty ri - ver, give her all she gets.___
```

Verse 2

```
C                    G               F   C   F   C
   What does she get for all the love she gave you
                 G            F       G*
There on the ladder of re - grets?
B♭   F/A  B♭    F    C         Am   Dm    G
Day - time nigh - time suffering    is all she gets.
```

Verse 3

```
C                    G               F   C   F   C
   Where all the prizes for the games she en - tered
            G                        F      G*
With little chance of much suc - cess?
B♭   F/A  B♭    F    C         Am   Dm    G
Day - time nigh - time suffering    is all she gets.
```

Chorus 1

Cm   Gm Cm   Gm
   Come on, river,   all the flow
Cm   Gm   A♭   A♭ Gm
   Let your love of you people show
Fm   Cm Fm   Cm
   Come on, river,   flow through me
Fm   Cm   D♭
   Let your love of you people be
G*   Cm Gm   Cm   Gm
You are the river,   I am the stream
            Cm Gm   Cm
Flow mighty river—— through me.

Verse 4

C   G   F   C F C
   What does it pay to play the lead - ing la - dy
              G   F   G*
When like the damsel in dis - tress?
B♭   F/A B♭   F   C   Am   Dm   G
Day - time nigh - time suffering   is all she gets.

Middle 8

   C   Cmaj7
No less (no less), no more (no more)
   C6   Cmaj7
No sea (no sea), no shore (no shore)
   F   C/E
No sand (no sand), no pail (no pail)
   D7   G7
No fairy tale anymore.

```
           Cm            Gm  Cm            Gm
Chorus 2     Come on, river,    flow through me
           Cm            Gm               A♭      A♭  Gm
             Don't be stopped by in - sanity
           Fm            Cm  Fm           Cm
             Come on, river,    over - flow
           Fm           Cm              D♭
             Let your love for your neighbours grow
           G*           Cm  Gm            Cm     Gm
           You are the river,   I am the stream——
                          Cm  Gm               Cm
           Flow mighty river—— through me.

           G            (F/C) (C)  (F/C) (C)  (F/C) (C)
Verse 5    Dom dom dom dom dom dom dom dom
                        (F/C) (C)  (F/C)
           Dom dom dom dom dom.——
           B♭     F/A  B♭     F    C        Am   Dm    G
           Day - time nigh - time suffering    is all she gets, whoa, whoa.

           B♭     F/A  B♭     F    C        Am   Dm    G
Outro      Day - time nigh - time suffering    is all she gets whoa, whoa
           B♭     F/A  B♭     F    C        Am   Dm    G
           Day - time nigh - time suffering    is all she gets
           C                                    F    Em Dm7 C
             What does she get for all the love she gave you?
```

Dear Friend

Words & Music by
Paul McCartney & Linda McCartney

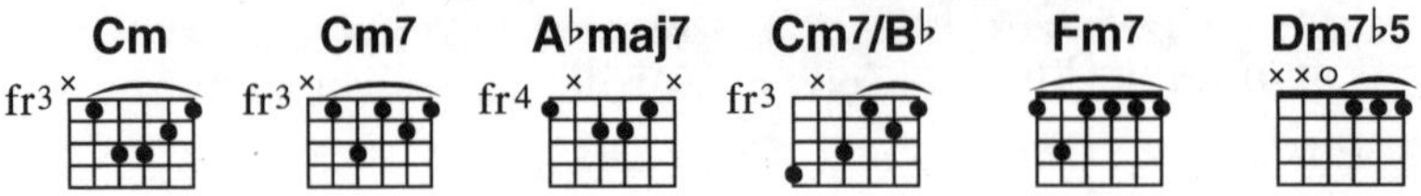

Verse 1

```
Cm              Cm7
   Dear friend,    what's the time?
A♭maj7
   Is this really the borderline?
Cm                  Cm7/B♭                A♭maj7
   Does it really          mean so much to you?
             Fm7  Dm7♭5            Cm
Are you a - fraid,        or is it true?___
```

Verse 2

```
(Cm)            Cm7
   Dear friend,    throw the wine
A♭maj7
   I'm in love with a friend of mine
Cm7                                 A♭maj7
   Really truly, young and newly wed
            Fm7  Dm7♭5          Cm
Are you a fool,       or is it true?___
```

Verse 3

```
| Cm    | Cm7/B♭ | A♭maj7 | A♭maj7 |

| Cm    | Cm7/B♭ | A♭maj7 | A♭maj7 |
              Ooh,  are___      are you
     Fm7  Dm7♭5          Cm
A - fraid,      or is it true?___
```

Interlude ||: Cm | Cm7/B♭ | A♭maj7 | A♭maj7 |

| Cm | Cm7/B♭ | A♭maj7 | A♭maj7 |

| Fm7 | Dm7♭5 | Cm | Cm :||

Verse 4

Cm Cm7/B♭
Dear friend, what's the time?
A♭maj7
Is this really the borderline?
Cm Cm7/B♭ A♭maj7
Does it really mean so much to you?
Fm7 Dm7♭5 Cm
Are you a - fraid, or is it true?___

Verse 5

Cm Cm7
Dear friend, throw the wine
A♭maj7
I'm in love with a friend of mine
Cm Cm7/B♭ A♭maj7
Really truly, young and newly wed
Fm7 Dm7♭5 Cm
Are you a fool, or is it true?___

Verse 6 As Verse 3

Outro | Cm | Cm7/B♭ | A♭maj7 | A♭maj7 |

| Cm | Cm7/B♭ | A♭maj7 | A♭maj7 |

| Fm7 | Dm7♭5 | Cm | Cm :||

| Cm | Cm | Cm (fermata) ||

Deliver Your Children

Words Music by
Paul McCartney & Denny Laine

Dm C G Am7 C/B F F/E Gm

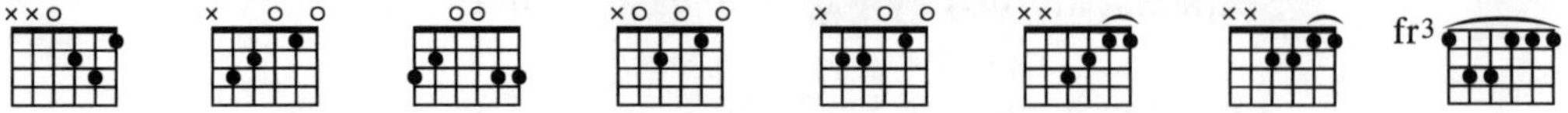

Capo seventh fret

```
Intro       |: Dm   | Dm   | Dm   | Dm   :|

                     Dm
Verse 1     Well, the rain was a-fallin'
                                     C
            And the ground turned to mud
                  Dm
            I was watching all the people
                                G
            Running from the flood
                 Dm
            So I started to prayin'
                                    C
            Though I ain't no prayin' man
                        Am7             Dm
            For the Lord to come a - helpin'
                          Am7         Dm
            Knowing he'd under - stand.

                   C          C/B              Am7
Chorus 1    De - liver your children to the good good life
            F                       F/E         Dm
            Give'em peace and shelter and a fork and knife
                        C            C/B            Am7
            Shine a light in the morning and a light at night
                        C     C/B  Am7                F      F/E    (Dm)
            And if a thing goes wrong you'd better make it       right.
            | Dm   | Dm   | Dm   | Dm   ||
```

Verse 2

```
          Dm
Well, I had me a woman
                      C
She was good and clean
    Dm                                   G
She spent all the day with the washing ma - chine
             Dm
But when it came to her lovin'
                      C
She was never a - round
           Am7         Dm
She was out getting dirty
Am7       Dm
All— over town.
```

Chorus 2 As Chorus 1

Link 1

```
| Dm    | Dm    | Dm    | Dm    ||
```

Verse 3

```
              Gm
Well, I was low on money
                         F
And my truck broke down
     Gm                         C
I was on my way to the lost and found
     Gm
So I took it to a dealer
                 F
I said make it run
         Dm        Gm
Well, I ain't got no money
       Dm     Gm
But I got me a gun.
```

Verse 4

Gm
I said you robbed me before
F
So I'm robbing you back
Gm
And if it don't put you straight
C
It'll put you on the right track
Gm F
Well, I ain't no devil and I ain't no saint
Dm Gm Dm Gm
But I can tell a dealer by the colour of his paint.

Chorus 3 As Chorus 1

Instrumental

Dm	Dm	Dm	C
Dm	Dm	Dm	G
Dm	Dm	Dm	C
Am7	Dm	Dm	Am7
Dm	Dm	

Chorus 4 As Chorus 1

Outro

Dm
If you want good eggs
C
You gotta feed that hen
Am7 Dm
And if you wanna hear some more
Am7 Dm Am7 Dm
Well, I'll sing it a - gain.

Distractions

Words & Music by
Paul McCartney

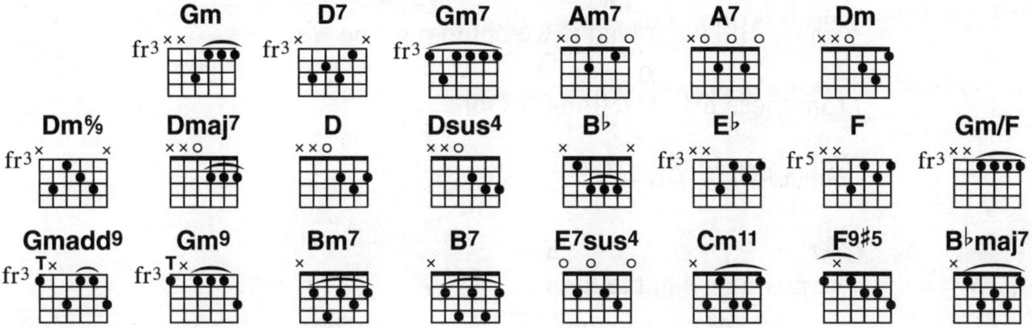

Verse 1

```
Gm7                       Am7           A7            Dm
   What is this thing in life that per - suades me to spend
                 Gm7
Time away from you?
                  Am7           A7                Dm  Dm6/9  D7
If you can answer this you can have the moon.——
```

Verse 2

```
Gm7                          Am7      A7             Dm
   This is the place to be,     any - way you can see
                Gm7
There's a lovely view.
                     Am7               A7          Dmaj7  Dsus4  D
Why are there always so many other things to do?
```

Chorus 1

B♭   E♭   F   Gm
Distractions, like butterflies are buzzing 'round my head
       Gm/F E♭   F
When I'm a - lone I think of you
                   Gm   Gm/F   E♭
And the life we'd lead if we could only be free
                  B♭   E♭   F
From these dis - tractions.   Ooh.——

| Gm(add9) | Gm9 |

Verse 3

Gm7   Am7
The postman's at the door
          A7   Dm   Gm7
While the telephone rings on the kitchen wall
                     Am7   A7   Dm
Pretend we're not at home and they - 'll disappear.   Ooh.

Verse 4

Gm7   Am7   A7   Dm
I want to be with you, tell me what I can do
                Gm7
Nothing is too small
                    Am7   A7   Dmaj7 Dsus4 D
Away from all this jazz we could do anything at all.

Chorus 2

B♭   E♭   F   Gm
Distractions, like butterflies are buzzing 'round my head
       Gm/F E♭   F
When I'm a - lone I think of you
                       Gm   Gm/F   E♭
And the things we'd do if we could only be through
                  B♭   E♭ F
With these dis - tractions.

| Gmadd9 | Gm9 |

Instrumental | Am7 | Bm7 B7 | E7sus4 | Am7 |

| Am7 | Bm7 B7 | E7sus4 | E7sus4 |

| Am7 | Bm7 B7 | E7sus4 | Am7 |

| Cm11 | F9#5 ‖

Gm7   Am7
   I'll find the peaceful place
          A7   Dm   Gm7
Far a - way from the noise of a busy day——
                                            Am7
Where we can spend our nights counting
A7   Dmaj7 Dsus4 D
Shooting stars.

B♭   E♭   F   Gm
Chorus 3   Distractions, like butterflies are buzzing 'round my head
          Gm/F E♭   F
When I'm a - lone I think of you
                                Gm   Gm/F   E♭
And the things we'd do if we could only be through
                              B♭   E♭
With these dis - tractions, like butterflies they're
F   Gm   Gm/F E♭   F
Buzzing 'round my head, when I'm a - lone I think of you
                              Gm   Gm/F   E♭
And the life we'd lead if we could only be free
                              B♭maj7
From these dis - tractions.

Don't Let It Bring You Down

Words & Music by
Denny Laine & Paul McCartney

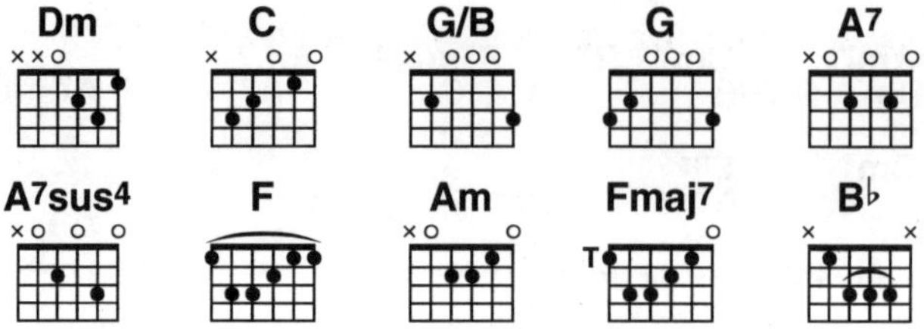

x3

Intro | 𝄆 Dm | Dm (C) | Dm | Dm (C) 𝄇 Dm | Dm ‖
| Dm C G/B | G | G | A7 | A7sus4 A7 |
| F G | A7 | Dm | Dm ‖

Verse 1
Dm C G/B G A7 A7sus4 A7
Though some things in life are hard to bear
F G A7 Dm
Don't let it bring you down.

Verse 2
Dm C G/B G A7 A7sus4 A7
Should the sand of time run out on you
F G A7 Dm
Don't let it bring you down.

Bridge 1
Am Fmaj7 Dm
Don't go down— don't go under - ground
Am B♭
Things seem strange, but they change
A7 A7sus4 A7
How they change.

Verse 3

```
Dm N.C.                  C   G/B  G        A7     A7sus4  A7
Up  and down your ca - rou - sel will go
    F     G    A7        Dm
So don't let it bring you down.
```

Instrumental

```
| Dm   C G/B | G        | G        | A7       | A7sus4  A7 |
| F  G       | A7       | Dm       | Dm       ||
```

Bridge 2

```
Am                  Fmaj7          Dm
Don't go down, don't get out of town
Am                     B♭
Get to know how it goes
          A7       A7sus4  A7
How it goes.
```

Verse 3

```
Dm N.C.                    C     G/B  G         A7     A7sus4  A7
When the price you have to      pay is high
F      G     A7          Dm
Don't let it bring you down.
```

Outro

```
| Dm   C G/B | G        | G        | A7       | A7sus4  A7 |
                                           Ooh, ooh.
F              G    A7          Dm
Ooh, don't let it bring you down.
                                    [1, 2, 3, 4.     ] [5.        ]
|: Dm       | Dm       | Dm       | Dm         :|| Dm (fermata) ||
```

Eat At Home

Words & Music by
Paul McCartney

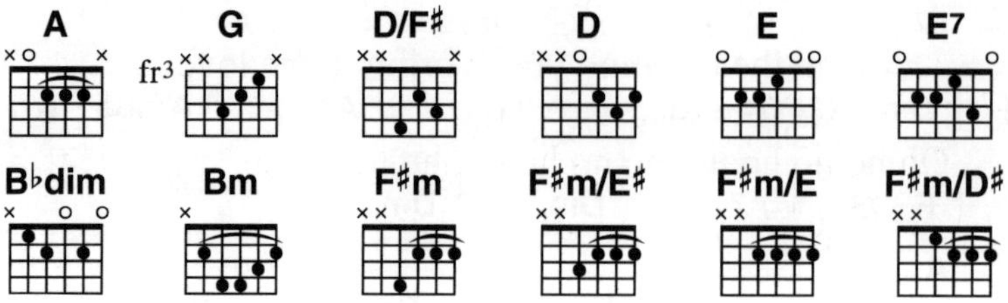


```
Intro        | A        | G  D/F♯   ||

             A                  D
Chorus 1       Come on little lady
                                  A
             Lady, let's eat at home______
                                D
             Come on little lady
                                  A
             Lady, let's eat at home______
                     E            A      | G  D/F♯   ||
             Eat at home, eat at home.

             A                  D
Chorus 2       Come on little lady
                                A
             Lady, let's eat in bed______
                                D
             Come on little lady
                                A
             Lady, let's eat in bed______
                     E          A     | G  D/F♯   ||
             Eat in bed, eat in bed.
```

Verse 1

E7
Bring the love that you feel for me
D   A
Into line with the love I see
E7   A
And in the morning you'll bring to me love
                     B♭dim   Bm   E
Oh ho ho ho ho, ho ho ho ho, ho ho ho ho.

Chorus 3

A   D
Come on little lady
                                A
Lady, now don't do that——
                        D
Come on little lady
                                A
Lady, now don't do that——
   E   F♯m
Do that, do that.

Bridge

(F♯m)   F♯m/E♯   F♯m/E   F♯m/D♯
Ooh, hoo hoo hoo, ooh hoo hoo, ooh hoo hoo.

| E7 | E7 | D | A | E7 | E7 |

A   B♭dim   Bm   E
Oh, ho ho ho ho, ho ho ho ho, ho ho ho ho.

Chorus 4 As Chorus 1

Solo

|: A | D | D | A :|

| E | A | G D/F♯ ||

Verse 2 As Verse 1

Chorus 5 As Chorus 3

Outro

(F♯m)   F♯m/E♯   F♯m/E   F♯m/D♯
Ooh ah, do that,—   do that, ow wow!

| E | E7 | D | A ||

Ebony And Ivory

Words & Music by
Paul McCartney

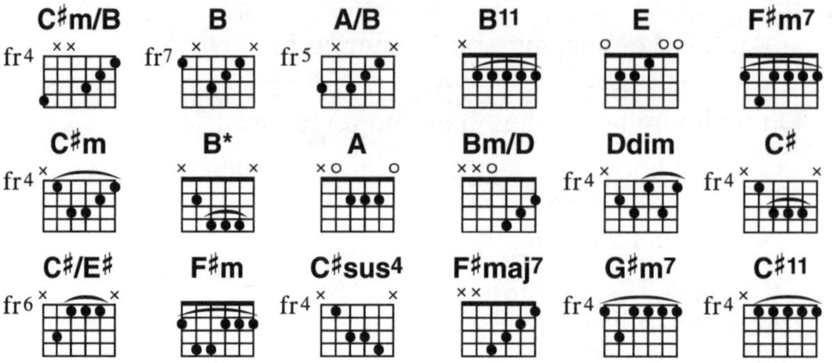

Intro ‖: C♯m/B B | A/B B11 :‖

Chorus 1

E F♯m7 B11 E F♯m7
Ebony and ivor - y live to - gether in perfect harmo - ny
B11 E F♯m7 B11 E C♯sus4 C♯
Side by side on my piano keyboard, oh Lord why don't we?

Verse 1

E C♯m B* A E
We all know that people are the same where ever you go
B*
There is good and bad in ev'ryone
Bm/D Ddim C♯ C♯/E♯
We learn to live, we learn to give
F♯m F♯m7 B11
Each other what we need to survive to - gether alive.

Chorus 2

E F♯m7 B11 E F♯m7 B11
Ebony and ivor - y live to - gether in perfect harmo - ny
E F♯m7 B11 E C♯sus4 C♯
Side by side on my piano keyboard, oh Lord, why don't we?

Bridge

| F#maj7 | G#m7 C#11 | F#maj7 | G#m7 C#11 ||

F#maj7 G#m7 C#11
Ebony, ivory living in perfect harmony

F#maj7 B11
Ebony, ivory, ooh.

Verse 2

E C#m B* A E
We all know that people are the same where ever you go

B*
There is good and bad in ev'ryone

Bm/D Ddim C# C#/E#
We learn to live, we learn to give

F#m F#m7 B11
Each other what we need to survive to - gether alive.

Chorus 3

E F#m7 B11 E F#m7 B11
Ebony and ivor - y live to - gether in perfect harmo - ny

E F#m7 B11 E C#sus4 C#
Side by side on my piano keyboard, oh Lord why don't we?

F#m7 B11
Side by side on my piano keyboard, oh Lord

E F#m7 B11 | E | F#m7 B11 |
Why don't we?——

Outro

| E | F#m7 B11 | E | F#m7 B11 |

E F#m7 B11
||: Ebony, ivory living in perfect harmony. :|| *Repeat to fade*

Every Night

Words & Music by
Paul McCartney

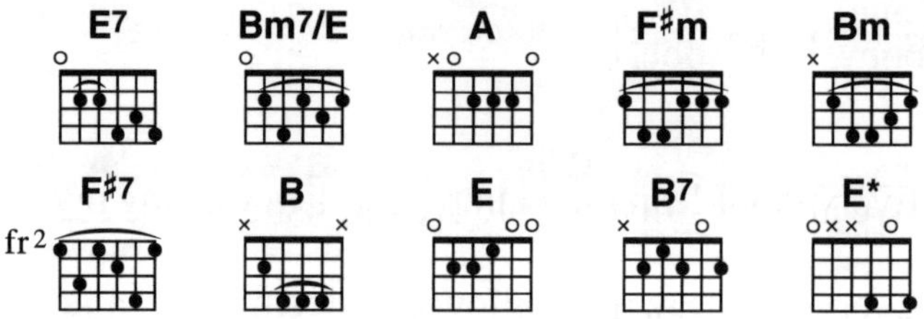

Intro | E7 | E7 | E7 | E7 ||

Verse 1

E7 Bm7/E
Every night I just wanna go out, get out of my head
E7 Bm7/E
Every day I don't want to get up, get out of my bed
A F#m Bm
Every night I want to play out
F#7 B E
And every day I want to do ooh ooh ooh ooh
(E)
But tonight I just want to stay in
F#m B
And be with you
N.C. | E* | E* |
And be with you.

```
           E           A    E            B7
Chorus 1     Ooh—— ooh, ooh—— ah na na
           E           A    E            B7
             Ooh—— ooh, ooh—— oh na na.

           | E7       | E7       |

           E7                                                    Bm7/E
Verse 2      Every day I lean on a lamp post, I'm wasting my time
           E7                                              Bm7/E
             Every day I lay on a pillow, I'm resting my mind
           A          F#m               Bm
             Every morning brings a new day
           F#7                          B                  E
             Every night that day is through ooh ooh ooh ooh
           (E)
           But tonight I just want to stay in
                       F#m   B
           And be with you
           N.C.                   | E*     | E*     |
           And be with you.

             E          A    E            B7
Chorus 2   ||: Ooh—— ooh, ooh—— ah na na (believe me mama)
                        A    E          B7
           Ooh—— ooh, ooh—— ah na na. :||  Repeat ad lib. to fade
```

Driving Rain

Words & Music by
Paul McCartney

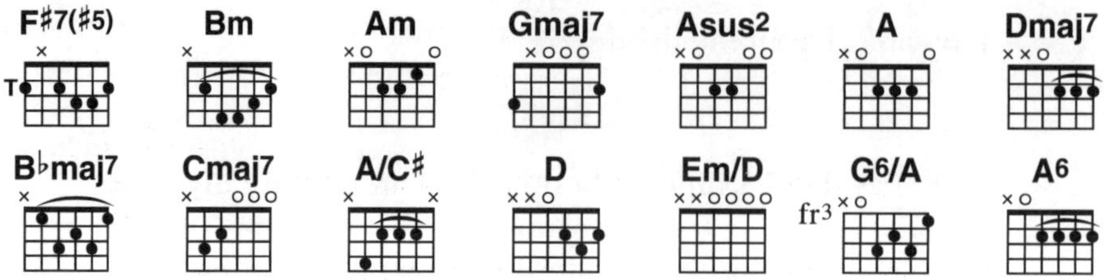


```
Intro      | N.C. (F♯7) | (F♯7)     | (F♯7)     ||

           F♯7♯5                             Bm
           One, two, three, four, five, let's go for a drive
           F♯7♯5
           Six, seven, eight, nine, ten,
           Bm                  Am          Gmaj7  Asus2  A
           Let's go there and back again,___      ooh.___

           Dmaj7                              Gmaj7
Verse 1      Something's open an' it's my heart
           Dmaj7                                 Gmaj7
             Something's missing it's when we're apart
           B♭maj7                               Cmaj7          A/C♯      D
             Something's good it's when were       back to - gether a - gain.

           Dmaj7                                  Gmaj7
Verse 2      A-nothing's wrong, it's just in - sane
           Dmaj7                        Gmaj7
             Nothing's right until your       back again
           B♭maj7                          Cmaj7
             Nothing's broken when it's        softly spoken
                A/C♯                           D
           And        walkin slowly down the lane.
```

Chorus 1

```
Em/D                          Dmaj7
Why don't we drive in the rain
Em/D                            Dmaj7
Straight throught eye of the hurricane
Em/D                    A       G6/A
Go for a ride in the driving rain.
```

Link 1

```
F#7#5                          Bm
One, two, three, four, five, let's go for a drive
F#7#5                         Bm
Six, seven, eight, nine, ten,     ooh, hoo
F#7#5                          Bm
One, two, three, four, five, let's go for a drive
F#7#5
Six, seven, eight, nine, ten
     Bm                 Am          Asus2  A
Yeah, let's go there and back again, baby,    baby.
```

Verse 3

```
Dmaj7                             Gmaj7
   You come walkin through my door
Dmaj7                         Gmaj7
   Like the one that I've been waiting for
Bbmaj7                   Cmaj7
   Letting sunshine in the darkest place when
A/C#                        D
   I've been going back there a - gain.
```

Chorus 2

Em/D Dmaj7
So why don't we drive in the rain
Em/D Dmaj7
Straight throught eye of the hurricane
Em/D Dmaj7
Why don't we drive in the rain
Em/D Dmaj7
Straight throught eye of the hurricane
Em/D A G6/A
Go for a ride in the driving rain.

Link 2

As Link 1

Bridge

A6
Ooh, the driving rain

Why do we drive in the driving rain?

Link 3

F♯7♯5 Bm
One, two, three, four, five, ooh, hoo
F♯7♯5 Bm
Six, seven, eight, nine, ten, oh let's go back again
F♯7♯5 Bm
One, two, three, four, five, let's go for a drive
F♯7♯5 Bm Am Gmaj7
A-six, seven, eight, nine, ten, yeah let's go back again———
Asus2 A
Ooh, hoo.

Outro

Dmaj7 Gmaj7
Who come walkin through my door
A6 N.C.(Gmaj7/A)
Like the one that I've been waiting for.

Famous Groupies

Words & Music by
Paul McCartney

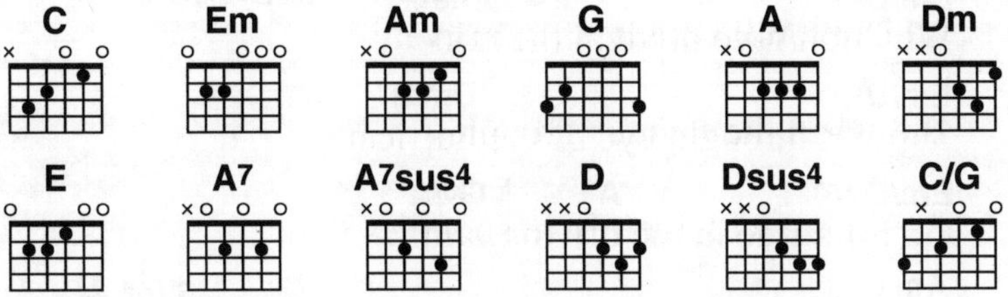

Intro

N.C.
One, two, one, two, three, four.

Chorus 1

C Em Am G
All stand back, let the people see
C Em Am G
Take a snap of the famous groupies for me.

Verse 1

A Dm
Be - hold the famous groupies

They are alike as two peas
E A7 A7sus4 A7
And where the other goes, the other goes
Am
But though the famous groupies
Bm Em
Are only paid in rupies
Am D Dsus4 D
Nobody knows what the famous groupies know
Am G
And nobody goes where the famous groupies go.

Verse 2

A Dm
There was a bongo player

Who kept an extra layer

E A7 A7sus4 A7
Of Dunlopillo mattress in his van

Am
But when the famous groupies

Bm Em
Ar - rived with their twin snoopies

Am D Dsus4 D
Nobody saw which way the poor boy ran

Am D Dsus4 D
As nobody does it like a famous groupie can.

Chorus 2

C Em Am G
We'll all stand back, let the people see

C Em Am G C/G G
Take a snap of the famous groupies for me.

Verse 3

A Dm
There was a lead guitarist

Who lived in Epping Forest

E A7 A7sus4 A7
And all he ever wanted was to blow

Am
But when the girls were with him

Bm Em
He never lost his rhythm

Am D Dsus4 D
And nobody knows what the famous groupies know

Am G
And nobody goes where the famous groupies go.

Instrumental ||: C | Em | Am | G :|| G ||

```
           A      Dm
Verse 4    There was a classic story

           Of a roadie nicknamed Rory
                                             E      A7   A7sus4 A7
           Who used to practice voodoo on the side
              Am
           But when the famous twosome
                Bm              Em
           Sug - gested something gruesome
           Am                                        D      Dsus4 D
           All that they found was a crater two miles wide
                  Am                                   D        Dsus4 D
           Which left the music business absolutely horrified.

           C        Em    Am          G
Chorus 3   All stand back, let the people see
           C      Em        Am
           Take a snap of the famous groupies (the famous groupies)

           The famous groupies ( the famous groupies)

           Ladies and gentlemen, those magnificent examples of

           Female pulchritude and luminosity, direct from their

           Global perambulations to the very boards of this

           Supremely magnificent proscenium arch - ladies and
                                Am           G
           Gentlemen; I give you famous group - ies!
```

Figure Of Eight

Words & Music by
Paul McCartney

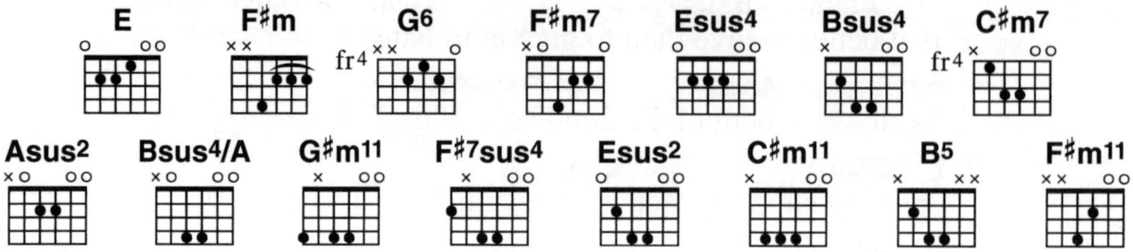

Intro ‖: E F#m E F#m | G6 F#m7 :‖

Verse 1

E   Esus4 E
Well, you've got me dancing in a figure of eight
                                                                    Esus4 E
Don't know if I'm coming or going, I'm early or late
Bsus4   C#m7
Round and round the ring I go
Asus2   Bsus4
   I wanna know, I wanna know, hey.

Verse 2

E   Esus4   E
   Why can't we travel a continuous line?
                                               Esus4 E
Make love reliable convenant all the time
Bsus4   C#m7
Up and down the hills I go
Asus2   Bsus4
   I got to know, I got to know.

Chorus 1

Asus2 Bsus4/A
Is it better to love one another
G♯m11 C♯m11
Than to go go for a walk in the dark?
Asus2 Bsus4/A G♯m11 F♯7sus4 Esus2
Is it better to love than to give in to hate?
Asus2 Bsus4/A
Yeah, we'd better take good care of each other
G♯m11 C♯m11
A - void slipping back off the straight and narrow
Asus2 B5 N.C.
It's better by far than getting stuck in a figure of eight.

Link

𝄆 E F♯m E F♯m | G6 F♯m7 𝄇

Middle 8

Bsus4 Asus2
Well, figure it out for your - self little girl
Esus4
It don't go nowhere at all
Bsus4 F♯m11 Bsus4 F♯m11 Bsus4
It's nothing more than a tape loop in a big dance hall.

Verse 3

E Esus4 E
Well, you got me running in a figure of eight
Esus4 E
Don't know if I'm coming or going, early or late (early or late)
Bsus4 C♯m7
Round and round I go
Asus2 Bsus4
I wanna know, I wanna know.

Chorus 2

Asus2 Bsus4/A
Say, is it better to love one another
G♯m11 C♯m11
Than to go go for a walk in the dark?
Asus2 Bsus4/A G♯m11 F♯7sus4 Esus2
Is it better to love than to give in to hate?
Asus2 Bsus4/A
Yeah, we'd better take good care of one another
G♯m11 C♯m11
A - void slipping back off the straight and narrow
Asus2 B5 N.C.
It's better by far than getting stuck in a figure of eight.

Outro

𝄆 E F♯m E F♯m | G6 F♯m7 𝄇 *Repeat to fade*

Flaming Pie

Words & Music by
Paul McCartney

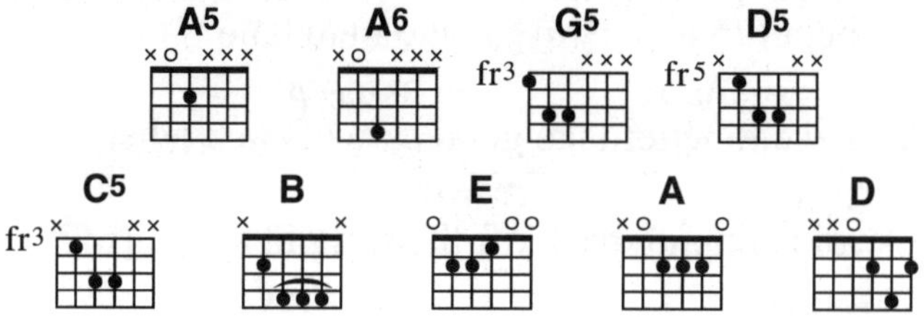

A5 riff

Intro | A5 A6 A5 A6 | A5 A6 A5 N.C. ||

Verse 1
A5 riff
Makin' love underneath the bed

Shooting stars from a purple sky
G5 D5 C5
I don't care how I do it
A5 riff
I'm the man on the flaming pie.

Verse 2
A5 riff
Stick my tongue out and lick my nose

Tuck my shirt in and zip my fly
G5 D5 C5
Go ahead, have a vi - sion
A5 riff
I'm the man on the flaming pie.

Bridge 1

```
                    B
Bridge 1            Everything I do has a simple explanation
                    E
                       When I'm with you, you could do with a vacation
                    A
                       I took my brains out and stretched 'em on the rack
                              D                         E                  | D  | E  N.C. ||
                    Now I'm not so sure I'm ever gonna get 'em back.

Link                | A5    | A5    | A5    | A5    ||

                    A5 riff
Verse 3                Cut my toes off to spite my feet

                    I don't know whether to laugh or cry
                    G5            D5               C5
                    Never mind, check my rhy - thm
                    A5                                  | G5  | D5  C5 |
                    I'm the man on the flaming pie
                    A5 riff
                    I'm the man on the flaming pie.

                          B
Bridge 2            Now everything I do has a simple explanation
                    E
                       When I'm with you, you could do with a vacation
                    A
                       I took my brains out and stretched 'em on the rack
                              D                            A5              | D  | E  N.C. ||
                    Now I'm not too sure I'm ever gonna get 'em back.            Ow!

Outro               ||: A5    | A5    | A5    | A5    :||  Repeat to fade
```

Flying To My Home

Words & Music by
Paul McCartney

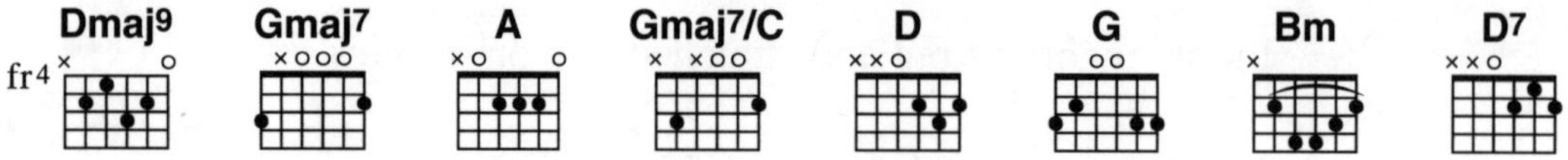

Intro

Dmaj9 Gmaj7
Flying to my home, home——

A Gmaj7 Gmaj7/C D
Flying to my home,——— home, home, home.

| D A | G | D A | G ||

Verse 1

D A G D
The sun is fading in the west

(D) A G
Out where the cattle roam

D A G D
I'm like a bird at the end of the day

Bm
Flying to my home

A G A
I'm flying to my home sweet majes - ty

D
I'm flying to my home.

Verse 2

D A G D
The sky is like a painted flag

(D) A G
Above a sea of chrome

D A G D
I've got a woman living in my life

Bm
Living in my home

A G A
I'm flying to my home sweet majes - ty

D D7
I'm flying to my home.

Bridge 1

```
G
   I haven't been back for so long
                    D
I don't know if I'm going to recognise it
G
   They gave the old place a new face
                        A
And I'm going to take some time

To size the situation up.
```

Solo

```
| D  A | G  D | D  A | G      |
| D  A | G  D | D    | Bm     |
| A    | G    | A    | D      | D7    ||
```

Bridge 2

As Bridge 1

Verse 3

```
D            A      G      D
The sun is fading in the west
(D)                  A     G
   Out where the cattle roam
D            A              G      D
   I've got a woman living in my life
                 Bm
Living in my home
A                    G                        A
   I'm flying to my home sweet majes - ty
                       D
I'm flying to my home.
```

Outro

```
                       Bm                     A
I'm flying to my home, (I'm flying to my home)
                       G                      D
I'm flying to my home, (I'm flying to my home)
                       Bm                     A
I'm flying to my home, (I'm flying to my home)
                       G                  A
I'm flying to my home sweet majes - ty
                       D
I'm flying to my home
   (D)
||: I'm flying to my home, I'm flying to my home. :||   Repeat to fade
```

Footprints

Words & Music by
Paul McCartney & Eric Stewart

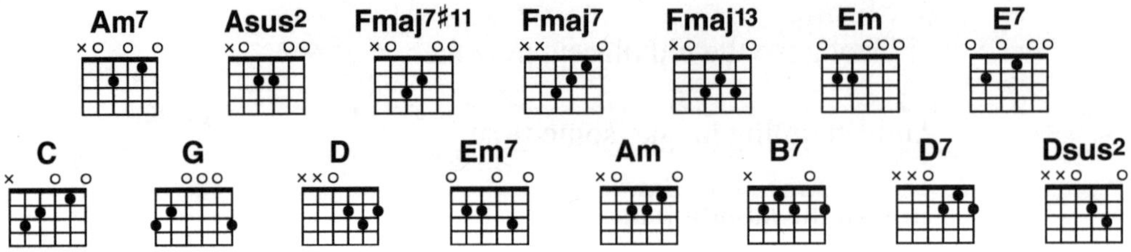

Intro | Am7 | Asus2 | Fmaj7♯11 Fmaj7 | Fmaj13 |
| Em | E7 | C G | D ||

Verse 1
Am7 Asus2
It's beautiful out - side
Fmaj7♯11 Fmaj7 Fmaj13
An old hand gathers wood——
Em Em7
Can he see me sitting here?
C G D
His mind is somewhere else.

Verse 2
C G Am7 Asus2
His friends have flown away
Fmaj7♯11 Fmaj7 Fmaj13
He's left out in the cold——
Em Em7
He won't sit by my fire
C G D
He says he likes it in the snow
Am Em C
Where footprints never go
D Am D
He likes it in the snow.

Verse 3

Am7 Asus2
It's getting dark outside
Fmaj7♯11 Fmaj7 Fmaj13
The old hand's going home
Em Em7
Has he someone waiting there
C G D
Or is he living on his own?
Am Em C
Where footprints never go
D Am D
He likes it in the snow.——

Chorus 1

C Dsus2 Em Am7 Em
Oh, white blanket, hiding the traces of tears she didn't see
C Dsus2 Em
Oh, white blanket covers the memory
Am7 Em
Of all that used to be
Am7 Em
All that used to be.

Bridge 1

B7 Em Am D7
But his heart keeps aching in the same old way
B7 Em Am D7 Am7
He can't help feeling that she might come back some - day.

Link

| (Am7) | Asus2 | Fmaj7♯11 Fmaj7 | Fmaj13 |
| Em | E7 | C G | D ‖

Verse 4

```
                  Am7    Asus2
It's beautiful out - side
   Fmaj7♯11                 Fmaj7  Fmaj13
A magpie looks for food.
    Em                        Em7
The old hand throws a crumb
       C          G       D
Do you think he's found a friend?
         Am          Em    C
Where footprints never go
   D       Am    D
He likes it in the snow.___
```

Chorus 2

```
C           Dsus2    Em                     Am7             Em
Oh, white blanket, hiding the traces of paths he didn't take
C           Dsus2   Em
Oh, white blanket covers the memory
   Am7                  Em
Of moves he didn't make___ (you go now)
C           Dsus2    Em                     Am              Em
Oh, white blanket, hiding the traces of tears she didn't see
C              Dsus2           Em
Snow white blanket simply covers the memory
   Am            Em
Of all that used to be.
```

Bridge 2

```
        B7           Em               Am        D7
But his heart keeps aching in the same old way
   B7          Em              Am            D7             Am7
He can't help feeling that she might come back some - day.
```

Outro

```
| (Am7)  | Asus2  | Fmaj7♯11   Fmaj7 | Fmaj13 |
| Em     | E7     | C  G | D          ||
```

From A Lover To A Friend

Words & Music by
Paul McCartney

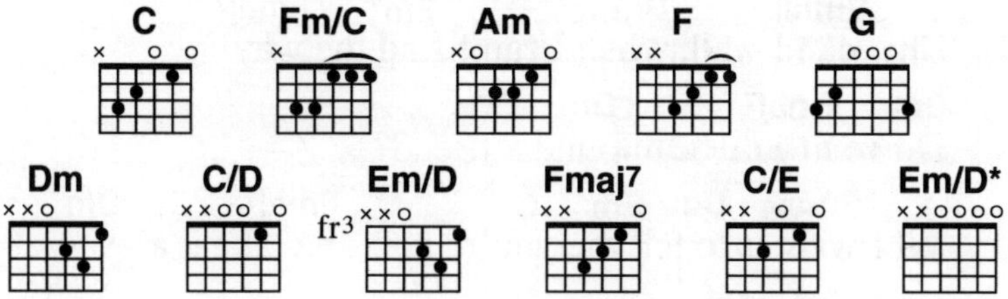

Intro
N.C.
La la la la la la...

Verse 1
C Fm/C
And when the time comes round
C Fm/C
We will be duty bound
C Fm/C C Fm/C
To tell the truth of what we've seen.——

Verse 2
C Fm/C
And what we haven't found
C Fm/C
Will not be going down
C Fm/C Am
Despite too easy ride to see. ——

Chorus 1
F C
From a lover to a friend
G
Take your own ad - vice
Dm
Let me love a - gain
F C
Now that you turned out to be
G
Someone I can trust
Dm
Someone I be - lieve.

Bridge 1

C/D Dm Em/D Dm Fmaj7 Dm
Ooh———

Dm Fmaj7 Dm
La la la la la la la

Fmaj7 Dm Fmaj7
How can I walk when I can't find the way

Dm Fmaj7 Dm
I'm in a dilemma

Fmaj7 Dm Fmaj7 Dm
All I want is to tell me you're gon - na take it a - way

Chorus 2

F C
From a lover to a friend

G
Take your own ad - vice

Dm
Let me love a - gain

F C
Now that you turned out to be

G
Someone I can trust

Dm
Someone I be - lieve.

Verse 3

C Fm/C
And what we haven't found

C Fm/C
Will not be going down

C Fm/C F C/E Am
Despite too easy ride to see.

```
            F                C
Chorus 3       From a lover to a friend
                             G
            You turned out to be
                           Dm    C/D  Dm
            Someone I be - lieve
            F                C
               From a lover to a friend
                                G
            Take your own ad - vice
                           Dm
            Let me love a - gain.

               C/D  Dm        C/D
Outro       Ooh——— la la la la la la la
            Dm          C/D
            La la la la la la la la.
            Dm              C/D              Dm                    C/D
               How can I walk when I can't find the way——
            Dm                 C/D
               I'm in a dil - emma
            Dm                C/D              Dm                          C/D      Dm  C/D
                All I want - ed is to tell me you're gonna take it away——
            Dm          C/D           Dm    C/D
               From a lover to a friend
            Dm          C/D           Dm    C/D
               From a lover to a friend
            Dm          C/D           Dm    C/D
               From a lover to a friend
            Dm   Em/D*
                 Let me love again.
```

Freedom

Words & Music by
Paul McCartney

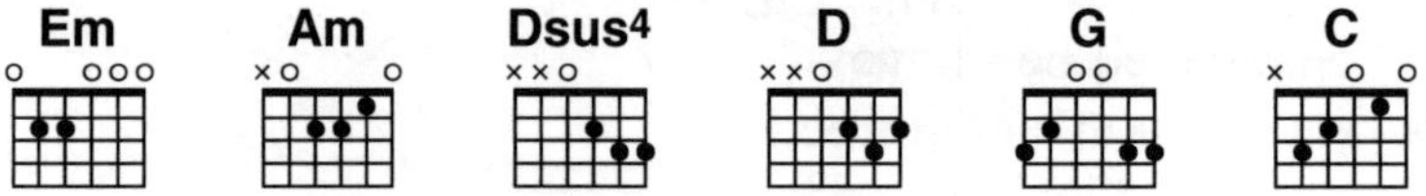

Verse 1

Em Am
This is my right, a right given by God
Dsus4 D G
To live a free__ life, to live in free - dom.

Chorus 1

(G)
We talkin' about freedom
Em
I'm talkin' about freedom
C D
I will fight for the right
G
To live in free - dom.

Verse 2

Em Am
Any - one, who tries to take it a - way
Dsus4 D G
Will have to ans - wer 'cause this is my right.

Chorus 2

(G)
We talkin' about freedom
Em
I'm talkin' about freedom
C D
I will fight for the right
G
To live in free - dom, yeah, oh.

Solo 1

| Em | Em | Am | Am |

| Dsus4 D | D | D G ||

Chorus 3

```
                  (G)
We're talkin' about freedom
                 Em
I'm talkin' about freedom
       C           D
I will fight for the right
                 G
To live in free - dom.
```

Chorus 4

```
                           (G)
Everybody talkin' about freedom
                  Em
We're talkin' bout freedom
        C           D
We will fight for the right
                 G
To live in free - dom.
```

Solo 2

| (G) | G | Em | Em | C |

| C | D | D | G ||

Chorus 5 As Chorus 3

Chorus 6

```
                 (G)
I'm talkin; about freedom
                  Em
We're talkin' about freedom
        C           D
We will fight for the right
                 G      C   G
To live in free - dom.
```

Get It

Words & Music by
Paul McCartney

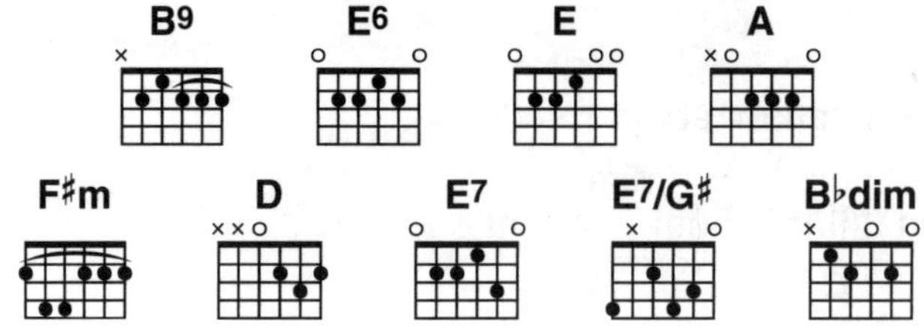

Intro ‖: B9 | B9 | E6 | E6 :‖

Chorus 1

                    B9
You've got to get it, mm mm

You've got to get it don't forget
          E6
It doesn't come around again
                    B9
You've got to get it, mm mm
                                                E   E6
You've got to get it and you've got to get it good.

Verse 1

A   B9
Once I had a little Spanish guitar
E6   F♯m
  The neighbours told me I could go pretty far
D   A
  Well I came and I went
B9   E   E6
  And my guitar got bent.

```
            A                                          B9
Verse 2        But I discovered that the people who love
            E6                                        F#m           D
               Are what we need if we're to get up above it all
                               A
            And that's that
            B9                                   E          E6 (E7)
               Unless the world is flat.

                       B9
Chorus 2    I wanna get it, mm mm

            I wanna get it just in case
                        E6
            It doesn't come around again
                       B9
            I wanna get it, mm mm
                                                        E6
            I wanna get it and I wanna get it good.

Link 1      | B9       | B9       | B9       | E6       |

            | B9       | B9       | B9       | E    E6  ||

            A                                      B9
Verse 3        Pardon me if I've been misunderstood
            E6                                     F#m
               I wanna get it while the going is good
            D                      A
               The telephone rang
            B9                     E      E6
               About a song I sang.
```

```
                A                          B9
Verse 4           The life of Cadillac and Ultra for sure
                E6                       F♯m
                  Is automatic for the Lady Demure
                D                   A
                  She came and she went
                B9                E      E6 (E7)
                  Without a single dent.


Chorus 3        As Chorus 1


Link 2          ‖: B9    | B9    | B9    | E6    :‖


                            B9
Chorus 4        Come on, let's get it, mm mm

                You've got to get it don't forget
                        E6
                It doesn't come around again
                           B9
                You've got to get it, mm mm

                You've got to get it and you've got to
                      E6   E7/G♯ | A  B♭dim | E N.C. | B9  E(fermata) ‖
                Get it good.
```

Get On The Right Thing

Words & Music by
Paul McCartney & Linda McCartney

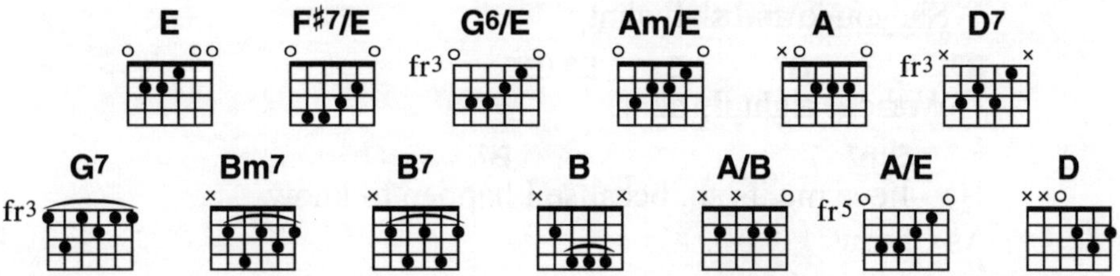

Intro | E | F♯7/E | G6/E | F♯7/E |
| Am/E | E | E | E |
| F♯7/E | G6/E | F♯7/E Am/E | E | E ||

Verse 1
(E) F♯7/E
All at once you get love on your mind
G6/E A
And your world is as kind as a penny.

Pre-chorus 1
D7 G7 D7 G7
Oh—— and you knew it all along, you did the right thing
Bm7 B7
Be - lieve me its true and it can happen to you.

Verse 2
E F♯7/E
All at once you get sound in your ears
G6/E A
And your cloud disappears into yellow.

Pre-chorus 2

```
D7
   Well, you know they were were wrong
             G7
Get on the right thing
                      D7
Well, you knew it all along
             G7
Get on the right thing
     Bm7                            B7
Be - lieve me its so, because I happen to know.
```

Chorus 1

```
E                                   A
   Try a little love, you can't go wrong

Get on the right thing

Get on the right thing
E
Get on the right thing
                                     A
Well, my little love you can't go wrong

Get on the right thing

Get on the right thing
E
   Get on the right thing
B     A/B                          E
Do,—— get on the right thing you.
```

Link

```
| (E)     | F#7/E   | G6/E    | A/E     |

| D       | D7      | E       | N.C.(E) ||
```

Verse 3

```
E                         F#7/E
   All at once we see things in our skies
                 G6/E                  A
And we both         realise it together.
```

```
                   D7
Pre-chorus 3  Well, you know they were wrong
                    G7
              Get on the right thing
                             D7
              Yes, you knew it all along
                    G7
              Get on the right thing
                     Bm7
              Well, be - lieve me it's so, (it's so babe)
                     B7
              Because I happen to know.

              E               A
Chorus 2        You can't go wrong

              Get on the right thing

              Get on the right thing
              E
              Get on the right thing
              (E)                                A
              Well, try a little love, it can't go wrong

              Get on the right thing

              Get on the right thing
              E
                Get on the right thing
              B     A/B                          E
              Do,—— get on the right thing you.

Link 2        | (E)      | F#7/E    | G6/E     | A/E      |

              | D        | D7       | E        | N.C.(E)  ||

                 E                                     A
Outro         ||:  Well, try a little love, it can't go wrong

              Get on the right thing

              Get on the right thing
              E
                Get on the right thing. :||  Repeat ad lib. to fade
```

Get Out Of My Way

Words & Music by
Paul McCartney

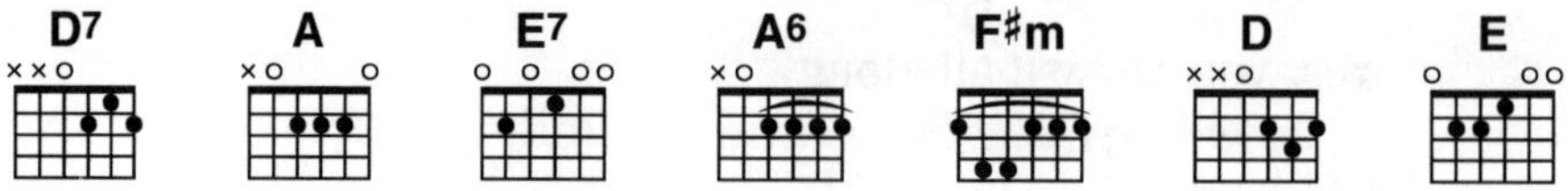

Intro | D7 | A | E7 | E7 ||

Verse 1

```
A
Crash bang wallop I'm a lover again
                D7
I've got my eyes on the road and I'm feeling no pain
                E7                                            A6
I've found a real fine woman, I'm heading to see her.
```

Verse 2

```
A
Bye bye melancholy listen to me
             D7
We had a long long ride but it isn't to be
                E7                                            A6
I've found a real fine woman, I'm heading to see her now.
```

Chorus 1

```
             F#m D                   A   E
Get out of my   way, get out of my life
                F#m          D                  A
I don't need anybody to tell me how to be right
                    F#m  D                 A     E
Ah, don't try to stop  me, I've got the ans - wer
                 F#m           D                   A
I won't need anybody ex - cept my woman to - night.
```

Solo

```
|: D7  | D7  | A  | A  |
 1, 2.                      3.
| E7  | E7  | A  | A  :|| E7  | D7  |
```

Verse 3

```
   A
    I can't help it if I'm starting to smile
            D7
I've got a full gas tank and it's only a mile
            E7                                        A6
'Til I'll be with my little woman, I'm ready to see her.
```

Verse 4

```
          A
So I say bye bye melancholy listen to me
            D7
We had a long long ride but it isn't to be
              E7                                       A
I've found a real fine woman, I'm heading to see her now.
```

Chorus 2 As Chorus 1

Chorus 3

```
                        F#m D                    A E
Yeah, get out of my   way, baby get out of my life
                          F#m             D                A
Yeah, I won't need anybody ex - cept my woman to - night

Tonight, yeah, yeah...
```

Outro

```
|: D7       | D7           | A        | A      |
    Yeah,          yeah, yeah,   yeah,
| E7      | E7      | A       | A       |

| D7      | D7      | A       | A       |

| E7      | D7   A || N.C.    | N.C.   :||
```

Getting Closer

Words & Music by
Paul McCartney

```
             A                    E    D    F♯               Bm      E (A)
*Verse 1*      Say you don't love him,—— my sala - mander
             A                 E    D
               Why do you need him?
             F♯                Bm      E     A
               Oh no, don't answer, oh no.

                              Bm/A
*Chorus 1*   I'm getting closer
                              Dm/A          A
             I'm getting closer to your heart.

             A                          E
*Bridge 1*   Keeping ahead of the rain on the road
             A                              E
             Watching my windscreen wipers
             A                    E
             Radio play me a danceable ode
             A                    E       | D    | D     E
             Cattle beware of snipers.

             A                    E   D    F♯            Bm        E (A)
*Verse 2*      When will you see me,—— my sala - mander?
             A                       E   D
               Now don't try to tell me
             F♯                Bm      E     A
               Oh no, don't answer, oh no.
```

Chorus 2

```
               Bm/A
I'm getting closer
               Dm/A        A
I'm getting closer to your heart.
```

Bridge 2

```
A                     E
Hitting the chisel and making a joint
A                       E
Glueing my fingers to - gether
A                 E
Radio play me a song with a point
A                 E   | D | D   E |
Sailor beware of weather.
```

Verse 3

```
A            E    D   F♯           Bm       E (A)
  I'm getting clo - ser,___ my sala - mander
A                     E D
  Well when will we be there?
F♯             Bm     E    A
  Ah no, don't answer, oh no.
```

Chorus 3

```
               Bm/A
I'm getting closer
               Dm/A        A
I'm getting closer to your heart
               Dm/A        A
I'm getting closer to your heart
               Dm/A        A
I'm getting closer to your heart.
```

Outro

```
||: Dm             | Dm    | A              | A     :||  Repeat to fade
  Closer, closer,            closer, closer.
```

Girl's School

Words & Music by
Paul McCartney

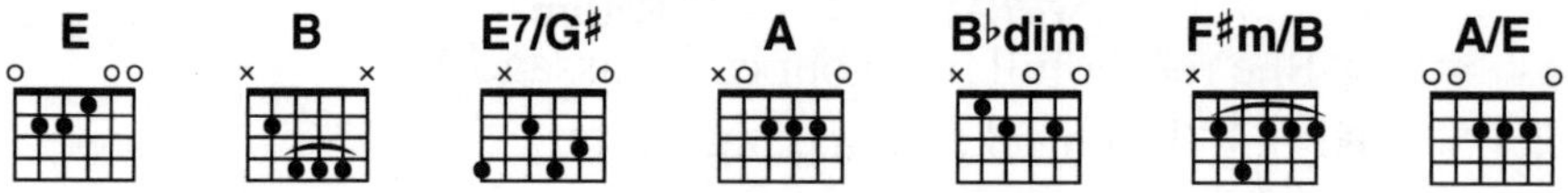

Intro | 𝄆 E | E | E | E 𝄇

Verse 1

E
Sleepy head, kid sister
B
Is lying on the floor
E E7/G♯ A B♭dim
Eighteen years and younger, boy
B
Well she knows what she's waiting for.

Link 1 | E | E | E | E ‖

Verse 2

E
Well, Yuki's a cool school mistress
B
She's an oriental princess
E E7/G♯ A B♭dim
Well, she shows films in the classroom, boy
B
They put the paper on the windows.

Chorus 1

F♯m/B | E A/E E | E A/E E |
Ah,— what can the sisters do
F♯m/B | E A/E E | E A/E E | E A/E E | E A/E E ‖
Ah,— girls' school. Ow!

Link 2 | 𝄆 E | E | E | E 𝄇

Verse 3

E
The head nurse is Sister Scala
B
Now she's a Spanish doll
E E7/G♯ A B♭dim
She runs a full body out call massage
B
Parlour from the teacher's hall.

Chorus 2

F♯m/B | E A/E E | E A/E E |
Ah,— what can the sister do
F♯m/B | E A/E E | E A/E E | E A/E E | E A/E E ‖
Ah,— girls' school.

Link 3

‖: E | E | E | E :‖

Verse 4

E
Well now, Roxanne's the woman trainer
B
She puts the kids to bed, bad move
E E7/G♯ A B♭dim
She gives them pills in a paper cup
B
And she knocks them on the head, yeah.

Chorus 3

‖: F♯m/B | E A/E E | E A/E E |
Ah,— what can a sister do
F♯m/B | E A/E E | E A/E E :‖
Ah,— girls' school.

Instr.

| E | E | E | B | B ‖

Verse 5

E E7/G♯ A B♭dim
She shows her films in the classroom, boy
B
They put the paper on the windows, yeah.

Chorus 4

As Chorus 3 *(with repeats)*

Outro

‖: E | E | E | E :‖ *Repeat to fade*

Give Ireland Back To The Irish

Words & Music by
Paul McCartney

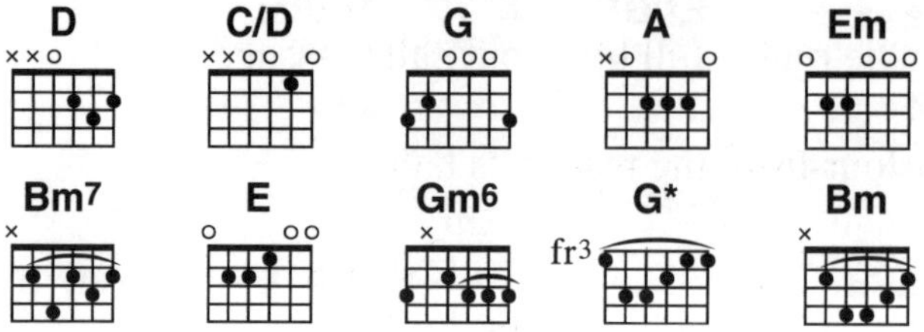

Intro | D | C/D ||

Chorus 1
D G
Give Ireland back to the Irish
D A
Don't make them have to take it a - way
D G
Give Ireland back to the Irish
D A D
Make Ireland Irish today.___

Verse 1
D Em
Great Britian you are tre - mendous
G D
And nobody knows like me
D Em
But really what are you doin'
G D
In the land across the sea.

Pre-chorus 1
Bm7 E
Tell me how would you like it
Gm6 D
If on your way to work
Bm7 E
You were stopped by Irish soliders?
G*
Would you lie down do nothing
A
Would you give in, or go ber - serk?

Chorus 2 As Chorus 1

Solo

| D | G | D | A |
| D | G | D A | D ||

Verse 2

```
     D                  Em
Great Britain and all the people
          G                D
Say that people must be free___
              D            Em
And mean - while back in Ireland
          G                      D
There's a man who looks like me.___
```

Pre-chorus 2

```
           Bm7                 E
And he dreams of God and Country
            Gm6         D
And he's feeling really bad
Bm7                  E
And he's sitting in a prison
              G*
Should he lie down, do nothing
                          A
Should he give in or go mad.___
```

Chorus 3 As Chorus 1

Chorus 4 As Chorus 1

Outro

| Bm | G* | Bm | G* | D (fermata) ||

Girlfriend

Words & Music by
Paul McCartney

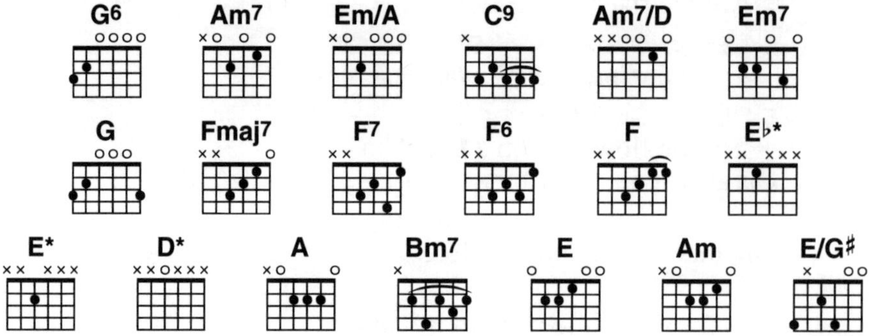

Intro | G6 | G6 | Am7 | Am7 Em/A | C9 ||

Verse 1

```
G6                              Am7       Am7/D
Girlfriend, I'm gonna tell your boyfriend, yeah
G6                            Am7   Am7/D
Tell him exactly what you're doin', yeah
G                        Em7
Tell him what you do to me
        Am7                    Fmaj7  | F7  F6  F |
Late at night when the wind is free
G6
Girlfriend.
```

| E♭* E* G6 | D7 E* G6 | E♭* E* G6 | D* E* G6 ||

Verse 2

```
G6                         Am7      Am7/D
Girlfriend, I'm show your boyfriend, yeah
G6                              Am7    Am7/D
Show him the letters I've been saving, yeah
G                           Em7
Show him how you feel in - side
          Am7                 Fmaj7      | F7  F6  F |
Then our love couldn't be de - nied, oh no
           Em7
And we're gonna have to tell him
       Am7                 C N.C. G6
You'll only be a girlfriend       of mine.
```

Link 1 |: G6 | Am7 :| G6 |

Do do do do, do do do do, do do do do. Do do do do.

Bridge

```
E♭* E*      G6   D* E*  G6
  Till the river stop a-flowin'
E♭* E*      G6          D*     E* G6
  Till the wind doesn't wan - na blow
E♭* E*      G6         D* E*   G6
  Till the flowers stop a - growin'
E♭* E*      G6             D*    E* G6
  Till my love doesn't wan - na know.
```

Link 2/Instr.

```
| A       | A       | Bm7  E || Am     |
| E/G♯    | Fmaj7   | N.C.(Fmaj7) | Am |
| E/G♯    | Am  Em7 | Fmaj7  | F7      |
```

```
      Em7
We're gonna have to tell him
      Am7                 C N.C. G6
You'll only be a girlfriend      of mine.
```

Verse 3

```
G6                                   Am7      Am7/D
Girlfriend we'd better tell your boyfriend, yeah
G6                                 Am7   Am7/D
Tell him exactly what we're doing, yeah
G                                Em7
Tell him what he needs to know
        Am7                  Fmaj7    | F7   F6  F |
Or he may never let you go
             Em7
Yes, we're gonna have to tell him
        Am7                      C N.C.  G6
You'll only be a girlfriend        of mine.
```

Outro

```
|: G6               | Am7                        :|
      Do do do do,   do do do do, do do do do.     Play 5 times
(Am7)       G6
Till the river    stops a-flowin'
Am7                        G6
   Till the wind doesn't wanna blow
Am7                G6
   Till the flowers stop a-growin'
Am7                  G6
   Till the ocean's a sea of snow,
                 Am7
(Sea of snow, sea of snow, sea of snow...)
                    |1 - 5.
|: G6               | Am7                        :|
      Do do do do,   do do do do, do do do do.
|6.
| Am7     | Am7   Em/A  | C9        |
                            Ah.
G6          G
Girlfriend.
```

Good Times Coming/ Feel The Sun

Words & Music by
Paul McCartney

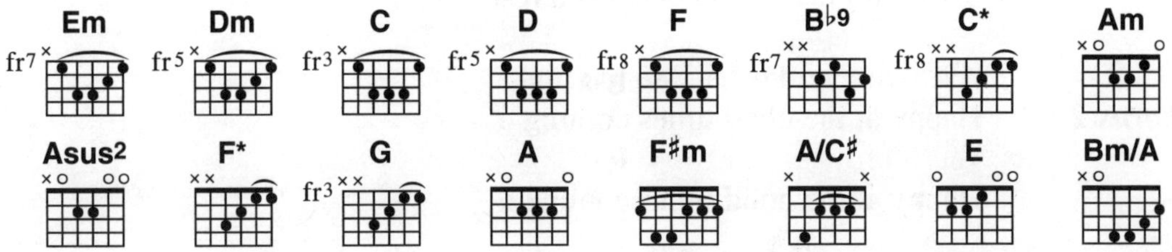

Intro
N.C.(B♭9)
𝄆 Good times coming,
(C)
Good times coming in. 𝄇 *Play 4 times*

Verse 1
Em Dm C D
I was thinking about that summer, so long a - go
Em Dm C D
Pack up your bags and yell "Ge - ronimo"
Em F Em F
That was a golden summer, wasn't it hot?
Em F
We laughed a lot that summer, laughed a lot.

Chorus 1
B♭9
Laughing at the good times coming
C*
Laughing at the good times coming in
B♭9
Good times coming
C*
Laughing at the good times coming in.

Verse 2

```
Em                          Dm                    C          D
There was something a - bout the weather,     what can I say?
Em               Dm        C        D
Nothing like any other holiday
Em            F            Em            F
That was a silly season,     was it the best?
Em           F
We didn't need a reason, just a rest.
```

Chorus 2

```
                            B♭9
Happy at the good times coming
                            C*
Happy at the good times coming in
                B♭9
Good times coming
                            C*
Happy at the good times coming in.
```

Link 1

```
| Am    | Am    | Am    | Am    |
| Asus  | F*    | F*    | F*    |
| F*    | G     ||
```

Bridge 1

```
Em                 Dm                    C                    D
I'm loving you,     I'm loving you,     I'm loving you now
Em                 Dm                    C                    D
I'm loving you,     I'm loving you,     I'm loving you now.
```

Verse 3

```
|: Em   | Dm   | C    | D    :|

Em  F                              Em        F
     There was a golden sum - mer be - fore the war
Em                    F
   They laughed a lot that summer, lah de dah.
```

Chorus 3

                         B♭9
Laughing at the good times coming
                         C*
Laughing at the good times coming in
             B♭9
Good times coming
                         C*
Laughing at the good times coming in
               B♭9
||: Good times coming, good, good
             C
Good times coming in, good, good :||
             B♭9
Good times coming
             A
Good times coming in.

Chorus 4

           F♯m   D   A/C♯   E
Feel the sun shine in, shine in, shine in
           F♯m   D   A   E
Feel the sun shining in on you
           F♯m   D   A/C♯   E
Feel the sun shine in, shine in, shine in
           F♯m   D   A
Feel the sun shining in on you.

Bridge 2

A   Bm/A
  All the beauty,   all the pain
A   Bm/A
  Will it ever be the same again?
D   A   D   A
  If you love me,   show me now
D   A   F♯m
  It's the only way that we know how.

Outro

               F♯m   D   A/C♯   E
||: Feel the sun shine in, shine in, shine in
           F♯m   D   A   E
Feel the sun shining in on you
           F♯m   D   A/C♯   E
Feel the shine in, shine in, shine in
           F♯m   D   A
Feel the sun shining in on you. :|| *Repeat to fade*

Golden Earth Girl

Words & Music by
Paul McCartney

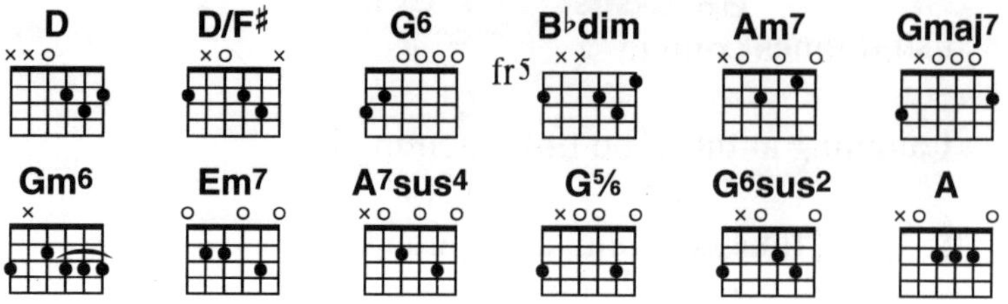

Intro

| D D/F♯ | G6 B♭dim | B♭dim | Am7 |
| G6 Gmaj7 | Gm6 | D/F♯ | Em7 A7sus4 ||

Verse 1

D D/F♯ G6 B♭dim
Golden earth girl, female animal
Am7 G6 Gmaj7 Gm6
Sings to the wind, resting at sunset, ooh
D/F♯
In a mossy nest
Em7 A7sus4
Sensing moonlight in the air
D
(Moonlight in the air).

Verse 1

D D/F♯ G6 B♭dim
Good clear water friend of wilderness
Am7 G6 Gmaj7 Gm6
Sees in the pool her own re - flection, ooh
D/F♯
In another world
Em7 A7sus4
Someone over there is counting.

Chorus 1

G5/6 G6sus2 G5/6 G6sus2
Fish in a sunbeam

G5/6 A
In eggshell seas

G5/6 G6sus2 G5/6 G6sus2
Fish in a sunbeam.

G5/6 A
Eggshell fi - nish.

Verse 3

D D/F♯ G6 B♭dim
Nature's lover climbs the primrose hill

Am7 G6 Gmaj7 Gm6
Smiles at the sky watching the sunset, ooh

D/F♯
From a mossy nest

Em7 A7sus4
As she falls a - sleep she's counting ...

Chorus 2

G5/6 G6sus2 G5/6 G6sus2
Fish in a sunbeam

G5/6 A
In eggshell seas

G5/6 G6sus2 G5/6 G6su2s
Fish in a sunbeam

G5/6 A
Eggshell fi - nish.

Instrumental

| D D/F♯ | G6 B♭dim | B♭dim | Am7 |

| G6 Gmaj7 | Gm6 | D/F♯ |

Em7 A7sus4
As she falls a - sleep she's counting...

Chorus 3 As Chorus 2

Great Day

Words & Music by
Paul McCartney

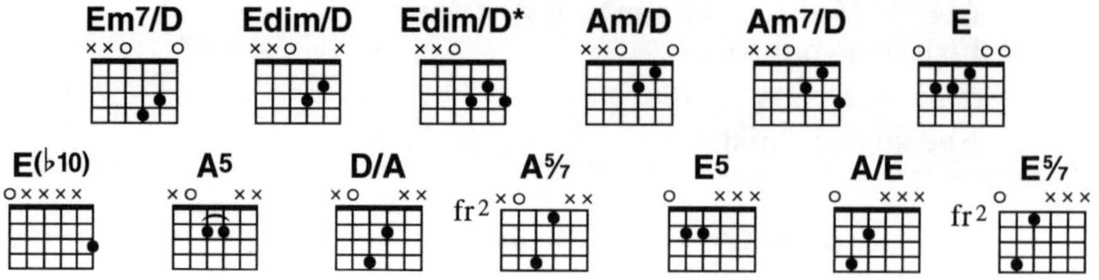

Intro | Em7/D | Em7/D | Edim/D | Edim/D* Edim/D |
| Am/D Am7/D | Am/D | E | E ||

Verse 1
Em7/D
When you're wide awake
Edim/D
Say it for goodness sake
Am/D E
It's gonna be a great day
Em7/D
While you're standing there
Edim/D
Get up and grab a chair
Am/D E E(♭10)
It's gonna be a great day.

Chorus 1
A5 D/A A5/7 D/A
And it won't be long, oh no it won't be long
E5 A/E E5/7 A/E
It won't be long, no no it won't be long
E5 A5 D/A A5/7 D/A
It won't be long, oh no it won't be long
Em7/D
It won't be long.

Link 1

| (Em7/D) | Em7/D | Edim/D | Edim/D |
(long.)
| Am/D | Am7/D Am/D | E | E |

| Em7/D | Em7/D | Edim/D | Edim/D |
Ooh,—— ooh,—— oh, yeah
| Am/D | Am/D | E E(♭10) | E(♭10) ||
Gonna be a great day.

Chorus 2 As Chorus 1

Link 1

| (Em7/D) | Em7/D | Edim/D | Edim/D |
(long.)—— ooh,—— ooh,——
| Am/D | Am/D | E | E ||
—— Ah, yeah.——

Verse 3

Em7/D
When you're wide awake
Edim/D
Say it for goodness sake
Am/D E
It's gonna be a great day
Em7/D
While you're standing there
Edim/D
Get up and grab a chair
Am/D E E(♭10)
It's gonna be a great day.

Goodnight Tonight

Words & Music by
Paul McCartney

Em C Emaj7 C♯m9 F♯m7 B7♭9 Em7 A6

Intro | Em | C | Em | C ||

|: N.C.(Em7) | (Em7) (A7) :| *Play 4 times*

|: Emaj7 C♯m9 | F♯m7 B7♭9 :|
Ooh,___ ooh.___

Verse 1

Emaj7 C♯m9 F♯m7 B7♭9
Don't get too tired for love
Emaj7 C♯m9 F♯m7 B7♭9
Don't let it end. ooh___
Emaj7 C♯m9 F♯m7 B7♭9
Don't say good - night to love
Em7 B7♭9 Emaj7
It may never be the same a - gain.

Chorus 1

Emaj7
Don't say it!
C♯m9
Don't say it!
F♯m7 B7♭9 Emaj7
Say anything but don't say goodnight to - night

Don't say it!
C♯m9
Don't say it!
F♯m7 B7♭9 Emaj7
Say anything but don't say goodnight to - night

Don't say it!
C♯m9
Don't say it!
F♯m7 B7♭9 E5
You can say anything but don't say goodnight to - night.

Link | (E5) | (A5) | (E5) | (A5) |

| (Emaj7) | (C♯m9) | (F♯m7) | (B7♭9) ‖

Chorus 2

Emaj7
Don't say it!
C♯m9
Don't say it!
F♯m7 B7♭9 Emaj7
Say anything but don't say goodnight to - night

Don't say it!
C♯m9
Don't say it!
F♯m7 B7♭9 Em7 B7♭9 Em7
Say anything but don't say goodnight to - night.

Link 2 ‖: (E5) | (A5) :‖ *Play 3 times*

| Em7 | C | Em7 | Em7 A6 ‖

Solo ‖: Em7 | Em7 A6 :‖ *Play 3 times*

| N.C.(Fmaj7) | (C♯m7) |

Play 3 times
‖: (Emaj7) | (C♯m9) | (F♯m7) | (B7♭9) :‖
3° Good - night, good - night, good...

Verse 2

```
Emaj7   C#m9   F#m7        B7♭9
   Don't get too tired for love
Emaj7   C#m9  F#m7  B7♭9
   Don't let it   end
Emaj7   C#m9       F#m7        B7♭9
   Don't say good - night to love
   Em7          C#m9            F#m7  B7♭9
   It's a feeling that may never end,   ooh.
```

Chorus 3

```
   Emaj7
‖:   Don't say it!
C#m9
Don't say it!
F#m7                  B7♭9                     Emaj7
   Say anything but don't say goodnight to - night

Don't say it!
C#m9
   Don't say it!
F#m7                  B7♭9                     Emaj7
   Say anything but don't say goodnight to - night

Don't say it!
C#m9
   Don't say it!
F#m7                          B7♭9                     Emaj7
   You can say anything but don't say goodnight to - night. :‖
```

Repeat to fade

Heart Of The Country

Words & Music by
Paul McCartney & Linda McCartney

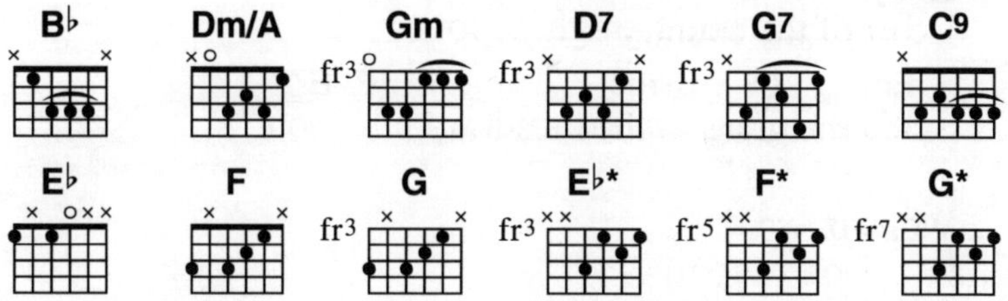

Tune 6th string to D

Verse 1

```
      B♭           Dm/A
I look high, I look low
            Gm
I'm lookin' everywhere I go
B♭          D7
Lookin' for a home
                 Gm
In the heart of the country.
```

Verse 2

```
           B♭                 Dm/A
I'm gonna move, I'm gonna go
           Gm
I'm gonna tell everyone I know
B♭          D7
Lookin' for a home
                 Gm
In the heart of the country.
```

Chorus 1

```
G7
Heart of the country
               C9
Where the holy people grow,
G7
Heart of the country
              C9
Smell the grass in the meadow,

Wo, wo, wo.
```

Interlude 1

```
| N.C.(Gm) | (Gm)  | (Gm)  | (Gm)  |

| (Gm)  | (Gm)  | Gm    | Cm    | E♭  F | G     ||
```

Verse 3

```
          B♭                Dm/A
Want a horse, I want a sheep
             Gm
I want to get me a good night's sleep
B♭           D7
Living in a home
                         Gm
In the heart of the country.
```

Verse 4

```
              B♭                 Dm/A
I'm gonna move, I'm gonna go
              Gm
I'm gonna tell everyone I know
B♭           D7
Living in a home
                         Gm
In the heart of the country.
```

Chorus 2

```
G7
Heart of the country
                 C9
Where the holy people grow,
G7
Heart of the country
                C9
Smell the grass in the meadow,

Wo, wo, wo.
```

Interlude 2

```
| N.C.(Gm) | (Gm) | (Gm) | (Gm) |
| (Gm) | (Gm) | Gm | Cm | E*♭  F* | G* ||
```

Verse 5

```
            B♭          Dm/A
Wanna horse, I gotta sheep
              Gm
I want to get me a good night's sleep
B♭             D7
Living in a home
                        Gm
In the heart of the country.
```

Verse 6

```
              B♭                   Dm/A
I'm gonna move, I'm gonna go
              Gm
I'm gonna tell everyone I know oh, oh,
B♭      D7
Ooh,——
                        Gm
In the heart of the country.
```

Chorus 3 As Chorus 2

Heather

Words & Music by
Paul McCartney

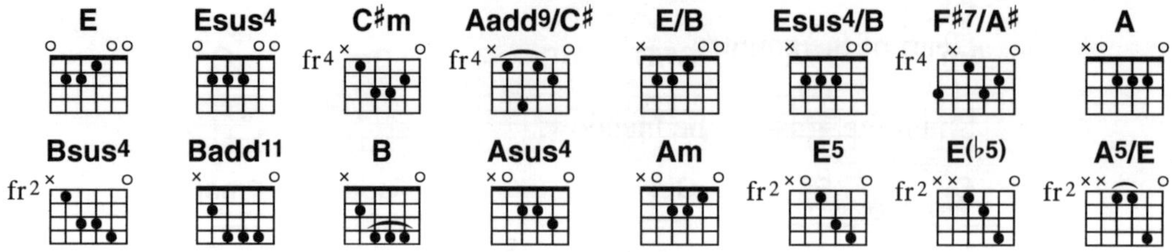

Instrumental 1 ‖: E Esus4 | Esus4 E | E Esus4 | Esus4 E |

| C♯m Aadd9/C♯ | C♯m | E/B Esus4/B | E/B |

| F♯7/A♯ | F♯7/A♯ | A | Bsus4 Badd11 :‖

‖: B A E B | B A E B E :‖

| Asus4 A | Am E5 | E(♭5) A5/E | Bsus4 B ‖

Instrumental 2 As Instrumental 1

Verse 1

```
E                         Esus4                      E
I'm gonna fly to the moon, check in outer space
                        Esus4                  E
Find me a suitable plot, build myself a place
C♯m                 Aadd9/C♯  C♯m
There I will stay for a       year and a day
           E/B              Esus4/B  E/B
Until the cares of my life blow    a - way
             F♯7/A♯
And I will dance to a runcible tune
          A             Bsus4 Badd11    E     Esus4
With a queen, of my heart,              um  -  mm
        E          Esus4  E
Hea - ther, ooh.___
```

Heaven On A Sunday

Words & Music by
Paul McCartney

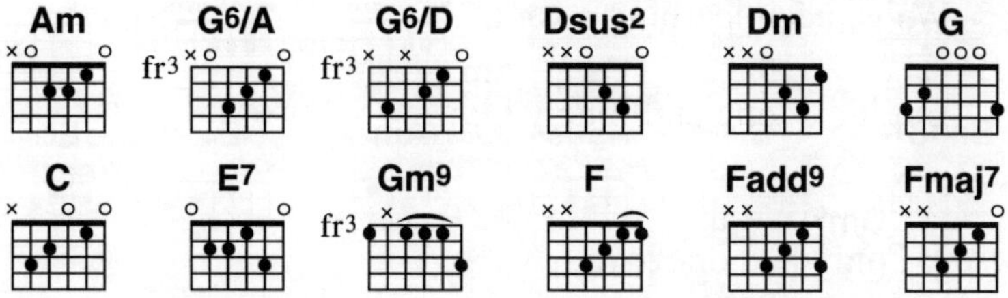


```
         | Am   G6/A  | G6/A           | Am   G6/A  | G6/A  ||
Intro         Ooh____      wow____       wow.____

          Am       G6/A                    G6/D  Dsus2
Verse 1   Peace - ful, like heaven on a Sun - day
          Am      G6/A                        Dsus2 Dm Dsus2
          Wish - ful, not thinking what to do
          G                     C
            We've been calling it love
                     E7                 Am
          But it's a dream we're going through.

                     Gm9       F
Chorus 1  And if I only had one love
          C                     E7       Am
          Yours would be the one I'd choose
                Gm9        F
          If I only had one love
          C                     E7       Am
          Yours would be the one I'd choose.
```

Verse 2

```
Am    G6/A                  G6/D  Dsus2
Rest - ful, like Devon on a Mon - day
Am    G6/A                   Dsus2 Dm Dsus2
Cool - ing my fingers in the bay
G                       C
We've been learning a song
           E7                Am
But it's a long and lonely blues.
```

Chorus 2

```
    Gm9      F
If I only had one love
C                      E7     Am
Yours would be the one I'd choose
    Gm9      F
If I only had one love
C                      E7     Am
Yours would be the one I'd choose
    Gm9      F
If I only had one love
C                      E7     Am
Yours would be the one I'd choose.
```

Solo

```
||: Am  | Am  | Am  | Am  |
| Dm    | Dm  | Am  | Am  :||
```

Verse 3

```
    Am     G6/A                       G6/D  Dsus2
It's peace - ful, like heaven on a Sun - day
Am    G6/A                       Dsus2 Dm Dsus2
Wish - ful, not thinking what to do
G                         C
   We've been calling it love
          E7                  Am
But it's a dream were going through.
```

Chorus 3

Gm9 F
And if I only had one love
C E7 Am
Yours would be the one I'd choose
Gm9 F
If I only had one love
C E7 Am
Yours would be the one I'd choose
Gm9 F
If I only had one love
C E7 Am
Yours would be the one I'd choose.
Gm9 F
||: If I only had one love
C E7 Am
Yours would be the one I'd choose
Gm9 F
If I only had one love
C E7 Am
You'd be the one I'd choose. :||
Gm9 Fadd9
If I only had one love...
Fmaj7 Am
(Yours'd be the yours'd be the... Heaven on a Sunday.)

Outro | **(Am)** | **Am** ||: **Am G6/A** | **Am G6/A** :|| *Repeat to fade*

Helen Wheels

Words & Music by
Paul McCartney & Linda McCartney

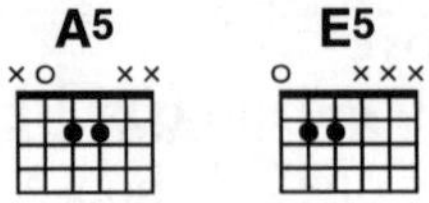

Intro | N.C.(A5) | N.C.(A5) | Drums 4 ||

Verse 1
```
A5
Said farewell to my last hotel, it was never much kind of abode
Glasgow town never brought me down when I was heading out on the road,
Carlisle city never looked so pretty and the Kendal freeway's fast
Slowdown driver, want to stay alive, I want to make this journey last.
```

Chorus 1
```
A5
Helen, hell on wheels, ain't nobody else gonna know the way she feels
                                E5                  A5
Helen, hell on wheels, and they never gonna take her a - way.
```

Verse 2
```
A5
M6 south down to Liverpool, where they play the west coast sound
Sailor Sam he came from Birmingham but he never will be found,
Doing fine when a London sign greets me like a long lost friend
Mister Motor won't you check her out, she's got to take me back again.
```

Chorus 2 As Chorus 1

Verse 3

```
A5
Got no time for a rum and lime, I wanna get my right foot down

Shake some dust off the old bus, I gotta get her out of town

Spend the day upon the motorway where the carburettors blast

Slow down driver, want to stay alive, I want to make this journey last.
```

Chorus 3

```
A5
Helen, hell on wheels, ain't nobody else gonna know the way she feels
                                 E5                   A5
Helen, hell on wheels, and they never gonna take her a - way.

Say 'Bye bye'! (Bye bye!)
```

Outro solo ‖: A5 | A5 | A5 | A5 :‖ *Repeat ad lib. to fade*

Here Today

Words & Music by
Paul McCartney

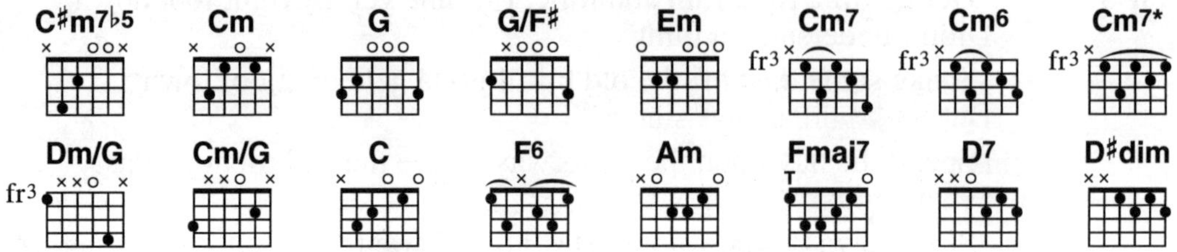


```
             C♯m7♭5     Cm
Verse 1        And if I said I really knew you well
                   G                        G/F♯
             What would your answer be
             Em
               If you were here today?
             Cm7    Cm6    Cm7*   Dm/G  Cm/G  G
             Ooh,— ooh,— ooh,— here   to  -  day.

             C♯m7♭5
Verse 2        Well knowing you——
             Cm                                   G                  G/F♯
               You'd probably laugh and say that we were worlds apart
             Em
               If you were here today
             Cm7    Cm6    Cm7*   Dm/G  Cm/G  G
             Ooh,— ooh,— ooh,— here   to  -  day.

             C
Verse 3        But as for me
             F6                      C
               I still remember how it was before,
             F6                            C     Am  Em
               And I am holding back the tears no   more
             C     Am     Em      Fmaj7    D7
             Ooh,— ooh,— ooh,— I love you, ooh.—
```

Middle

G
What about the time we met, (what about the time)
D♯dim Em
Well I suppose that you could say that we were playing hard to get

Didn't understand a thing
Am D7 | Em |
But we could always sing.
Em
What about the night we cried,
E♭dim Em
Because there wasn't any reason left to keep it all inside

Never understood a word
Am D7 Em
But you were always there—— with a smile.

Verse 4

C♯m7♭5 Cm
And if I say—— I really loved you
G G/F♯
And was glad you came along——
Em
And if you were here today
Cm7 Cm6 Cm7* Dm/G Cm/G G
Ooh,— ooh,— ooh,— for you were in my song
Cm7 Cm6 Cm7* Dm/G Cm/G G
Ooh,— ooh,— ooh,— here to - day.

Hope Of Deliverance

Words & Music by
Paul McCartney

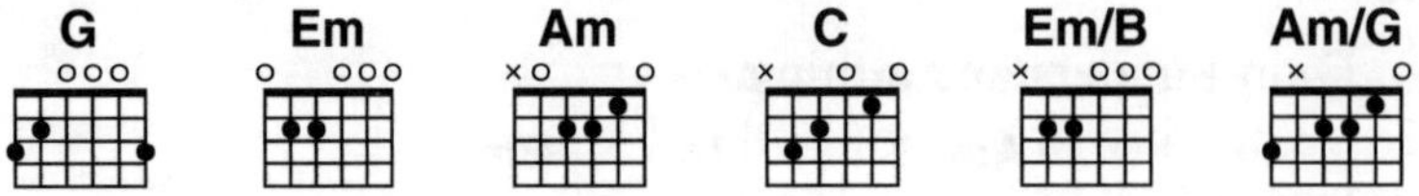

Capo fifth fret

Intro

```
| G         | Em        | G         | Em        ||
```

Verse 1

```
(Em)          G  Em       Am
I will always be hoping, hoping
                G  Em       Am
You will always be holding, holding

My heart in your hand
               G      | Em   | G    | Em   ||
I will under - stand.          Ooh.
```

Verse 2

```
(Em)           G     Em       Am
I will under - stand someday, one day
                 G     Em
You will under - stand always,
Am
Always from now until then.
```

Pre-chorus 1

```
                Em       Am
When it will be right, I don't know
                Em      Am
What it will be like, I don't know
           C       Em/B                 Am                  Am/G
We live in hope of deliverance from the darkness that sur - rounds us.
```

Chorus 1

```
C            Em         C            Em
Hope of de - liverance, hope of de - liverance
C            Em/B               Am                  Am/G
Hope of de - liverance from the darkness that sur - rounds us.
```

Link

```
| G         | Em        | G         | Em        ||
```

Verse 3

(Em) G Em Am
And I wouldn't mind knowing, knowing

G Em Am
That you wouldn't mind going, going along with my plan.

Pre-chorus 2

Em Am
When it will be right, I don't know

Em Am
What it will be like, I don't know

C Em/B Am Am/G
We live in hope of de - liverance from the darkness that sur - rounds us.

Chorus 2

C Em C Em
Hope of de - liverance, hope of de - liverance

C Em/B Am Am/G
Hope of de - liverance from the darkness that sur - rounds us.

Solo

| G | Em | Am | Am |

| G | Em | Am | Am |

| Am | Am | Em | Am |

| Em | Am | C | Em/B |

| Am | Am/G | Am/G ||

Chorus 3

C Em C Em
Hope of de - liverance, hope of de - liverance

C Em/B Am Am/G | Am/G ||
Hope of de - liverance from the darkness that sur - rounds us.

Outro

||: G | Em | G | Em :|| *Play 4 times*
Hope of deliverance, hope of deliverance.

| G ||

Hi, Hi, Hi

Words & Music by
Paul McCartney & Linda McCartney

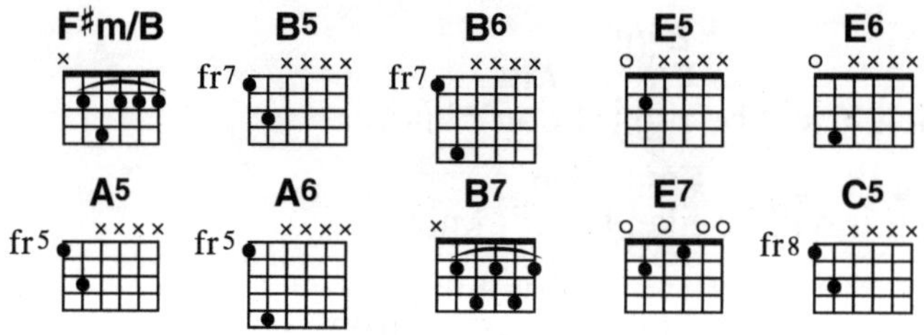

Intro | F♯m/B | F♯m/B |: B5 B6 B5 B6 | B5 B6 B5 B6 |
(B5 riff)

| E5 E6 E5 E6 | 1. E5 E6 E5 E6 :| 2. E5 N.C. ||
(E5 riff)

Verse 1

B5riff
Well, when I met you at the station
E5riff
You were standing with a bootleg in your hand
B5riff
I took you back to my little place
E5riff
For a taste of a multicoloured band.
(A5 riff)
A5 A6 A5 A6 A5 A6
We're gonna get hi,—— hi,—— hi——
E5riff
The night is young
B5riff
She'll be my funky little mama
E5riff E5 N.C.
Gonna rock it and we've only just be - gun.

Chorus 1

```
(N.C.)              B5riff
We're gonna get hi, hi, hi
                   E5
With the music on
                  B5riff
Won't say bye-bye bye-bye bye-bye bye-bye
                      E5riff
'Til the night is gone
                      A5riff
I'm gonna do it to you, gonna do you
                                     E5riff
Sweet banana, you'll never give up
                   B5riff                   E5riff  E5 N.C.
We're gettin' hi, hi, hi in the midday sun.
```

Link

```
||: B7      | B7       | E7       | E7       :||
              Ooh,—                  woah!—
```

Verse 2

```
                B5riff
Well well, take off your face
                                        E5riff
Recover from the trip you've been on
                   B5riff
I want you to lie on the bed
                                   E5riff
Get you ready for my poly - gon,
                      A5riff
I'm gonna do it to you, gonna do it
                                         E5riff
Sweet banana, you've never been done
                    B5riff
Yes, and like a rabbit, gonna grab it
                                     E5riff  E5 N.C.
Gonna do it 'til the night is done.
```

Chorus 2

```
(N.C.)              B5riff                   E5riff
We're gonna get hi, hi, hi with the music on
                  B5riff
Won't say bye-bye bye-bye bye-bye bye-bye
                    E5
'Til the night is gone
                    A5riff
I'm gonna do it to you, gonna do you
                                 E5riff
Sweet banana, you'll never give up
                    B5riff                    C5
We're gonna get hi, hi, hi, we're gonna get hi, hi, hi
                    B5riff                  E5riff  E5 N.C.
We're gonna get hi, hi, hi in the midday sun.       Ooh, babe.
```

Outro
(double tempo)

```
| B5      | B5      | E5      | E5      |

| B5      | B5      | E5      | E5      |

| A5      | A5      | E5      | E5      |

| B5      | B5      | C5      | C5      |
  Hi, hi,   hi,       hi, hi,   hi,
| B5      | B5 N.C.             | E5
  Hi, hi,   hi, in your midday    sun.
```

I Do

Words & Music by
Paul McCartney

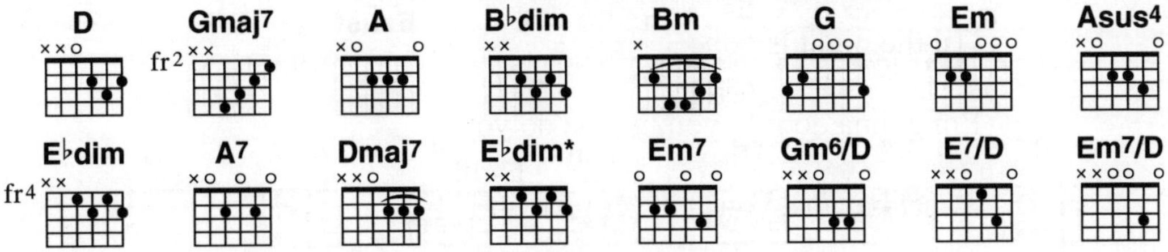

Verse 1

D Gmaj7 A B♭dim Bm
If you only knew how much it meant to me
G D Em | Asus4 A |
You'd under - stand and I would feel your love was true
E♭dim Em A7 D Dmaj7
This is all I want, this is all I need
E♭dim* Em Em7 | Asus4 A ||
This all I long for, I do.

Verse 2

D Gmaj7 A B♭dim Bm
Just re - member this after a time is through
G D Em | Asus4 A |
And never more will there be days for me and you
E♭dim Em A7 D Dmaj7
This is all I ask all I ask of you
E♭dim* Em Em7 Asus4 A D
Please remember darling, I do love you.

Bridge

Gm6/D D Gm6/D D
And days go by so quickly, when you're having fun
E7/D Em7/D G A
Life is never ea - sy even in the sun.

Verse 3

D Gmaj7 A B♭dim Bm
But please re - member this after a time is through
G D Em | Asus4 A |
And never more will there be days for me and you
E♭dim Em A7 D Dmaj7
This is all I want, this is all I need——
E♭dim* Em Em7 Asus4 A D
Darling please remem - ber, I do, love you
D Gmaj7 A
If you only knew.

I Am Your Singer

Words & Music by
Paul McCartney

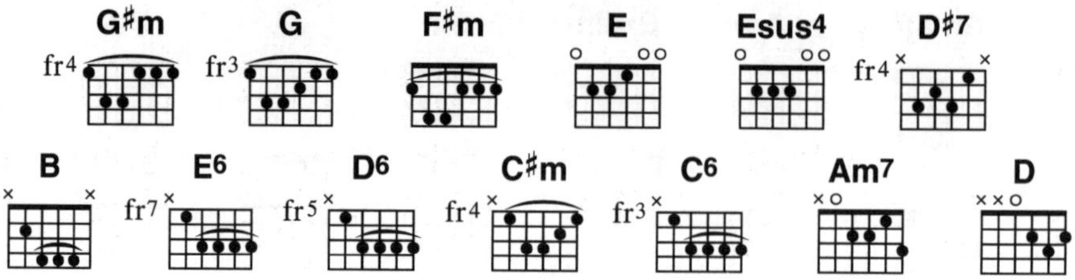

Verse 1

G♯m G
You are my love
F♯m
You are my song, linger on
You are my song
E Esus4 | E D♯7 ||
I am your singer.

Verse 2

G♯m G
You are my one
F♯m
You are my own melo - dy
You are my song
E Esus4 | E ||
I am your singer.

Chorus 1

B E
Someday when we're singing
B E6 D6 | C♯m C6 |
We will fly away, going wing - ing
F♯m Am7 D E Esus4 | E N.C. D♯7 ||
Sing, singing my love song___ to you.

Instrumental | G♯m | G♯m | G | G |

| F♯m | F♯m | E Esus4 | E ||

Chorus 2 As Chorus 1

G♯m
Verse 3 My song is sung
G F♯m
When day is done, harmo - nies will linger on.
E
I am your singer,
C♯m E6 D6 | C♯m C6 |
I am your singer——
F♯m Am7 D E Esus4 | E (fermata) ||
Singing my love song—— to you.

I Lost My Little Girl

Words & Music by
Paul McCartney

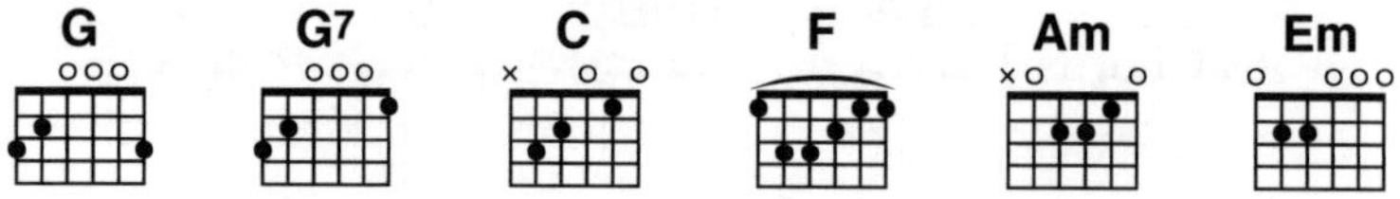

Intro | G G7 | C | G G7 | C ||

Verse 1

```
             G          G7       C
Well, I woke up late this morning
       G           G7  C
My head was in a whirl
G     G7     C            (C)  N.C.
Only then I realised I lost my little girl
                  C
Ah-hah, hah— hah-hah.
```

Verse 2

```
                G          G7      C
Well, her clothes are not ex - pensive
      G           G7      C
Her hair didn't always curl
  G             G7     C
I don't know why I love her
         F             G    N.C.
But I love my little girl
                  C
Ah-hah, hah— hah-hah.
```

Middle 8

```
          Am
Well, gather 'round people let me tell you the story
           Em                 Am
Of the very first song I wrote

Well, gather 'round people let me tell you the story
           G                    C  N.C.
Of the very first song I wrote.
```

Verse 3

As Verse 1

```
      G C
I said.
```

I Owe It All To You

Words & Music by
McCartney

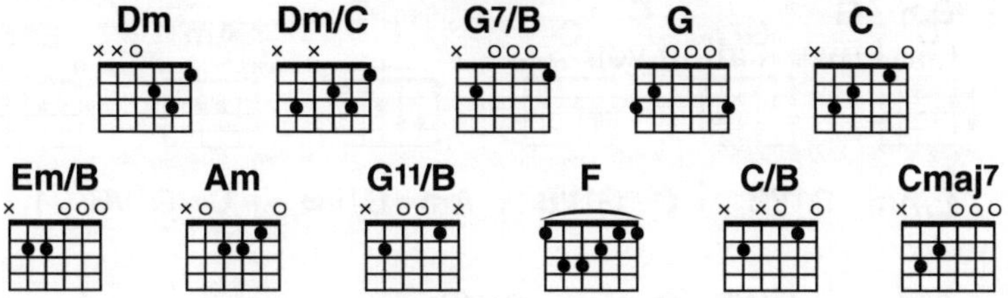

Intro

```
| Dm  Dm/C | G7/B  G | C  Em/B | Am |
| Dm  Dm/C | G7/B    | Am      | Am (fermata) ||
||: Am  G11/B | C  G11/B :||
```

Verse 1

```
Am           G11/B C           G11/B
Last night you   helped me through
Am                  G11/B  C     G11/B
Took me to the lovers  zone
Am    G11/B  C     G11/B
I saw there, ima - ges
      Am          G       F
Pro - jected on a wall of stone.
```

Pre-chorus 1

```
(F)                   C
   I stood inside E - gyptian temples
F                    C
   I looked into e - ternal gardens
F                          Am
   Lay on the shores of distant islands
G                  F
Listening to the sea birds' song of joy.
```

Chorus 1

Dm G C
Oh, I owe it all to you
C/B Am
You make me happy
Dm G C
Oh, I owe it all to you.

Link

𝄆 **Am G^{11}/B | C G^{11}/B | Am G^{11}/B | C G^{11}/B** 𝄇

Verse 2

Am G^{11}/B C G^{11}/B
Late last night we were right
Am G^{11}/B C G^{11}/B
Into some ex - otic scene
Am G^{11}/B C G^{11}/B
Every - where, ima - ges
Am G F
Appearing on a giant screen.

Pre-chorus 2

F C
I stood inside a glass cathedral
F C
I looked into the golden canyon
F Am
Lay by the lakes of holy water
G F
Glistening like a diamond in the light.

Chorus 2

Dm G C
𝄆 Oh, I owe it all to you
C/B Am
You make me happy
Dm G C
Oh, I owe it all to you. 𝄇

```
Verse 3     | Am  G11/B | C  G11/B | Am  G11/B | C  G11/B |

            | Am  G11/B | C  G11/B | Am  G        | F         ||
                                    I  owe it all to  you

            F     C
              E - gyptian temples
            F     C
              E - ternal gardens
            F  Am
              Distant islands
            G               F
            Listening to the sea birds song of joy.

            Dm   G           C
Chorus 3    Oh, I owe it all to you
            C/B  Am
            You make me happy
            Dm   G             Am
            Oh, I owe it all to you.

Outro       |: Am  G11/B | C  G11/B | Am  G11/B | C  G11/B |
                                    1 - 3.
            | Am  G11/B | C  G11/B | Am  G11/B | C     G11/B  :||
            4.                                  I  owe it all to you.
            | Am    G11/B | Cmaj7   ||
              owe it all to   you.
```

I'm Carrying

Words & Music by
Paul McCartney

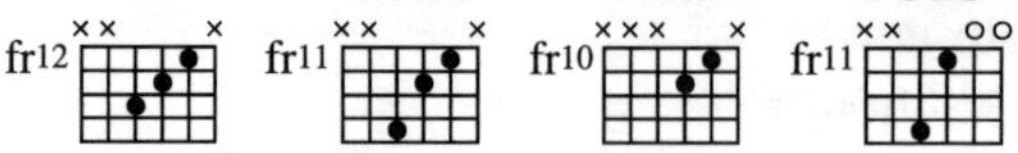

Verse 1

```
E                  Edim              F♯m7          Bsus4
  By dawn's first light I'll come back to your room a - gain
E                Edim          F♯m7          Bsus4
  With my car - nation hidden by the packa - ges
```

Chorus 1

```
    E        F♯m7  Bsus4
I'm carrying
E         F♯m7  Bsus4
Something
    E        F♯m7      Bsus4   E
I'm carrying something—— for you.
```

Verse 2

```
E                Edim        F♯m7               Bsus4
  Ah, long time no see baby, sure has been a while
E             Edim         F♯m7             Bsus4
  And if my reappearance lacks a sense of style
    E        F♯m7  Bsus4
I'm carrying
E         F♯m7  Bsus4
Something
    E        F♯m7      Bsus4   E
I'm carrying something—— for you.
```

|: E | Edim | F#m7 | Bsus4 :|

Verse 3 Ah.___

E F#m7 Bsus4
I'm carrying

E F#m7 Bsus4
Can't help it

E F#m7 Bsus4 E
I'm carrying something___ for you.___

|: (E) | Edim | F#m7 | Bsus4 :|

Verse 4 Ooh.___

E F#m7 Bsus4
I'm carrying, ooh___

E F#m7 Bsus4
Something, ooh___

E F#m7 Bsus4 E
I'm carrying something___ for you.

I've Had Enough

Words & Music by
Paul McCartney

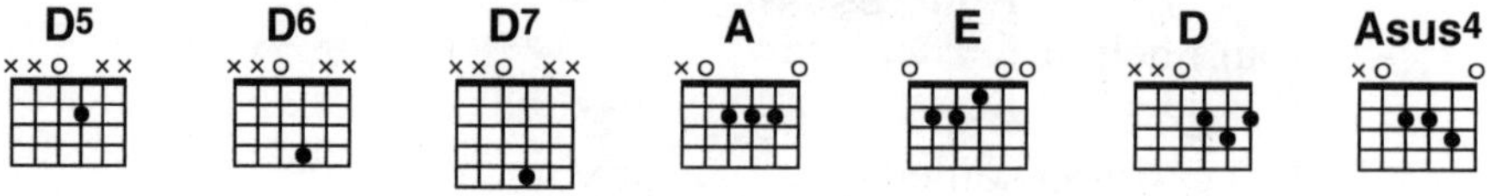

D5 riff

Intro ‖: D5 D6 D7 D6 | D5 D6 D7 D6 | D5 D6 D5 D6 | D5 D6 D5 :‖

Verse 1

A E
You're talking to me from the back of my car
D
And I can't get nothing right
A E
And then you wonder why stand at the bar
A Asus4
Day and night.

Chorus 1

D5 riff
(Well,) I've had e - nough
I can't put up with any more
No no, no, no no no
D5 riff
I've had e - nough
I can't put up with any more
No no, no, no no no.

Verse 2

A E
You stand behind me with a watch in your hand
D
And I can't get nothing done
A E
Well, people tell me you're punctual man
A Asus4
But come on, come on.

Chorus 2   As Chorus 1

```
             A                                                    E
*Verse 3*       I earn the money and you take it away
                       D
             When I don't know where you're from
             A                                                        E
                I should be worried but they say
                                  A              Asus4
             It'll pay for a bomb, oh.
```

Chorus 3   As Chorus 1 *w/ad lib. vocal*

Instrumental | A | E | D | A |

| A | E | A | Asus4 ||

Chorus 4   As Chorus 1 *w/ad lib. vocal*

```
             A           E                                   D
*Verse 4*       Baby, you know sometimes you get a little weary
             A
                But if it ever happens honey
             E                                        A
                You just come along to me
                                        Asus4
             Because you know.
```

Chorus 5   As Chorus 1 *w/ad lib. vocal*

```
                            D5riff
*Chorus 5*   I've had e - nough

             I can't put up with anymore

             No no— no, no no no,no no no
             D5riff
             No———

             I can't put up with anymore
                                          D5 N.C.
             No baby, I've had e - nough.
```

If You Wanna

Words & Music by
Paul McCartney

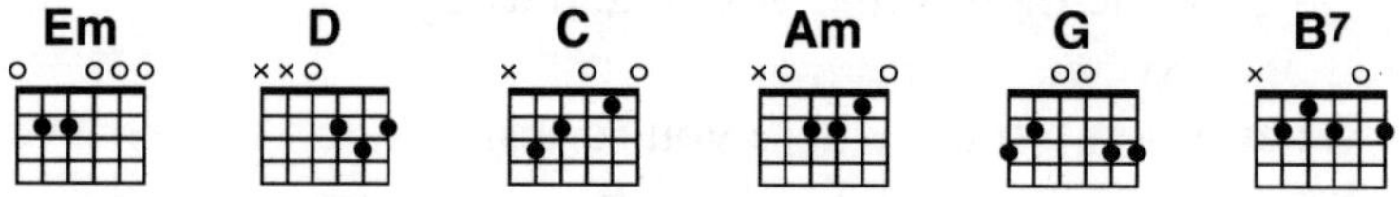

Intro | Em D | Em D | Em D | Em D Em ‖

Verse 1

Em D
If you wanna

Em D
If you wanna

Em D Em D Em
If you wanna love me a - gain

C Am Em
I'll take you for a ride in my Cadil - lac

C Am Em
He'll be in the front, we'll be in the back.

Chorus 1

| Em D | Em
When you're ready

| Em D | Em
Let me know

| Em D | Em
I'll be waiting

| Em D | A
To make arrangements for the trip

To make arrangements for the trip

To make arrangements for the trip.

Link | Em D | Em D | Em D | Em D Em ‖

Verse 2

```
Em                D
   And if you wanna
Em       D
   If you wanna
Em       D        Em      D  Em
   If you wanna do it a - gain
C                      Am                  Em
   I'll take you to the coast for a holi - day
C                   Am                     Em
   You can be my guest, you can let me pay, yeah.
```

Chorus 2

```
| Em  D | Em
              When you're ready
| Em  D | Em
              Well, let me know
| Em  D | Em
              I'll be waiting
| Em  D | A
              To make arrangements for the trip
```

To make arrangements for the trip

To make arrangements for the trip.

Link 2

```
| Em  D | Em  D                | Em  D | Em  D  Em ||
           Whenever you're       ready.
```

Bridge 1

```
D                  G
   When you wanna love me
Em                 Am
   This is what you need
D               G
   To be thinking of me
B7                          Em
   When you plant the seed of love.
```

Link 3 | Em D | Em D | Em D | Em D Em ||

Solo | Em D | Em D | Em D | Em D Em |
| C | Am | Em | Em |
| C | Am | Em | Em ||

Chorus 3 As Chorus 1

Link 4 | Em D | Em D | Em D | Em D Em ||

Bridge 2

```
D                         G
   Well if you want to love me
Em                      Am
   This is what you need
D                    G
   To be thinking of me
B7                                          Em
   When you plant the seed, the seed of love.
```

Link 5 | Em D | Em D | Em D | Em D Em ||

Verse 3

```
Em        D
   If you wanna
Em        D
   If you wanna
Em        D        Em  D  Em
   If you wanna do it a - gain
C                       Am                  Em
   I'll take you for a ride in my Cadil - lac
C                    Am                   Em
   He'll be in the front, we'll be in the back.
```

Chorus 4 As Chorus 1

Outro | Em D | Em D | Em D | Em D Em ||

Jet

Words & Music by
Paul McCartney & Linda McCartney

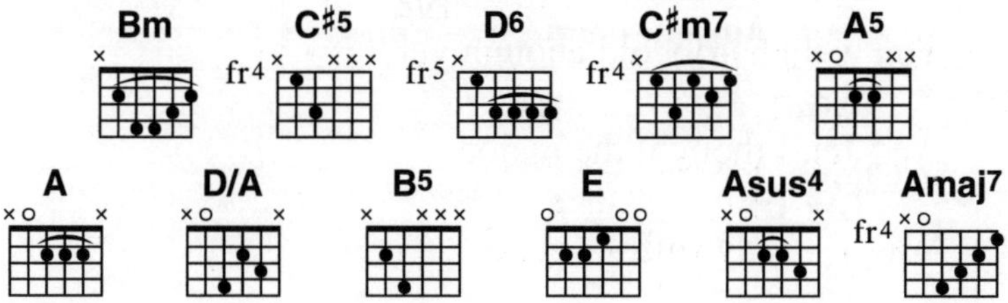


```
Intro     |: Bm   C#5 D6 | D6   | Bm   C#5 D6 | D6   | C#m7 | C#m7 :|

          |  Bm   C#5 D6 | D6   | A5       | A5   | A5        | A5   ||
                                     Jet!                Jet!

          A                                          D/A      A
Verse 1     Jet! I can almost remember their funny fa - ces

          That time you told them that
                                              D/A
          You were going to be marrying soon
               C#m7            Bm
          And Jet, I thought the only
                C#5 D6                  A5
          Lone - ly    place was on the moon

          Jet! Ooh___

          Jet! Ooh.___
```

Verse 2	**A** Jet! Was your father as bold as a **D/A** sergeant ma - **A** jor?

```
A                                        D/A        A
  Jet! Was your father as bold as a sergeant ma - jor?

Well, how come he told you that
                                   D/A
You were hardly old enough yet?
    C#m7            Bm
And Jet, I thought the major
   C#5  D6          A
Was a   lady suffra - gette

Jet! Ooh___

Jet! Ooh.___
```

Bridge 1

```
B5                        E
Ah, mater, want Jet to always love me?
B5                        E
Ah, mater, want Jet to always love me?
B5              A      Asus4  A
Ah, mater, much la     -      ter.
```

Link 1

```
| A5     | A5     | A5     | A5     ||
```

Instrumental

```
| A5     | A5     | D/A  A | A      ||

| A5     | A5     | D/A    | D/A    ||
```

Verse 3

```
    C#m7            Bm
And Jet, I thought the major
   C#5  D6              A
Was a       lady suffre - gette

Jet! Ooh___

Jet! Ooh.___
```

Bridge 2 As Bridge 1

Link 2 As Link 1

Verse 4

```
A                                          D/A        A
   Jet! With the wind in your hair of a thousand la - ces

Climb on the back and we'll
                      D/A
Go for a ride in the sky
     C#m7             Bm
And Jet, I thought the major
     C#5 D6            A
Was a     lady suffra - gette

Jet! Ooh——

Jet! Ooh.——
     C#m7               Bm
And Jet, d'you know I thought you
     C#5 D6            A
Was a     lady suffra - gette

Jet! Ooh.
```

Outro

```
| Bm   C#5 D6  | D6             | Bm   C#5 D6
                 A little lady,
| D6           | C#m7   | C#m7  |
  my little lady  yeah!
| Bm     | Bm     | C#m7   | Amaj7  ||
```

Junior's Farm

Words & Music by
Paul McCartney & Linda McCartney

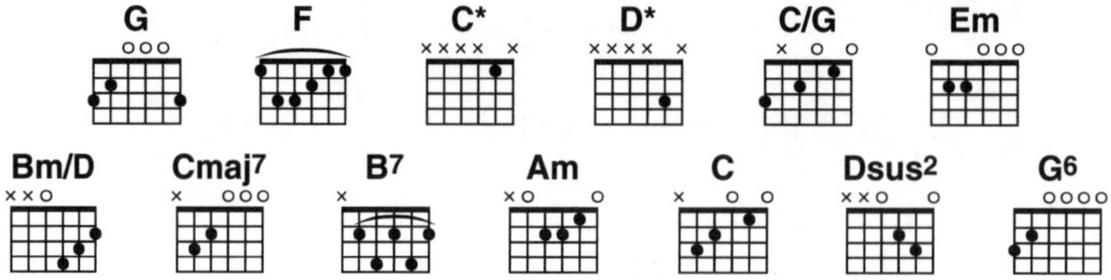

Intro ‖: G | G | F C* D* | G :‖

| G | G C/G | G | G C/G ‖
Ah!

Verse 1
G C/G G
You should have seen me with the poker man
I had a honey and I bet a grand
F Em
Just in the nick of time I looked at his hand.

Verse 2
G C/G G
I was talking to an Eskimo,
Said he was hoping for a fall of snow
F Em
When up popped a sea lion ready to go.

Chorus 1
G
Let's go, let's go, let's go, let's go
F G
Down to Junior's farm where I want to lay low
Low life, high life, oh, let's go
F G
Take me down to Junior's farm, take me down Jimmy.

```
Solo       | G     | G     | F     | G     |

           | G     | G     | F     | G     ||

           G                                   C/G  G
Verse 3      I took my bag into a grocer's store

           The price is higher than the time before
           F              Em
           Old man asked me why is it more.

             G                                            C/G  G
Verse 4    I said, "You should have seen me with the poker man

           I had a honey and I bet a grand
           F                        Em
           Just in the nick of time I looked at his hand."

                G
Chorus 2   Let's go, let's go, let's go, let's go
           F                         G
           Down to Junior's farm where I want to lay low

           Low life, high life, oh, let's go
            F                      G
           Take me down to Junior's farm
                              F                         G
           Let's go, let's go, down to Junior's farm where I want to lay low

           Low life, high life, oh, let's go
            F                      G
           Take me down to Junior's farm
           F          G
           Ev'rybody tag a - long
           F                        Em  | Em  | N.C.(G) | (G) ||
           Take me down to Junior's farm.

Outro      | Em    | Bm/D  | Em    | Bm/D  |

           | Cmaj7 | B7    | Am    | Am        |
                                       Take me back.
           | Em    | Bm/D  | Em         | Bm/D      |
                             Take me back.___  I wanna
           | Cmaj7  | B7        | Am       | C  Dsus2 | G6    ||
             Go back,  yeah, yeah___  yeah,   yeah, yeah.___
```

Junk

Words & Music by
Paul McCartney

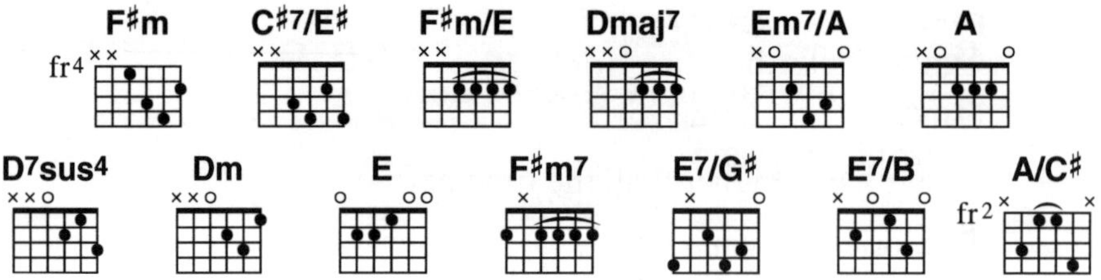

Verse 1

F♯m C♯7/E♯
Motor cars, handle bars
F♯m/E Dmaj7
Bicycles for two
Em7/A A
Broken hearted jubi - lee.

Verse 2

F♯m C♯7/E♯
Parachutes, army boots
F♯m/E Dmaj7
Sleeping bags for two
Em7/A A
Sentimental jambo - ree.

Chorus 1

D7sus4 Dm A
Buy,——— buy
E F♯m7 E7/G♯ A E7/B A/C♯
Says the sign in the shop win - dow
D7sus4 Dm A
Why,——— why
E F♯m7 E7/G♯ A
Says the junk in the yard.

Link

| F♯m | C♯7/E♯ | F♯m/E | Dmaj7 |
Da da da...
| Dmaj7 | Dmaj7 | Em7/A | A ||

Verse 3

F♯m C♯7/E♯
Candlesticks, building bricks
F♯m/E Dmaj7
Some old and new
Em7/A A
Memories for you and me.

Chorus 2

D7sus4 Dm A
Buy,——— buy
E F♯m7 E7/G♯ A E7/B A/C♯
Says the sign in the shop win - dow
D7sus4 Dm A
Why,——— why
E F♯m7 E7/G♯ F♯m
Says the junk in the yard.

Outro

| (F♯m) | C♯7/E♯ | F♯m/E | Dmaj7 | A ||
Da da da...

Let 'Em In

Words & Music by
Paul & Linda McCartney

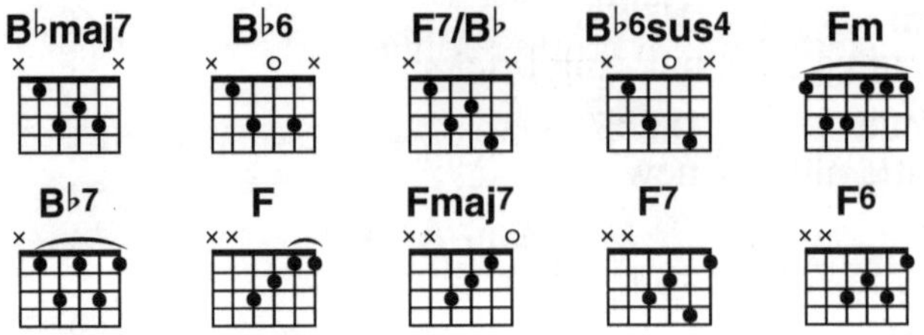

Intro | B♭maj7 | B♭6 | B♭maj7 | B♭6 |

| F7/B♭ | B♭6sus4 | B♭maj7 | B♭6 ||

Verse 1
B♭maj7
Someone's knockin' at the door
B♭6
Somebody's ringin' the bell
B♭maj7
Someone's knockin' at the door
B♭6
Somebody's ringin' the bell
F7/B♭
Do me a favour
B♭6sus4 B♭maj7 B♭6
Open the door and let 'em in, ooh, yeah.

Verse 2 As Verse 1

Interlude 1 | B♭maj7 | B♭6 | B♭maj7 | B♭6 |

| F7/B♭ | B♭6sus4 | B♭maj7 | B♭6 ||

Bridge 1
Fm B♭7
Sister Suzie, brother John
Fm B♭7
Martin Luther, Phil And Don
Fm B♭7
Brother Michael, Auntie Gin
Fm F | Fmaj7 F7 | F6 F ||
Open the door and let 'em in.___

Instrumental | B♭maj7 | B♭6 | B♭maj7 | B♭6 |

| F7/B♭ | B♭6sus4♭ | B♭maj7 | B♭6 ||

Bridge 2

Fm Bb7
Sister Suzie, brother John
Fm Bb7
Martin Luther, Phil And Don
Fm Bb7
Uncle Ernie, Auntie Gin
Fm F | Fmaj7 F7 | F6 F ||
Open the door and let 'em in.—— oh yeah.

Verse 3

B♭maj7
Someone's knockin' at the door
B♭6
Somebody's ringin' the bell
B♭maj7
Someone's knockin' at the door
B♭6
Somebody's ringin' the bell
F7/B♭
Do me a favor
E♭add9/B♭ B♭maj7 B♭6
Open the door and let 'em in, ooh, yeah, yeah, let 'em in now.

Interlude 2 As Interlude 1

Bridge 3

Fm Bb7
Sister Suzie, brother John
Fm Bb7
Martin Luther, Phil And Don
Fm Bb7
Uncle Ernie, Uncle Ian
Fm F | Fmaj7 F7 | F6 F ||
Open the door and let 'em in.——

Verse 4 As Verse 3

Outro | B♭maj7 | B♭6 | B♭maj7 | B♭6 |

| F7/B♭ | B♭6sus4 | B♭maj7 | B♭6 ||

||: F7/B♭ | B♭6sus4 | B♭maj7 | 1. B♭6 :|| 2. B♭maj7 B♭6 ||

Let Me Roll It

Words & Music by
Paul McCartney & Linda McCartney

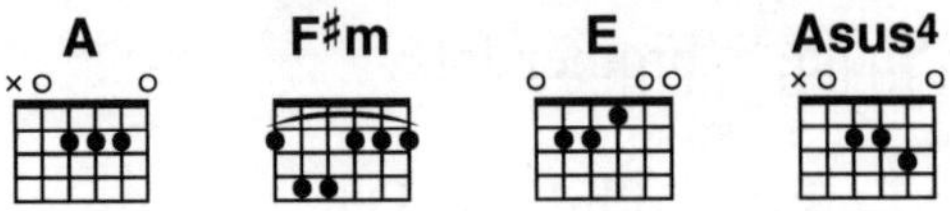

Intro | A F♯m | A F♯m | E Asus4 A | E Asus4 A |
| E Asus4 A | E Asus4 A | E | E N.C. ||
| F♯m | E | F♯m ||

Verse 1
E
You gave me something
F♯m
I understand
E
You gave me loving
F♯m
In the palm of my hand.

Pre-chorus 1
A F♯m A
I can't tell you how I feel
F♯m E
My heart is like a wheel.

Chorus 1
A
Let me roll it
E A
Let me roll it to you
E A
Let me roll it
E A E
Let me roll it to you.

Link 1 | F♯m | E | F♯m ||

Verse 2

```
E
  I want to tell you
F♯m
  And now's the time
E
  I want to tell you that
       F♯m
You're going to be mine
```

Pre-chorus 2

```
A      F♯m       A
I can't tell you how I feel
    F♯m          E
My heart is like a wheel.
```

Chorus 2

```
       A
Let me roll it
E      A
  Let me roll it to you
E      A
  Let me roll it
E      A          E
  Let me roll it to you.——
```

Link 2 | F♯m | E | F♯m | E | F♯m | E | F♯m ‖

Pre-chorus 3 As Pre-chorus 1

Chorus 3 As Chorus 2

Link 3 | F♯m | E | F♯m ‖

Verse 3 As Verse 1

Pre-chorus 4 As Pre-chorus 2

Chorus 4 As Chorus 2

Outro ‖: F♯m | E | F♯m | E :‖ *Repeat to fade*

Letting Go

Words & Music by
Paul McCartney & Linda McCartney

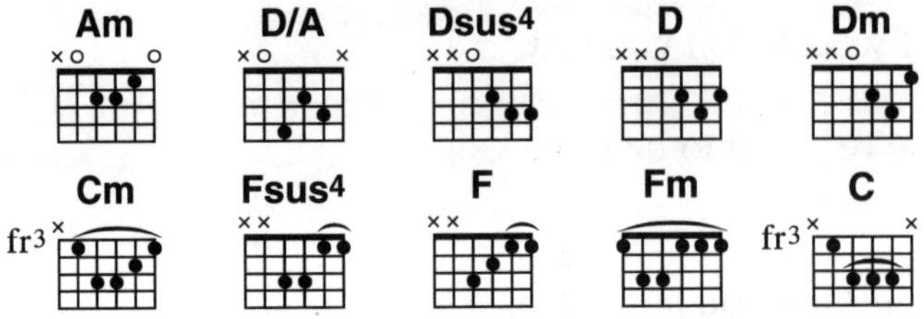

Intro | Am | Am D/A | Am | Am D/A |

|: Am | Am | Am | Am :| *Play 3 times*

Verse 1

Am
Ah, she tastes like wine
Dsus4 D
Such a human being so divine
Am
Oh, she feels like sun
Dsus4 D
Mother nature look at what you're done.

Chorus 1

Dm Am
Oh, I feel like letting go
Dm Am D
Oh, I feel like letting go.

Verse 2

Am
Oh, she looks like snow
Dsus4 D
I want to put her in a Broadway show
Am
Ah, she'll dance and dine
Dsus4 D
Like a Lucifer she'll always shine.

Chorus 2

```
Dm                       Am
Oh, I feel like letting go
Dm                       Am
Oh, I feel like letting go.
```

Interlude ‖: (Am) | Am Dm | Dm | Dm Am :‖ Am D ‖

Solo ‖: Am | Am | Dsus4 | D :‖

Chorus 3

```
Dm                       Am
Oh, I feel like letting go
Dm                       Am    | Am ‖
Oh, I feel like letting go.
```

Verse 3

```
Cm
Ah, she sings it so
Fsus4                        F
   I want to put her on the radio
Cm
   One day and there you are
Fsus4
   Ladies and gentlemen
 F
A brand new star.
```

Chorus 4

```
Fm                       Cm
Oh, I feel like letting go
Fm                       Cm
Oh, I feel like letting go.
```

Chorus 4 ‖: (Cm) | Cm Fm | Fm | [1-3.] Fm Cm :‖ [4.] Fm C |

‖: Cm | Cm Fm | Fm | [1.] Fm Cm :‖ [2.] Fm C :‖ *Repeat to fade*

Listen To What The Man Said

Words & Music by
Paul McCartney & Linda McCartney

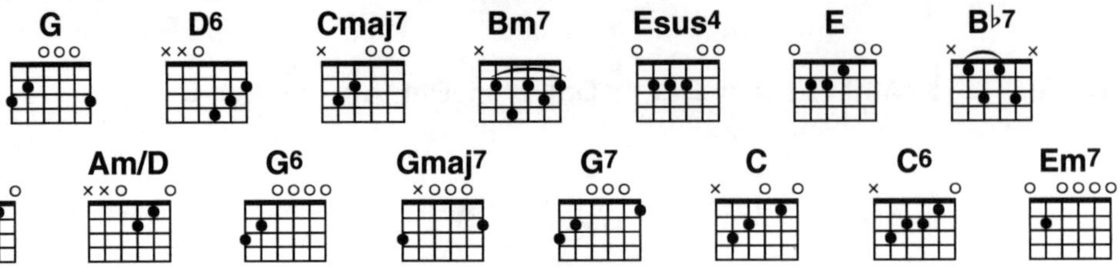

Intro | G | G | G | G :|

Verse 1

D6 Cmaj7
Any time, any day
Bm7 Esus4 E
You can hear the people say——
B♭7 Am
That love is blind
Bm7
Well, I don't know
Cmaj7
But I say love is kind.

Link 1

|: G | G :|
Do do do— do do do do do.—

Verse 2

D6 Cmaj7
Soldier boy kisses girl
Bm7 Esus4 E
Leaves behind a tragic world——
B♭7 Am Bm7
But he won't mind, he's in love
Cmaj7
And he says love is fine.

Link 2

|: G | G :|
Do do do— do do do do do.—

Bridge 1

```
   Am/D
Oh,—— yes, indeed we know

That people will find a way to go
   G                 G6   Gmaj7  G7
No matter what the man said
    C                C6
And love is fine for all we know
   Cmaj7               C6
For all we know, our love will grow
G                  G6   Gmaj7  G6
   That's what the man said
                                  G6   Gmaj7  G6
So won't you listen to what the man said,—— he said....
```

Link 3

```
| G      | G      | G      | G                 ||
                             Ah, take it away!
```

Solo

```
| D6     | Cmaj7  | Bm7    | Esus4  E  B♭dim  |
| Am     | Bm7    | Cmaj7  | Cmaj7  ||
```

Link 4

```
| G      | G      | G      | G      ||
```

Bridge 2 As Bridge 1

Link 5

```
| G      | G      | G      | G      ||
```

Bridge 3 As Bridge 1

Outro

```
| G      | G      | G      | G      ||
     G
The wonder of it all baby, the wonder of it all baby

The wonder of it all baby, yeah, yeah, yeah, yeah.——

| G      | G (fermata) || Bm7  | Em7    | Bm7    |
| Em7    | Bm7    | Esus4  | E      ||
```

segue "Treat Her Gently (Lonely Old People)"

Little Willow

Words & Music by
Paul McCartney

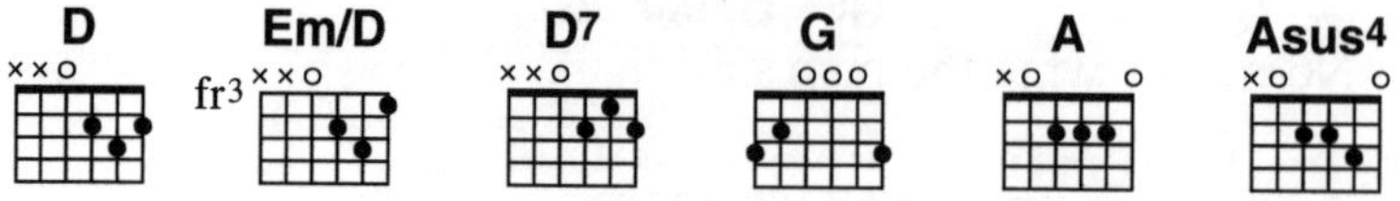

Intro | D Em/D | D Em/D ||

Verse 1

```
D         Em/D
  Bend,        little willow
D         Em/D
  Wind's       gonna blow you
D                Em/D     D      Em/D
  Hard and cold to - night
D        Em/D
  Life,        as it happens
D
  Nobody warns you
D              Em/D     D      D7
  Willow, hold on tight.
```

Bridge 1

```
G                         A
  Nothing's gonna shake your love
                       D
Take your love a - way
G                      A
  No one's out to break your heart
                                 Asus4
It only seems that way,— hey.
```

Verse 2

D Em/D
Sleep little willow
D Em/D
Peace gonna follow
D Em/D D Em/D
Time's gonna heal your wounds
D Em/D
Grow to the heavens
D Em/D
Now and forever
D Em/D D Em/D
Always came too soon.

Interlude

|: D Em/D | D Em/D | D Em/D |1. D Em/D :|2. D D7 ||
Ah.— Ah.— Ah.— Little willow.

Bridge 2

As Bridge 1

Verse 3

D Em/D
Bend, little willow
D Em/D
Wind's gonna blow you
D Em/D D Em/D
Hard and cold to - night
D Em/D
Life, as it happens
D Em/D
No - body warns you
D Em/D D Em/D
Willow, hold on tight.

Outro

| D Em/D | D Em/D | D Em/D | D Em/D |
Ah.— Ah.— Ah.— Little willow.
| D Em/D | D Em/D | D Em/D | D ||
Ah.— Ah.— Ah.— ooh, little willow.

Little Woman Love

Words & Music by
Paul McCartney & Linda McCartney

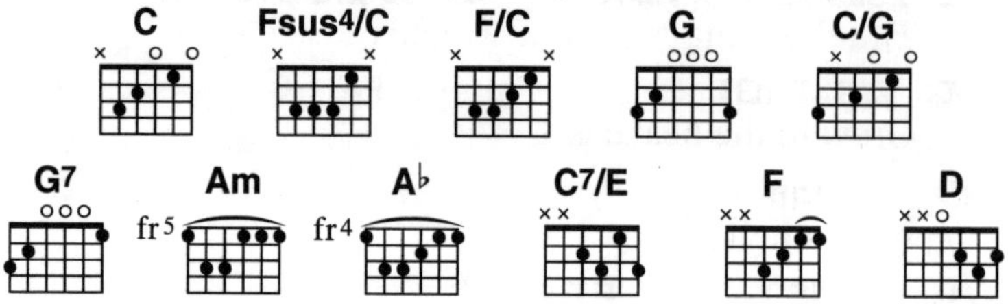

Intro

N.C.

Verse 1

C Fsus4/C F/C C
I got a little woman I can really love
Fsus4/C F/C C
My woman fit me like a little glove
G C/G G7
You know I'll always love
G C Fsus4/C F/C | C N.C. ||
My little woman love.

Verse 2

C Fsus4/C F/C C
I take her home most ev'ry night
C Fsus4/C F/C C
My woman love to hold me tight
G C/G G7
You know I feel al - right
G C Fsus4/C F/C | C ||
My little woman mine.

Bridge 1

Am A♭ Am
Oh yeah, oh yeah
C C7/E F F G
Oh,— oh, oh,— oh——
A♭ Am
Oh yeah, oh yeah
C D G N.C.
Oh,— oh, oh,— oh.

Verse 3 As Verse 1

Solo
| C Fsus4/C F/C | C | C Fsus4/C F/C | C |
| G C/G | G7 G | C Fsus4/C F/C | C ||

Bridge 2
```
A♭          Am
Oh yeah, oh yeah
C      C7/E      F    F G
Oh,— oh, oh,— oh——
A♭          Am
Oh yeah, oh yeah
C      D         G N.C.
Oh,— oh, oh,— oh.
```

Verse 4 As Verse 2

Outro
| C Fsus4/C F/C | C | C Fsus4/C F/C | C |
| G C/G | G7 G | C Fsus4/C F/C | C N.C. ||

Live And Let Die

Words & Music by
Paul & Linda McCartney

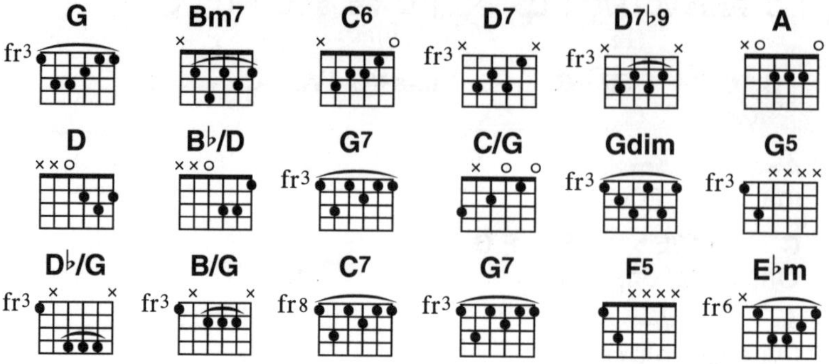

Verse 1

G   Bm7
When you were young
C6   D7   D7♭9
And your heart was an open book
G   Bm7   C6
You used to say live and let live
D7   D7♭9   G
(You know you did, you know you did, you know you did)
Bm7   C6
But if this ever changin' world
A
In which we live in
D   B♭/D
Makes you give in and cry.

Chorus 1

G7 C/G
Say live and let die——
Gdim G7
Live and let die
G7 C/G
Live and let die
Gdim G5
Live and let die.

Interlude | ‖: (G5) | G5 | G5 | G5 :‖

| D♭/G | D♭/G | B/G | B/G |

‖: (G5) | G5 :‖ *Play 3 times*

‖: (G5) | G5 | G5 | G5 ‖

Middle 8

C7
What does it matter to ya
G7
When you got a job to do
D7
You got to do it well
F5
You got to give the other fella hell.

Link 1 | ‖: G5 | G5 | G5 | G5 :‖

Verse 2 | G Bm7 | C6 D7 D7♭9 |

G Bm7 C6
You used to say live and let live
D7 D7♭9 G
(You know you did, you know you did, you know you did)
Bm7 C6
But if this ever changin' world
A
In which we live in
D B♭/D
Makes you give in and cry.

Chorus 2

G7 C/G
Say live and let die——
Gdim G7
Live and let die
G7 C/G
Live and let die
Gdim G5
Live and let die.

Outro ‖: (G5) | G5 | G5 | [1, 2, 3.] G5 :‖ [4.] E♭m (fermata) ‖

Little Lamb Dragonfly

Words & Music by
Paul McCartney & Linda McCartney

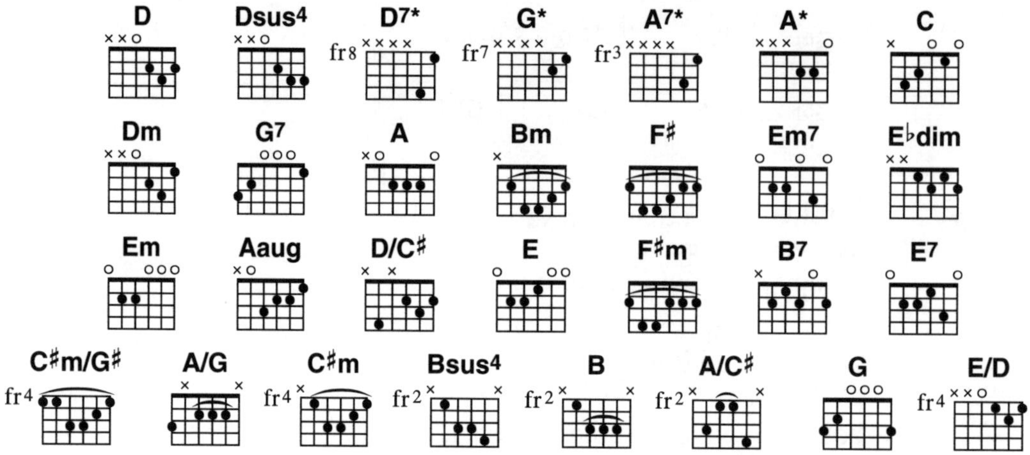

Intro | D Dsus4 D | D7* G* A7* A* | D ‖

‖: C | Dsus4 D | Dm G7 | C :‖ Dsus4 D A ‖

Verse 1

```
Bm                              F♯
   I have no answer for you little lamb

I can help you out
Em7     A                D
   But I cannot help you in
E♭dim                              Em
Sometimes you think that life is hard
A            Aaug         D      D/C♯
   And this is only one of them
Bm                                F♯
My heart is breaking for you little lamb

I can help you out
Em7             A          D
But we may never meet a - gain.
```

Link 1 | D Dsus4 D | D7* G* A7* A* | D ‖

Chorus 1

𝄆 C | Dsus4 D | Dm G7 |
La, la la la— la la la, la la la la— la la
| C 𝄇 E | E ‖
la.

Verse 2

E F♯m
Dragonfly fly by my window
B7 E E7
You and I still have a way to go
A C♯m/G♯ A/G F♯m C♯m
Don't know why_______ you hang a - round my door
Em7 A D
I don't live here any more.

Bridge 1

F♯m B7
Since you've gone I never know
F♯m B7 | E | E |
I go on, but I miss you so.

Verse 3

E F♯m
Dragonfly don't keep me wait - ing

(I'm waiting, can't you see me? I'm waiting)
B7 E E7
When we try, we'll have a way to go
A C♯m/G♯ A/G F♯m C♯m
Dragon - fly,_______ you've been a - way too long
Em7 A D
How did two rights make a wrong?

Bridge 2

F♯m B7
Since you've gone I never know
F♯m B7
I go on but I miss you so
F♯m Bsus4 B
In my heart I feel the pain——
Dsus4 D A/C♯ Bm | F♯ | G A | D ‖
Keeps coming back a - gain.

Link 2 | D Dsus4 D | D7* G* A7* A* | D | E/D ||

Verse 4

E F#m
Dragonfly fly by my window

(I'm flying, can't you see me? I'm flying)

B7 E E7
You and I can find a way to see

A C#m/G# A/G F#m C#m
Dragon - fly,_______ the years a - head will show

Em7 A D
How little we really know.

Bridge 3

F#m B7
Since you've gone its never right

F#m B7
They go on the lonely nights,

F#m Bsus4 B | Dsus4 D A/C# |
Come on home and make it right.___

Verse 5

Bm F#
My heart is aching for you little lamb

I can help you out

Em7 A D Dsus4 D | D7* G* A7* A* | D ||
But I cannot help you in.

Outro

||: C | Dsus4 D | Dm G7 |
La, la la la— la la, la la la la— la la

| C :||
La. *Repeat to fade*

London Town

Words & Music by
Denny Laine & Paul McCartney

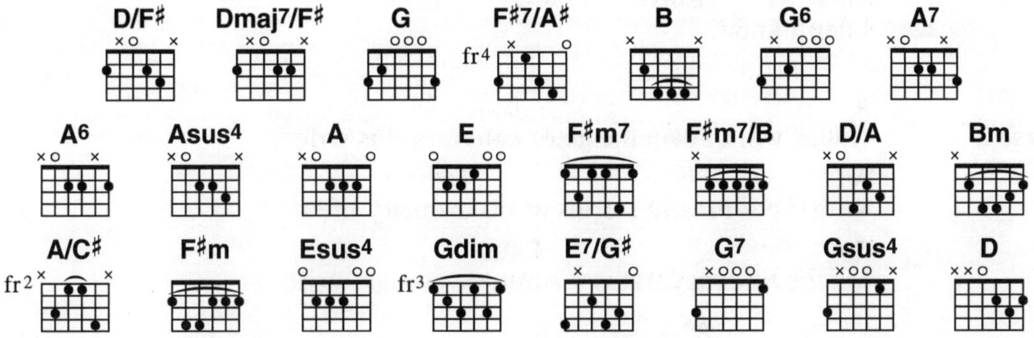

Intro

| D/F♯ Dmaj7/F♯ G | F♯7/A♯ B ‖
| A7 A6 Asus4 A | E | D/F♯ Dmaj7/F♯ G |
| F♯7/A♯ B | B G6 F♯m7 ‖

Chorus 1

E
Walking down the sidewalk on a purple afternoon
F♯m7 F♯m7/B E
I was ac - costed by a barker playing a simple tune up - on his flute
D/A A E
Toot, toot, too, toot
B
Silver rain was falling down
A7 A6 Asus4 A E | A | E ‖
Up - on the dirty ground of London Town.

Verse 1

A Bm
People pass me by on my i - maginary street
A/C♯ F♯m
Ordinary people it's im - possible to meet
Bm Esus4 E
Holding conversations that are always incom - plete
A
Well I don't know.

Bridge 1

F♯m7 Gdim E7/G♯ A
Oh, where are there places to go?
F♯m7 Gdim E7/G♯ A
Someone, somewhere has to know
D/F♯ G E7/G♯
I don't know.

Verse 2

A Bm
Out of work again,the actor entertains his wife
A/C♯ F♯m
With the same old stories of his ordinary life
Bm Esus4 E
Maybe he exaggerates the trouble and the strife
A
Well, I don't know.

Bridge 2

F♯m7 Gdim E7/G♯ A
Oh, where are there places to go?
F♯m7 Gdim E7/G♯ A | D/F♯ Dmaj7/F♯ G | F♯7/A♯ B ||
Someone, somewhere has to know.

Interlude 1

| A | E | D/F♯ Dmaj7/F♯ G | F♯7/A♯ B | B G6 F♯m7 ||

Chorus 2

E
Crawling down the pavement on a Sunday afternoon
F♯m7
I was ar - rested by a rozzer
F♯m7/B E
Wearing a pink balloon a - bout his foot
D/A A E
Toot, toot, toot, toot
B
Silver rain was falling down
A7 A6 Asus4 A E | A | E ||
Up - on the dirty ground of London Town.

| A | Bm | A/C♯ | F♯m |

Interlude 2 Ooh, ooh— ooh,— ooh,——

| Bm | Esus4 E | A ||

ooh.————

Solo | A | A | F♯m | F♯m |

| A | A | F♯m7 Gdim | E7/G♯ A ||

```
        F♯m7      Gdim        E7/G♯  A
Outro   Someone, somewhere has to know

        Silver rain was falling down
             G7       G6    Gsus4  G  D              A
        Up - on the dirty ground of London Town.
```

Lonely Road

Words & Music by
Paul McCartney

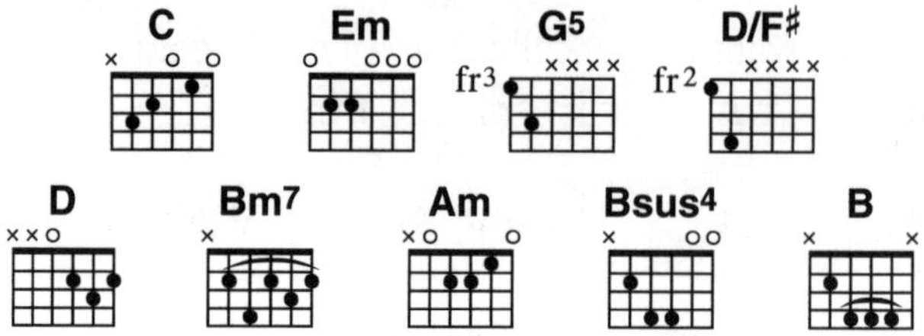

Intro | N.C.(C) | (Em) | (C) | (Em) ||

Verse 1

C   Em
  I tried to get over you
C   Em
  I tried to find something new
C   G5 D/F♯ Em
  But all I could ev - er   do
     D   C   Bm7   Am
Was fill my time with thoughts of you.

Verse 2

C   Em
  I tried to go somewhere old
C   Em
  To search for my pot of gold
C   G5 D/F♯ Em
  But all I could ev - er   hold
    D   C   Bm   Am
In - side my mind were thoughts of you.

Chorus 1

Em   Am
  I hear your music and it's driving me wild
Em   Am
  Familiar rhythms in a different style
Em   Am
  I hear your music and it's driving me wild
          Bsus4
Again,— oh.——

Chorus 2

```
Em                       Am
   Don't want to let you take me down
Em                        Am
   Don't want to get hurt second time around
Em                           Am               B
   Don't want to walk that lonely road again.——
```

Solo

```
| C       | Em      | C       | Em      |
  Yeah.
| C       | G  D/F♯ Em | D       |
| C       | Bm7     | Am      | Am      ||
```

Chorus 3 As Chorus 1

Chorus 4 As Chorus 2

Chorus 5 As Chorus 2

Outro

```
    Em                        Am
||: I don't want to walk that lonely road, no
Em                            Am
   Don't wanna, don't wanna walk that lonely road
Em                     Am
Don't wanna walk that lonely road
Am                    Bsus4
I don't wanna walk, no no no no no no. :||  Repeat w/ad lib. vocal
Em
I don't wanna walk that lonely road, oh no, oh no.
```

Long Haired Lady

Words & Music by
Paul McCartney & Linda McCartney

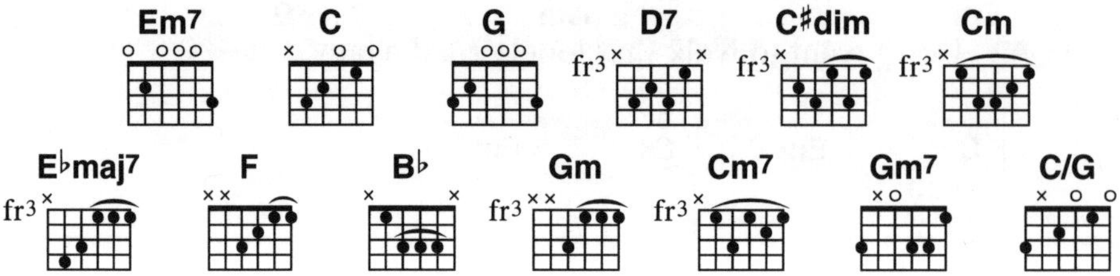

Verse 1

Em7 N.C.
Well, well, well, well, well
C G
Do you love me like you know you ought to do?
Em7 N.C.
Well, well, well, well, well
C G
Or is this the only thing you want me for?
D7 C♯dim
Well, I've been meaning to talk to you about it for sometime
Cm E♭maj7 G
Sweet little lass, you are my long haired lady.

Verse 2

F B♭ D7 Gm
Who's the lady that makes that brief oc - casional laughter?
F B♭ D7 Gm
She's the lady who wears those flashing eyes
F B♭ D7 Gm
Who'll be taking her ome when all the dancing is over?
F B♭ D7 Gm
I'm the lucky man she will hypno - tize.

Chorus 1

Cm7 G
Long haired lady
Cm7 G
Long haired lady.

Verse 3

F B♭ D7 Gm
Bees are buzzing about my sweet de - lectable baby

F B♭ D7 Gm
Birds are humming about their big sur - prise

F B♭ D7 Gm
Who's your favourite person, dear phe - nomenal lady?

F B♭ D7 Gm
I be - long to the girl with the flashing eyes.

Chorus 2

As Chorus 1

Interlude

| G | Gm7 | C/G | G |

G Gm7 C/G G
Ah, my love is long, love is long, love is long

Gm7 C/G G
Ah, sing your song, love is long, love is long

Gm7 C/G G
Ah, when you're wrong, love is long, love is long

G Gm7 C/G G
Win or lose it, winter summer, love is long, love is long
(Ah, when you're wrong———love is long, love is long.)

Verse 4

As Verse 1

Outro

G Gm7 C/G G
Ah, love is long, love is long, love is long

Gm7 C/G G
Ah, sing your song, love is long, love is long

Gm7 C/G G
Ah, when youre wrong, love is long, love is long

Gm7 C/G G
Ah, when youre wrong, love is long, love is long

Gm7 C/G G
Ah, sing your song, love is long, love is long

G Gm7 C/G G
𝄆 Ah, love is long, love is long, love is long. 𝄇 *Repeat ad lib. to fade*

Looking For Changes

Words & Music by
Paul McCartney

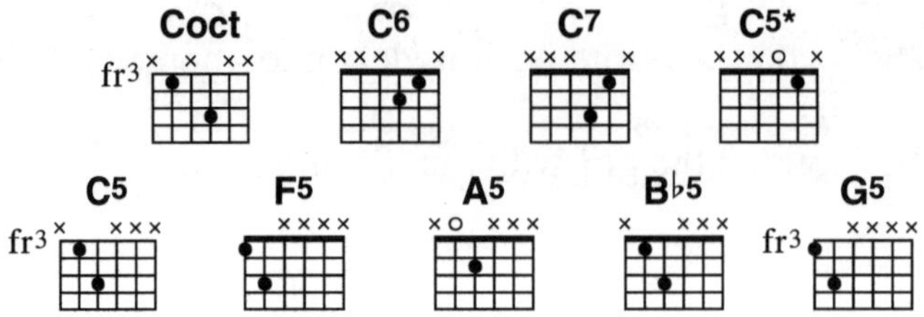

Intro | N.C. Coct C6 | C7 C5* ||

Verse 1

C5
I saw a cat with a machine in his brain
F5
The man who fed him said

He didn't feel any pain
C5
I'd like to see that man take out that machine
F5
And stick it in his own brain
Coct C6 | C7 C5* |
You know what I mean.

Verse 2

C5
I saw a rabbit with its eyes full of tears
F5
The lab that owned her had

Been doing it for years
C5
Why don't we make them pay for every last eye
F5
That couldn't cry its own tears
C5
Do you know what I mean.

Chorus 1

```
C5         A5              B♭5
When I tell you that we'll all be
                            F5
Looking for chan - ges
C5              A5                B♭5                  F5
   Changes in the way we treat our fellow crea - tures
C5        A5        B♭5         G5
   And we will learn how to grow.
```

Solo

```
| C5     | C5     | F5     | F5     |
| C5     | C5     | F5     | F5     ||
```

Chorus 2

```
C5           A5           B♭5
   Well I tell you that we'll all be
                      F5
Looking for changes
C5              A5                B♭5                  G5
   Changes in the way we treat our fellow crea - tures
C5        A5        B♭5         G5
   And we will learn how to grow
                                F5
When we're looking for changes.
```

Link

```
||: (F5)  | G5     | F5     | G5     :||
```

Verse 3

```
C5
   I saw a monkey that was learning to choke
F5
   A guy beside him gave him cigarettes to smoke
C5
   And everytime that monkey started to cough
     F5
The bastard laughed his head off
                                C5
Do you know what I mean?
```

Chorus 3

```
C5        A5             B♭5
When I tell you that we'll all be
                              F5
Looking for chan - ges
C5            A5             B♭5                      G5
   Changes in the way we treat our fellow crea - tures
C5       A5        B♭5         G5
   And we will learn how to grow
                                  F5
When we're looking for changes.
```

Outro

```
G5                  F5
We're looking for changes
G5                  F5
We're looking for changes
G5                    F5            G5
   We're looking for changes in the way we are.

| C5  A5 | B♭5    | F5     ||
```

Loveliest Thing

Words & Music by
Paul McCartney

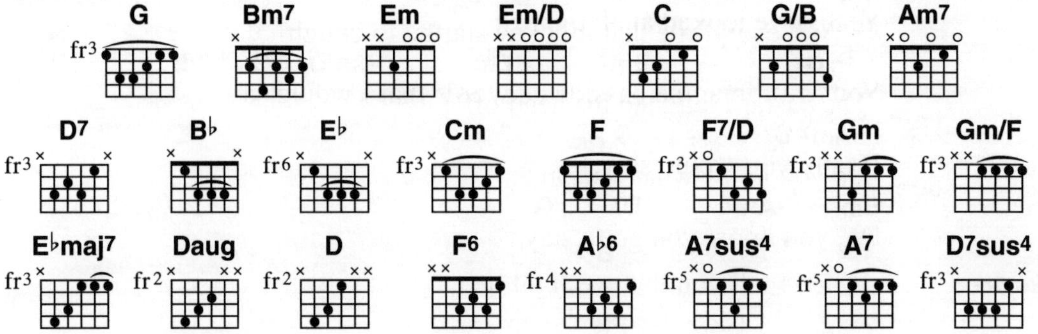

Intro One, two, one...

```
          G                    Bm7       Em          Em/D    C     G/B
Verse 1   To me you are the loveliest thing I've seen all day
              Am7         D7      G
          You can't take that a - way
          Bm7      Am7        D7       G
          No, you can't take that a - way
          G                Bm7                  Em          Em/D   C    G/B
          All my life, I wondered why it couldn't be this way
                       Am7     D7      G
          That was up un - til to - day
          Bm7              D7         G
          Oh. it had to be this way.

            G      B♭   E♭                 Cm        F           F7/A
Chorus 1  To - day,—— wait until the morning comes
              B♭                    D7
          Be - fore you slip a - way
          Gm          Gm/F        E♭maj7
             With - out per - mission
          Gm          Gm/F        E♭maj7
             With - out sus - picion
          Gm          Gm/F        E♭maj7  Daug   D
             With - out per - mission giv  -  en.
```

Verse 2

G Bm7 Em Em/D C G/B
You seem to have a friendlier smile than all the rest

Am7 D7 G
Well I looked and you were best

Bm7 Am7 D7 G
Yeah, I've looked at all the rest

G Bm7 Em Em/D C G/B
You can't imagine passionate words that I would say

Am7 D7 G
If only you would stay

Bm7 Am7 D7 G
Oh, you know you gotta stay.

Chorus 2

As Chorus 1

Middle

E♭maj7 F6
You used to be and early bird

Gm A♭6 Gm F
But how was I to know you would leave without shedding a tear

E♭maj7 F6
I only want to love you

Gm A♭6 A7sus4 A7
I'll make a wish and suddenly I'm glad that I have you here

A7sus4 A7
Oh, I'm glad I have you here

G
Ooh, today.——

Solo

| (G) B♭ | E♭ Cm | F F7/A | B♭ D7 |

| Gm Gm/F E♭maj7 | Gm Gm/F E♭maj7 |

| Gm Gm/F E♭maj7 | Daug D ‖

```
            G                Bm7      Em        Em/D  C   G/B
*Verse 3*   To me you are the loveliest thing I've seen all day

               Am7       D7    G
            And you can't take that away

            Bm7    Am7      D7    G
            No, you can't take that away

            G             Bm7               Em      Em/D  C    G/B
            All my life, I wondered why it couldn't be this way

                    Am7   D7    G
            That was up until today

            Bm7   Am7  D7    G
            Yeah, it had to be this way.


               G   B♭  E♭         Cm      F      F7/A
*Chorus 3*  To - day,___ wait until the morning comes

               B♭            D7
            Be - fore you slip a - way,

               G   B♭  E♭ Cm F F7/A
            To - day,___ oh,_______

               B♭            D7
            Be - fore you slip a - way

            Gm      Gm/F   E♭maj7
              With - out per - mission

            Gm  Gm/F     E♭maj7
            A  -  bove sus - picion

            Gm      Gm/F   E♭maj7  Daug  D        Gm  D7sus4  D7  G
              With - out per - mission giv - en to you, ah,________ ah.
```

Love In Song

Words & Music by
Paul McCartney & Linda McCartney

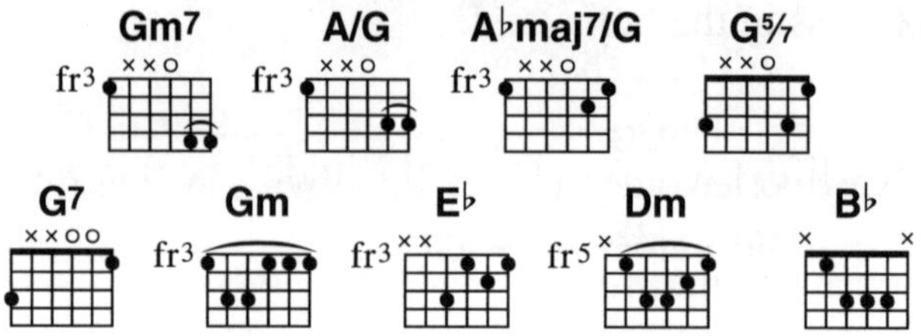

Intro | Gm7 | A/G | A♭maj7/G | G5/7 |

G7 riff

| G7 G5/7 G7 G5/7 G7 G5/7 G7 | G7 riff ||

Verse 1

Gm7 A/G
My heart cries out for love
A♭maj7/G G5/7
And all that goes with loving
G7riff G7riff
Love in song, love in song.

Verse 2

Gm7 A/G
My, you're so fine
A♭maj7/G G5/7
When love is mine I can't go wrong
G7riff G7riff
Love in song, love in song.

Pre-chorus 1

Gm E♭
I can see the places that
Dm Gm
We used to go to now.

```
             B♭                 Dm
Chorus 1     Happiness in the homeland
             | Gm      | E♭      | Dm      | Gm      |
             B♭                 Dm
             Happiness in the homeland.

             Gm7              A/G
Verse 3        My eye cries out
                        A♭maj7/G      G7
             A tear still born misunder - standing
                     G7riff       G7riff
             Love in song, love in song.

             Gm          E♭
Pre-chorus 2 I can see the places that
                Dm          Gm
             We used to go to now.

             B♭                 Dm
Chorus 2     Happiness in the homeland
             | Gm      | E♭      | Dm      | Gm      |
             B♭                 Dm
             Happiness in the homeland.

             Gm7               A/G
Verse 4        My, you're so fine
                          A♭maj7/G     G7
             When love is mine I can't go wrong
                     G7riff       G7riff        G7riff   Gm
             Love in song, love in song, love in song.
```

The Lovers That Never Were

Words & Music by
McCartney & Declan MacManus

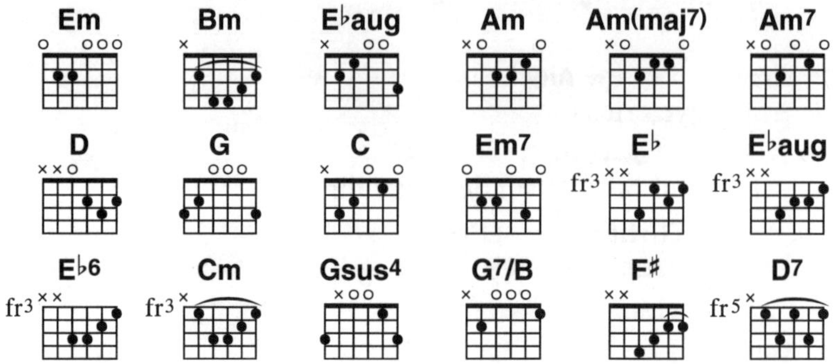

Piano cue

Intro | Em7 | (Em7)N.C. ||

Verse 1
Em Bm E♭aug Am Am(maj7) Am7
I have always needed some - body girl——
D G C D G
But I close the doors to keep out the world.

Pre-chorus 1
Em Em7 G
But for you, I would be here all a - lone
Locked in a photograph.

Chorus 1
E♭ Cm
All of the clocks have run down
E♭ E♭aug
Lover be - ware
E♭6 Cm G N.C.
We'll be the lovers that never were.

Verse 2
Em Bm E♭aug Am Am(maj7) Am7
I hang patiently on every word you send ——
D G C D G
Will we ever be much more than just friends?

Pre-chorus 2

Em G
As for you, you sit there playing this game

Gsus4 G
You keep me waiting.

Chorus 2

E♭ Cm
When all of the clocks have run down

E♭ E♭aug
All over the world

E♭6 Cm G G7/B
We'll be the lovers that never were. ___

C E♭6 G G7/B C E♭6 G G7/B
For as long as the sun shines in somebody's eyes

C E♭6 G G7/B C E♭6 G G7/B
I be - lieve in you ba - by, ___ so don't tell me lies

C E♭6 G C E♭6 G G7/B
For as long as the trees throw down blossoms and leaves___

C E♭6 G Bm F♯ Bm D7
I know there will be ___ a pa - rade of unpainted dreams.

Verse 3

Em Bm E♭aug Am Am(maj7) Am7
And I know dear, how much it's going to hurt___

D G C D G
If you still re - fuse to get your hands dirty.

Pre-chorus 3

Em Em7 G
So you, you must tell me something, I love you

Say goodbye or anything.

Chorus 3

E♭ Cm
All of the clocks have run down

E♭ E♭aug
Time's at an end

E♭6 Cm G G7/B | C E♭6 | G G7/B |
If we can't be lovers we'll never be friends.___

C E♭6 G G7/B C E♭6 G G7/B
For as long as the sun shines in somebody's eyes

C E♭6 G G7/B C E♭6 G G7/B
I be - lieve in you ba - by, so don't tell me lies

C E♭6 G G7/B C E♭6 G G7/B
For as long as the trees ___ throw down blossoms and leaves ___

C E♭6 G Bm F♯ Bm D7 N.C.
I know there will be ___ a pa - rade of unpainted dreams

E♭ Cm G
Ooh.______

The Lovely Linda

Words & Music by
Paul McCartney

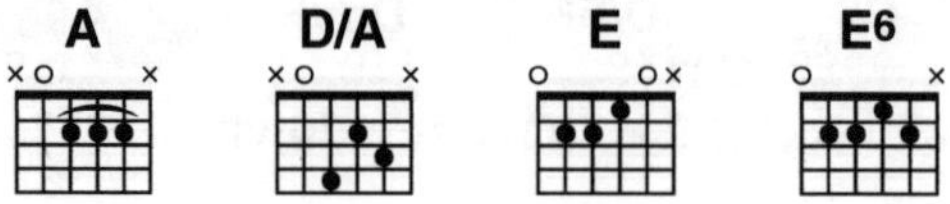

Capo first fret

Intro | A D/A ||

Verse 1

```
E                                   E6  A  D/A   A D/A
  La, la, la,— la,— la,— the love - ly  Lin - da
E                              E6 A    D/A A D/A
  With the lovely flowers in her hair——
E                                   E6  A  D/A   A D/A
  La, la, la,— la,— la,— the love - ly  Lin - da
E                              E6 A    D/A A D/A
  With the lovely flowers in her hair.——
```

| E E6 | E6 E E6 | A D/A (fermata) ||

Mama's Little Girl

Words & Music by
Paul McCartney & Linda McCartney

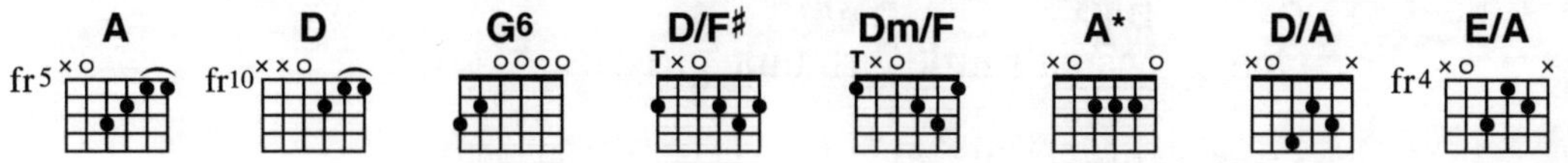

Intro

A	A	D	A
A	A	D	A
G6	G6	D/F♯	Dm/F
A	A	D	A	

Verse 1

```
A
Looking like a rag doll
D                 A
Mama's little girl
A
Singing like a skylark
D                 A
Mama's little girl
     G6
You better give me some time for this heart of mine
        D/F♯               Dm/F
Cause I just can't take it all in
A
Still I will remember
D                 A
Mama's little girl.
```

Chorus 1

| A | A | D | A |

| A | A | D | A |

G6 D/F♯ Dm/F A
Ooh,— Mama's little girl, little girl

D A
Mama's little girl.

Verse 2

A
Looking like a rosebud

D A
Mama's little girl

A
Pickin' up a mountain

D A
Mama's little girl

G6
You better give me some time for this heart of mine

D/F♯ Dm/F
Cause I just can't take it all in

A
Still we will remember

D A
Mama's little girl.

Chorus 2

| A | A | D | A |

| A | A | D | A |

G6 D/F♯ Dm/F A
Ooh,— Mama's little girl, little girl

D A
Mama's little girl.

Link

||: D/A | E/A | A* | A* :||

| D/A | E/A | A | A ||

Bridge

```
D/A          E/A   A
   Looking like a rag doll
D/A         E/A   A
   Singing like a skylark
D/A          E/A   A
   Growing like a rosebud
D/A        E/A    A
   Pickin' up a mountain
D/A         E/A  A
   Mama's little girl
D/A         E/A  A   | N.C.   | N.C.  ||
   Mama's little girl.
```

Verse 3

```
| A      | A      | D      | A      |

| A      | A      | D      | A      |

             G6
You better give me some time for this heart of mine
          D/F♯                 Dm/F
Cause I just can't take it all in
A
Still I will remember
D                   A
Mama's little girl.
```

Outro

```
A
Still we will remember
D                   A
Mama's little girl
A
Still we will remember
D                   A
Mama's little girl
          D/F♯          Dm/F     A
Ooh,— Mama's little girl, little girl
D              A
Mama's little girl.
```

Magic

Words & Music by
Paul McCartney

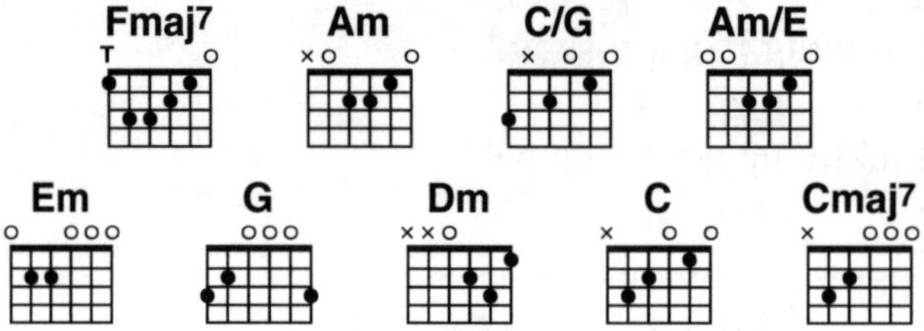

Verse 1

Fmaj7 Am
It must have been ma - gic
C/G Fmaj7
The night that we met
Am/E Em
If I hadn't stopped you
G(Dbass) Dm
I'd always re - gret.

Verse 2

Fmaj7 Am
A few minutes la - ter
C/G Fmaj7
You'd had been out that door
Am/E Em
I'd have been lonely
G(Dbass) Dm G C
Forever - more, forever - more.

```
            Fmaj7                    Cmaj7
Bridge 1    Oh, what made us do it
            Fmaj7                 Cmaj7
            Under what holy spell
            Fmaj7           Am
            Nature's mother knew it
                    Dm   G
            Only too well.

            Fmaj7                      Am
Verse 3     She reached out her fingers
            C/G                   Fmaj7
              To point at the sky
            Am/E              Em
              Leaving me helpless
            G(Dbass)              Dm    G
              Not knowing why.

            Fmaj7              Am
Verse 4     And this is the hour
            C/G                              Fmaj7
              That we turn out the light
            Am/E           Em
            Nothing but memories
            G(Dbass)        Dm   G            C
              Burning so bright, burning so bright.

Bridge 2    As Bridge 1

Verse 5     As Verse 1

              Fmaj7                          Am
Outro       ||: It must have been ma - gic :||  Play 3 times
            C/G                       C
              The night that we met.
```

Mamunia

Words & Music by
Paul McCartney & Linda McCartney

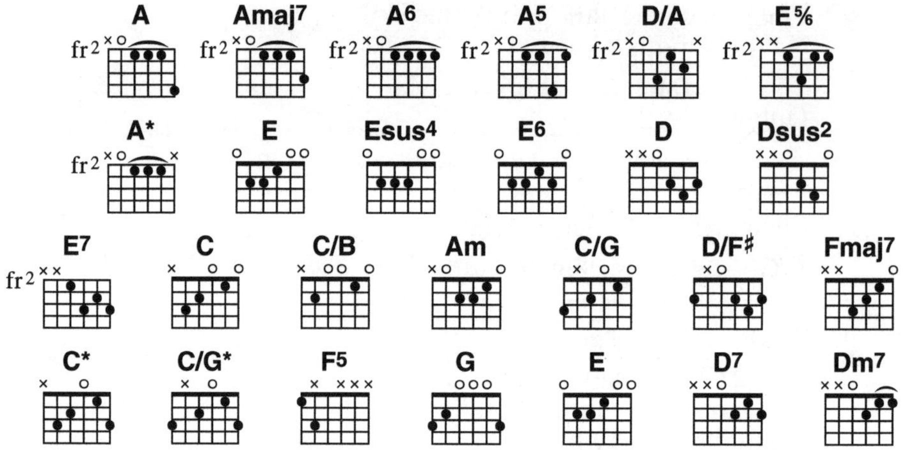

Intro

| A | Amaj7 | A6 | A5 |
| D/A | A6 | E6/9 | A* ‖

Chorus 1

```
A                 Amaj7              A6              A5
  Mamunia,          Mamunia,          Mamunia,        oh, oh, oh
D/A                A6                E6/9            A*
  Mamunia,         Mamunia, oh, oh,— oh.
```

Link 1

| E | Esus4 | E | E6 |
| D | Dsus2 | D | E7 ‖

Chorus 2 As Chorus 1

Verse 1

C C/B Am C/G
The rain comes falling from the sky
D/F♯ Fmaj7 C* C/G*
To fill the stream that fills the sea
C* C/B Am C/G D/F♯ N.C. (F5)
And that's where life be - gan for you and me.

Verse 2

C C/B Am C/G
So the next time you see rain it ain't bad
D/F♯ Fmaj7 C* C/G*
Don't com - plain it rains for you
C* C/B Am C/G
The next time you see L.A. rainclouds
D/F♯ Fmaj7 C* C/B
Don't complain it rains for you and me.

Chorus 2 𝄆 As Chorus 1 𝄇

Verse 3

C C/B Am C/G
It might have been a bright blue day
D/F♯ Fmaj7 C* C/G*
But rainclouds had to come this way
C C/B Am C/G D/F♯ N.C. (F5)
They're watering every - thing that they can see.

Verse 4

C C/B Am C/G
A seed is waiting in the earth
D/F♯ Fmaj7 C* C/G*
For rain to come and give him birth
C C/B Am C/G D/F♯ N.C. (F5)
It's all he really needs to stay and breathe, ah.

Verse 5

C C/B Am C/G
So the next time you see L.A. rainclouds
D/F♯ Fmaj7 N.C.
Don't complain, it rains for you.

Bridge

G C
So lay down your umbrel - las
E Am
Strip off your plastic macs
D7
You've never felt the rain my friend
Dm7 G
Till you've felt it running down your back.

Verse 7 As Verse 2

Chorus 4 𝄆 As Chorus 1 𝄇

Link 2 As Link 1

Chorus 5 𝄆 As Chorus 1 𝄇

The Man

Words & Music by
Michael Jackson & Paul McCartney

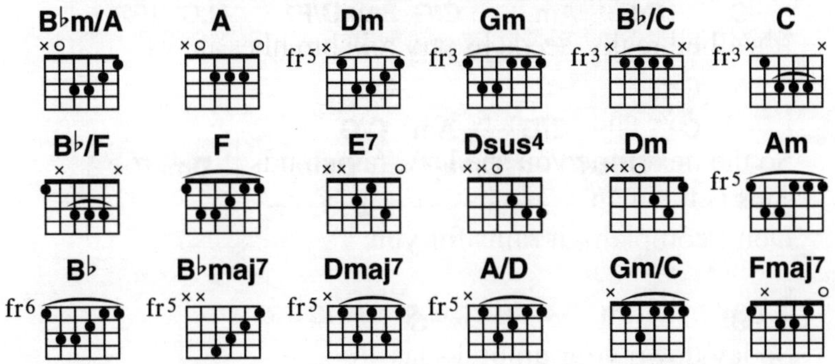

Intro

| B♭m/A | A ‖

| Dm | Gm | B♭/C C | B♭/C C |

| B♭/F F | E7 B♭m/A A | Dsus4 | Dm ‖

Verse 1

F
There's a man
Gm Am B♭
Who plays the game of life so well, ooh
F
There's such a man
Gm Am B♭
His thoughts you can never tell, ooh.

Pre-chorus 1

B♭maj7 Am
And it's just the way he thought it would be
B♭maj7 Am
'Cause the day has come for him to be free
B♭maj7 Am
Then he laughs, he kicks and rolls up his sleeves
B♭maj7 Am
I'm a - live and I'm here for - ever
Dmaj7 A/D | Dmaj7 A/D ‖
This is the man.——

Chorus 3

```
          Gm                Am
And it's just the way he thought it would be
              Gm                 Am
'Cause the day has come for him to be free
          Gm                  Fmaj7
Then he laughs, he kicks and rolls up his sleeves
        Gm                    Am
I'm a - live and I'm here for - ever
              Dmaj7  | Dmaj7  | Dmaj7  | Dmaj7  ||
This is the man.______________________
```

Solo

```
||: Dm    | Gm     | B♭/C  C | B♭/C  C |

| B♭/F  F | E7  B♭m/A  A | Dsus4 | Dm   :||
```

Verse 3

```
          F         Gm              Am     B♭
Did you know this man can do any - thing? Ooh
               F
There's such a man
  Gm                    Am    B♭
I wish that we could bring, ooh.
```

Pre-chorus 2

```
          B♭maj7          Am
And it's just the way she thought it would be
        B♭maj7              Am
As he says, something has happened to me
          B♭maj7               Am
Then he laughs, he kicks and rolls up his sleeves
      B♭maj7               Am
I'm alive and I'm here for - ever
              Dmaj7  A/D | Dmaj7  A/D ||
This is the man.______
```

Chorus 3

```
               Gm              Am
And it's just the way he thought it would be
                 Gm                Am
'Cause the day has come for him to be free
          Gm                         Fmaj7
Then he laughs, as he smiles and rolls up his sleeves
     Gm                     Am
I'm alive and I'm here for - ever
                  Dmaj7 | Dmaj7 | Dmaj7 | Dmaj7 ||
This is the man.________________________

| B♭m/A | A ||
```

Solo

```
|: Dm | Gm | B♭/C  C | B♭/C  C |

| B♭/F  F | E7  B♭m/A  A | Dsus4 | Dm :|
```

Verse 3

```
               F           Gm               Am    B♭
Did you know, this man can do any - thing? Ooh.
                       F
There's such a man
  Gm                     Am    B♭
I wish that we could bring, ooh.
```

Pre-chorus 3 As Pre-chorus 1

Chorus 4 As Chorus 2

Outro

```
                 Dmaj7
This is the man______

This is the man.______
```

Man We Was Lonely

Words & Music by
Paul McCartney

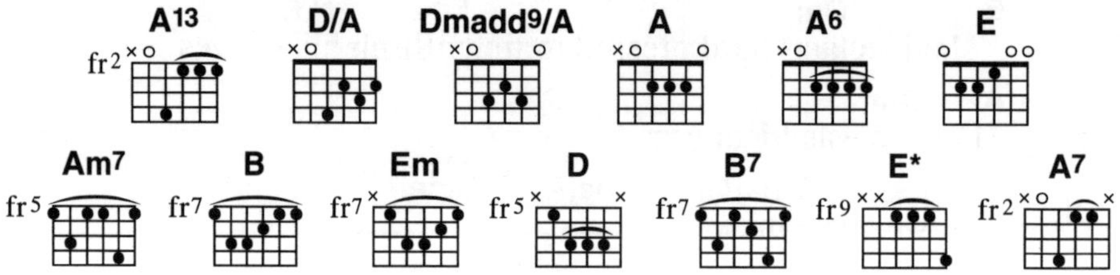

Intro ‖: A13 | D/A | Dmadd9/A |1. A :‖2. A6 | A6 N.C. ‖

Chorus 1

A6
Man, we was lonely

Yes, we was lonely
E   N.C.
And we was hard pressed to find a smile
A6
Man, we was lonely

Yes, we was lonely
E   A
But now were fine all the while.

Verse 1

Am7   B   E
I used to ride on my fast city line
Am7   B   Em
Singing songs that I thought were mine a - lone
Am7   D   Em   Am7   B7
Now let me lie with my love for the time I am home, home
E*   N.C.
Home._____

Chorus 2

```
A6
Man, we was lonely

Yes, we was lonely
E                                      N.C.
   And we was hard pressed to find a smile
A6
Man, we was lonely

Yes, we was lonely
E                          A
   But now we're fine all the while.
```

Verse 2

```
| Am7 B | Em | Am7 B | Em |
Am7          D           Em                        Am7   B7
   Now let me lie with my love for the time I am home, home
E*          N.C.
Home.____
```

Chorus 3

```
A6
Man, we was lonely

Yes, we was lonely
E                                      N.C.
   And we was hard pressed to find a smile
A6
Man, we was lonely

Yes, we was lonely
E                          A
   But now were fine all the while
E                          A
   But now were fine all the while
E                          A
   But now were fine all the while.
```

Outro

```
                                       1.          2.
||: A13 | D/A | Dmadd9/A | A7 :|| A ||
```

Mary Had A Little Lamb

Words & Music by
Paul McCartney & Linda McCartney

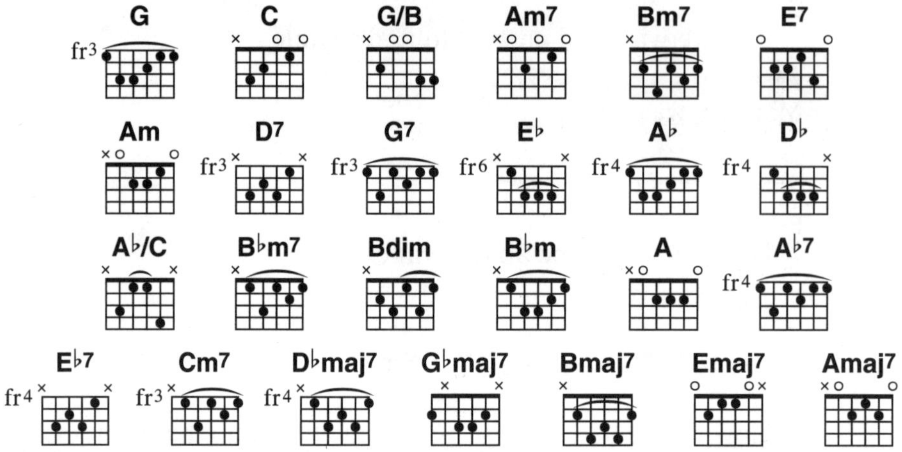

Verse 1

G
Mary had a little lamb
C G/B Am7 G
Its fleece was white as snow
C Bm7 E7
And ev'ry - where that Mary went
Am D7 G
That lamb was sure to go
G7
And you could hear them singing:

Chorus 1

C G/B Am7 D7 G G7
La, la, la, la, la, la, la, la, la, la
C Bm7 E7 Am D7 G
La, la, la, la, la, la, la, la, la, la.

Link 1

| (G) | E♭ | G | E♭ ||

Verse 2

G
He followed her to school one day
C G/B Am7 G
It was a - gainst the rules
C Bm7 E7
It made the children laugh and play to

cont.

Am D7 G
See a lamb at school
G7
And you could hear them singing.

Chorus 2 As Chorus 1

Link 2 | (G) | E♭ | G | E♭ ||

Verse 3

G
And soon the teacher turned it out
C G/B Am7 G
But still it lin - gered near
C Bm7 E7
Waited patient - ly about till
Am D7 G
Mary did ap - pear
G7
You could hear them singing:

Chorus 3 As Chorus 1

Link 3 | (G) | E♭ | G | E♭ ||

Verse 4

A♭
"But the lamb loved Mary so"
D♭ A♭/C B♭m7 A♭
The eager child - ren cry
D♭ A♭/C Bdim B♭m7
"And Mary loves the lamb, you know"
A A♭
The teacher did re - ply
A♭7
And you could hear them singing:

Chorus 4

D♭ A♭/C B♭m7 E♭7 A♭ A♭7
La, la, la, la, la, la, la, la, la, la (Ev'ry body singing)
D♭ Cm7 F7 B♭m E♭7 A♭
La, la, la, la, la, la, la, la, la, la, la, la, la, la
| A♭ D♭maj7 | G♭maj7 Bmaj7 | Emaj7 Amaj7 | A♭ (fermata) ||
(La,) la, la, la, la, la, ooh.

Maybe I'm Amazed

Words & Music by
Paul McCartney

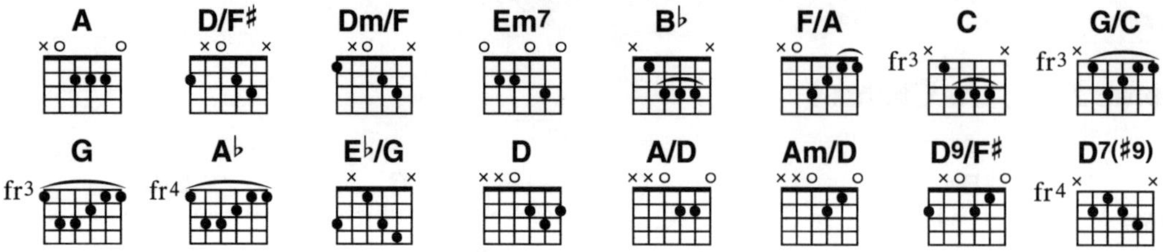

Intro | A | D/F♯ Dm/F | Em7 A(fermata) ||

Verse 1

B♭ F/A C G/C
Baby, I'm a - mazed at the way you love me all the time
B♭ F/A C N.C.
And maybe I'm a - fraid of the way I love you
B♭ F/A C G
Baby, I'm a - mazed at the the way you pulled me out of time
B♭ F/A
And hung me on a line
A♭ E♭/G C
Maybe I'm amazed at the way I really need you.

Chorus 1

D A/D Am/D
Baby, I'm a man and maybe I'm a lonely man
D9/F♯
Who's in the middle of something
G D D7(♯9)
That he dosen't really under - stand
D A/D Am/D
Baby, I'm a man and maybe you're the only woman
D9/F♯
Who could ever help me
G D/F♯ Dm/F | Em7 A ||
Baby, won't you help to me under - stand? Ooh.

Solo 1 | B♭ F/A | C G/C | B♭ F/A | C N.C. |

| B♭ F/A | C G | B♭ F/A | A♭ E♭/G | C ||

Chorus 2 As Chorus 1

Verse 2

```
B♭                F/A                        C              G/C
   Baby, I'm a - mazed at the way you're with me all the time
B♭                   F/A                 C          N.C.
   Maybe I'm a - fraid of the way I leave you
B♭                 F/A                 C                    G
   Baby, I'm a - mazed at the way you help me sing my song
     B♭                      F/A
You right me when I'm wrong
A♭                                E♭/G          C
Maybe I'm amazed at the way I really need you.
```

Instr. Chorus

```
| D  A/D   | Am/D    D9/F♯ | G             | D   D7(♯9) |
  Oh,  oh,        oh,___         hey.__
| D  A/D   | Am/D    D9/F♯ | G             | D/F♯   Dm/F | Em7   A ||
  Oh,    oh,      oh,___         hey.___
```

Solo 2 | B♭ F/A | C G/C | B♭ F/A | C N.C. |

| B♭ F/A | C G | B♭ F/A | A♭ E♭/G | C ||

Outro As Instr. Chorus *to fade*

The Mess

Words & Music by
Paul McCartney

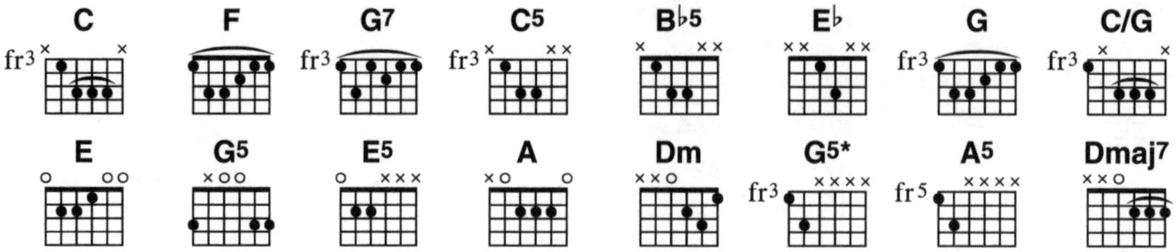

Intro ‖: C | F | C | F :‖

Verse 1

C F
You sailed away one night in June
C F
I heard you say you would be back soon
C F
But since that day it's been one long loon
G7 F C5 B♭5 E♭5 | C5 N.C. ‖
Woah, sweet darling, what a mess I'm in.

Verse 2

C F
I spoke to Jimmy with the big tattoo
C F
Said had he seen any sign of you
C F
He looked at me and then laughed at you
G7 F
See, no just wait a minute, sweet darling,
C5 B♭5 E♭5 | C5 N.C. ‖
What a mess I'm in.

Solo | C | F | C | F | C | F | G7 | G7 |

| G | G C/G | G | G C/G | G | G | E G5 ‖

Link 1 | G5 | N.C.(G5) | G5 | G5 | G5 | N.C.(C5) ‖

Bridge 1

```
E5               G5 A
When I want ya?
E5               G5 A
  Do I get you?
E5           G5 A
All I needed
E5           G5 A
Your number
E5               G5 A
Will you give me
E5                  G5 A  N.C.
Your home number?
```

Link 2

```
|: C    | F    | C    | F    :|
```

Chorus

```
G         F
Oh, sweet darling
G        F
Oh, sweet darling
G         F                      C
Oh, sweet darling what a mess I'm in
F               C            F
What a mess I'm in, since you left me
                C    F
What a mess I'm in, oh yeah
G   Dm  C   E
Oh,—— oh——
G   Dm  C   E               G5
Oh,—— oh,—— c'mon. c'mon.
```

Link 3

```
| G5    | N.C.(G5) | G5    | G5    | G5    | N.C.(C5) ||
```

Bridge 2

```
E5                     G5* A5
  When you're near me
E5                G5* A5
  Can you hear me
E5              G5 (A)
  I can't see ya
E5                  G5 (A)
  Well, I can feel ya
E5                     G5 A
  When you're near me
E5                G5 A
  Can ya hear me?
```

Outro

```
                       |1, 2, 3, 4.        |5.
|: E    | G5   A  | E      | G5   A  :| A      | Dmaj7 ||
                      w/vocal ad lib.
```

Motor Of Love

Words & Music by
Paul McCartney

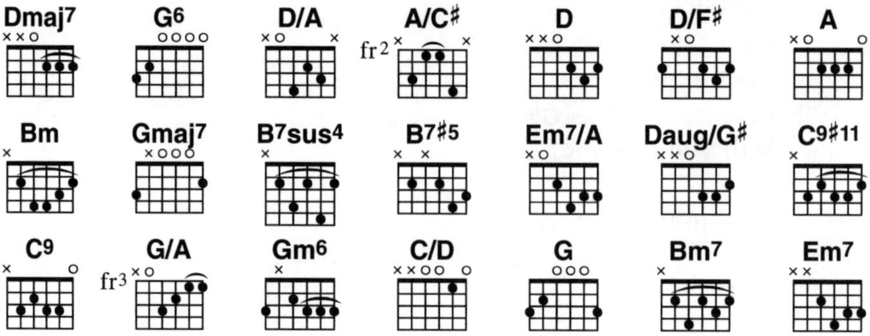

Intro
| Dmaj7 | G6 | Dmaj7 | G6 ||
Ooh,— Ooh,— Ooh,— Ooh,—

Verse 1

G6 D/A A/C♯
I can't get over your love

D D/F♯
No matter how hard life seems

G6 A
There's a light in my dreams

D Bm
Thanks to you.

Gmaj7 D/A A/C♯
My friends keep asking me why

D D/F♯
There's such a smile on my face

G6 A
There's a home at my place

B7sus4 B7♯5
Thanks to you.—

Pre-chorus 1

Em7/A A Em7/A A
I don't want anything from you

Emaj7/A A Emaj7/A
Turn on your motor of love.

```
            D                Daug/G#
Chorus 1    Motor of love, motor of love
            Gmaj7                    C9#11          C9
            Heavenly Father look down from a - bove
            D                       Daug/G#  G/A      Dmaj7
            I can't get over your powerful motor of love.—
            | (Dmaj7) | Gmaj7   | Dmaj7            | Gmaj7     ||
                        Ah, oh.— (Your motor of love....)

            G6         D/A       A/C#
Verse 2       I can't get over your love
                      D         D/F#
            No matter how lost I feel
                    G6        A
            I know my love is real
                      D    Bm
            Thanks to you
            Gmaj7       D/A              A
              You simply reached out your hand
                                D                 D/F#
            And touched me deep in my soul—
                       G6          A
            I came in out of the cold
                       B7sus4  B7#5
            Thanks to you.—

              Em7/A        A          Em7/A     A
Pre-chorus 2  I won't steal anything from you
              Emaj7/A      A              Em7/A     A
              You give me more than e - nough.—

            D                Daug/G#
Chorus 2    Motor of love, motor of love
            Gmaj7                    C9#11          C9
            Heavenly Father look down from a - bove
            D                       G6        Gm6      C/D      G
            I can't get over your powerful motor of love, oh.—
```

Middle

```
               Bm7
There was a time
                                         Em7
When I was down and counted out
                                 Bm7
Well I remember I felt so bad

I nearly threw away
       A/C#                        A
Nearly threw away the keys, ah no no, no no.
```

Chorus 3

```
D              Daug/G#
Motor of love, motor of love
Gmaj7                    C9#11        C9
Heavenly Father look down from a - bove
D              Daug/G#
Motor of love, motor of love
Gmaj7                    C9#11        C9
Heavenly Father look down from a - bove
D                        Daug/G#  G/A      Dmaj7
I can't get over your powerful motor of love.
```

Outro

```
||: (Dmaj7) | Gmaj7    | Dmaj7  | Gmaj7   :||  w/ad lib.
              (Ooh,—     ooh,     ooh.— )     Vocal to fade
```

Mrs. Vandebilt

Words & Music by
Paul McCartney & Linda McCartney

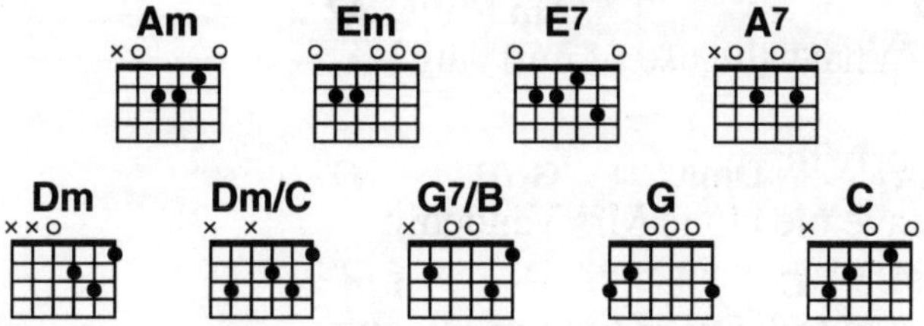

Intro | Am | Em | E7 | Am ||

Verse 1

Am
Down in the jungle living in a tent
Em
You don't use money, you don't pay rent
E7
You don't ever know the time
Am
'Cause you don't mind.

Chorus 1

Am Em
Ho, hey ho
E7 Am
Ho, hey ho
Em
Ho, hey ho
E7 Am
Ho, hey ho.

Verse 2

Am Em
When your light is on the blink
E7 Am
You never think of worrying
E7 Am
What's the use of worrying?

Verse 3

Am Em
When your bus has left the stop
E7 Am
You'd better drop your hurry - ing
E7 Am A7
What's the use of hurrying?

Bridge 1

Dm Dm/C G7/B G
Leave me alone Mrs Vandebilt
C Em
I've got plenty of time of my own.

Link 1

| Dm | Dm | Am | Am N.C. ‖

Pre-chorus 1

E7 Am
What's the use of worrying?
E7 Am
What's the use of hurrying?
E7 Dm Am
What's the use of an - y - thing?

Chorus 2

Am Em
Ho, hey ho
E7 Am
Ho, hey ho
Em
Ho, hey ho
E7 Am | A7 ‖
Ho, hey ho.

Link 2

| Dm | Dm/C | G7/B | G |

| C | C | Em | Em |

| Dm | Dm | Am | Am N.C. ‖

Pre- chorus 2 As pre-chorus 1

Chorus 3 As Chorus 1

Verse 3

```
                   Am              Em
When your pile is one the wane
                        E7                   Am
You don't com - plain of robbe - ry
E7                    Am
   Run away don't bother me
E7                      Am
   What's the use of worrying?
E7                      Dm Am          | A7      |
   What's the use of an - y - thing?
```

Bridge 2

```
Dm              Dm/C         G7/B         G
   Leave me alone Mrs Washington
               C                        Em
I've done plenty of time on my own .
```

Link 3 As link 1

Pre-chorus 3 As Pre-chorus 1

Outro Chorus 𝄆 As Chorus 1 𝄇 *Repeat to fade*

Mull Of Kintyre

Words & Music by
Paul McCartney & Denny Laine

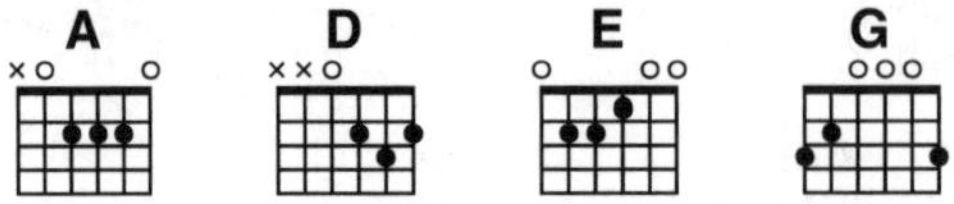

Intro | A | A | A | A ||

Chorus 1

A
Mull of Kintyre
D A
Oh, mist rolling in from the sea
D
My desire is always to be here
A
Oh, Mull of Kintyre.

Verse 1

A
Far have I travelled and much have I seen
D A
Dark distant mountains with valleys of green

Past painted deserts the sunset's on fire
D E A
As he carries me home to the Mull of Kin - tyre.

Chorus 2 As Chorus 1

Instrumental 1 | D | D | G | G |

| D | D | G | G |

| D | D | D | D ||

Verse 2

D
Sweep through the heather like deer in the glen
G D
Carry me back to the days I knew then

Nights when we sang like a heavenly choir
G A D
Of the life and the times of the Mull of Kin - tyre.

Chorus 3

D
Mull of Kintyre
G D
Oh, mist rolling in from the sea
G
My desire is always to be here
D
Oh, Mull of Kintyre.

Instrumental 2

| D | D | A | A |

| D | D | A | A ||

Verse 3

A
Smiles in the sunshine and tears in the rain
D A
Still take me back where my memories remain

Flickering embers growing higher and higher
D E A
As they carry me back to the Mull of Kin - tyre.

Chorus 4 As Chorus 1

Chorus 5 As Chorus 3

Outro

D A
𝄆 Mull of Kintyre, oh, Mull of Kintyre. 𝄇 *Repeat to fade*

Must Do Something About It

Words & Music by
Paul McCartney & Linda McCartney

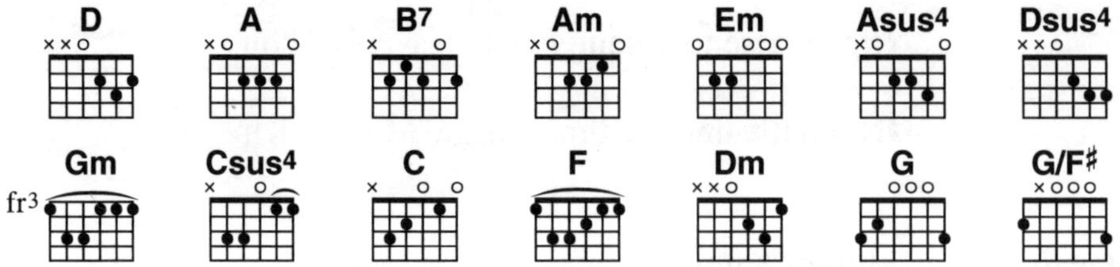

Capo first fret, tune flat

Intro | **(Em)** | **(D)** |
Synth cue

Verse 1

```
D                          A                B7
I've just seen another sunset on my own
Am       B7              Em
All day long I've been alone
        Asus4                   A
And I must do something about it
        Asus4                   A
Yes, I must do something about it.
```

Verse 2

```
D                          A                         B7
Played another losing card game with my - self
Am       B7        Em
Lonely joker on a shelf
        Asus4                   A
And I must do something about it
        Asus4                   A
Yes, I must do something about it.
```

Bridge 1

```
Am                       Dsus4 D
No one on the party line
Gm                             Csus4  C
No one seems to need a dime
F                            Dm                Asus4  A
No one even knows that I'm feeling this way.
```

Bridge 2

Am Dsus4 D
No one seems to need my vote
Gm Csus4 C
No one has to change a note
F Dm
No one here to hold my coat
Asus4 A
Oh, what a day, oh.

Verse 3

D A B7
I've just watched another movie on T.V.
Am B7 Em
No one's in the house but me
Asus4 A
And I must do something about it
Asus4 Dsus4 D
Yes, I must do something about it.
(D) G G G/F# Em Asus4 A
Oh, — oh, —— something a - bout— it.

Verse 4

D A B7
I've just dialled another number on my phone
Am B7 Em
All day long I've been alone
Asus4 A
And I must do something about it
Asus4 A
Yes, I must do something about it.

Verse 5

As Verse 1

Outro

Asus4 A
I must do something about it
Asus4 A
Yes, I must do something about it.

𝄆 Asus4 | A 𝄇 D | (D) G |
Play 3 times

Tag

| A D A G | F G A D | D | (D) G |

| A D A G | D G A D | D | D ||

My Love

Words & Music by
Paul McCartney & Linda McCartney

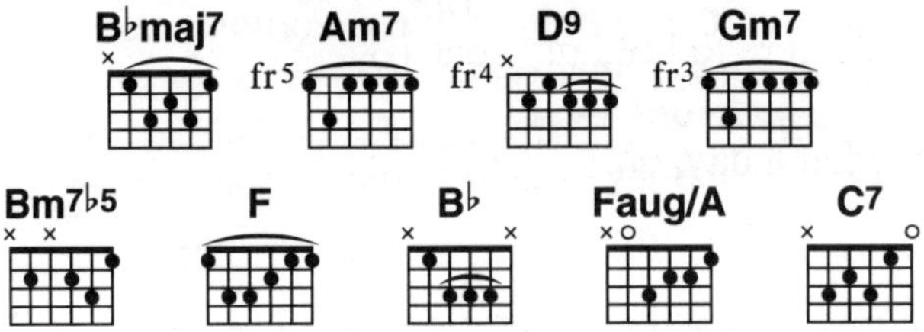

Verse 1

B♭maj7
And when I go away
Am7 D9
I know my heart can stay with my love, it's under - stood
Gm7 Am7 B♭maj7 Bm7♭5
It's in the hands of my love and my love does it good
F Gm7
Wo-wo-wo-wo, wo-wo-wo-wo
B♭ F
My love does it good.

Verse 2

B♭maj7
And when the cupboards bare
Am7
I'll still find something there with my love
D9 Gm7
It's under - stood, it's everywhere with my love
Am7 B♭maj7 Bm7♭5
And my love does it good
F Gm7
Wo-wo-wo-wo, wo-wo-wo-wo
B♭ F
My love does it good.

Bridge

```
   Gm7  C7          F        Faug/A
Oh, I love,— oh wo— my love
      B♭                C7     F   Faug/A
Only my love holds the other key— to me
   Gm7    C7             F    Faug/A
Oh, my love,— oh wo— my love
      Gm7          C7     F
Only my love does it good to me.
```

Solo

```
| B♭maj7 | B♭maj7 | Am7     | D9     |
| Gm7    | Am7  B♭maj7 | Bm7♭5 |
```

```
          F               Gm7
Wo-wo-wo-wo, wo-wo-wo-wo
B♭                F
My love does it good.
```

Verse 3

```
B♭maj7
   Don't ever ask me why
                          Am7
I never say goodbye to my love
              D9                                Gm7
It's under - stood, it's everywhere with my love
     Am7       B♭maj7  Bm7♭5
And my love does it  good
          F               Gm7
Wo-wo-wo-wo, wo-wo-wo-wo
B♭                F
My love does it good.
```

Outro

```
   Gm7      C7               F     Faug/A
Oh, my love,— oh wo— my love
      B♭              C7     F
Only my love does it good to me
Faug/A             B♭     C7       F
Wo-wo-wo-wo, wo-ho, wo-ho, wo.
```

Name And Address

Words & Music by
Paul McCartney

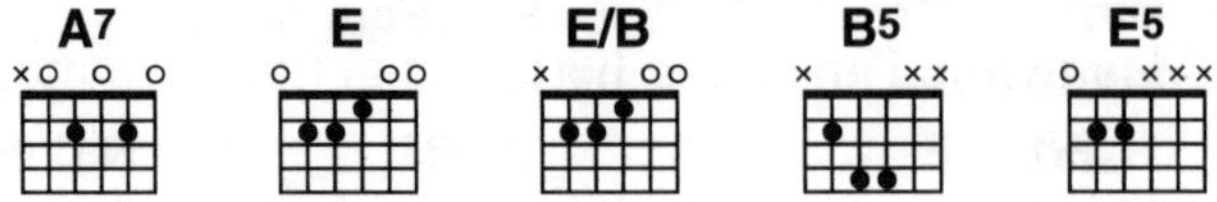

Intro

| A7 | A7 | A7 | A7 |

| E | E | E | E ||
Ooh.—

Verse 1

A7 E
Our love affair was over on the second day
A7 E
You packed a bag and like a birdie flew away
A7
Meanwhile I'm sitting here, I'm getting in a mess
E/B E B5 N.C. (E5)
If you want my love, leave your name and ad - dress.

Verse 2

A7 E
Well, I used to love you baby, when I was your man
A7 E
But maybe loving you is something no one man can do
A7
Meanwhile I'm sitting here, I'm getting in a mess
E/B E B5 N.C. (E5)
If you want my love, leave your name and ad - dress.

Bridge

A7 E
I'd love to feel the tingle of your heavenly caresses
A7 E
I'd love to intermingle, a lonely single without addresses
E/B E B5 N.C. (E5)
If you want my love, leave your name and ad - dress.

Verse 3

```
A7                                E
   But if it's all over baby, you know I'll understand
A7                              E
   Maybe I'll hate to think of you with another man
A7
   Meanwhile I'm sitting here, I'm getting in a mess
        E/B  E                     B5              N.C (E5)
If you want my love, leave your name and address.
```

Solo 1

```
| A7     | A7     | A7     | A7     |
| E      | E      | E      | E      :|| E5       ||
                                         Ooh. —
```

Verse 4

As Verse 3

```
| A7     | A7     | E      | E      |
| A7     | A7     | E      | E      |
| A7     | A7     | A7     | A7
| E/B E  | E      | B5     | E5     | E5       |
```

Outro

```
A7                               E
   But if it's all over baby, you know I'll understand....
```

Nineteen Hundred & Eighty-Five

Words & Music by
Paul McCartney

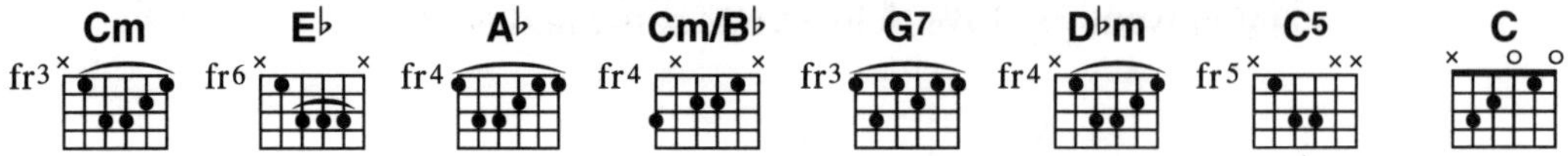

Intro | Cm | Cm | Cm | Cm |

|: E♭ | E♭ | Cm | Cm :|

| A♭ | A♭ | Cm | Cm |

| Cm | Cm | Cm | Cm |

Verse 1

E♭
Ah, no one left alive in nineteen hundred and eighty five
Cm
Will ever do
E♭
She may be right, she may be fine
Cm
She may get love but she won't get mine 'cos I got you
A♭ Cm
Woah,— I,— oh,— I—
(Cm)
Well I just can't enough of that sweet stuff

My little lady gets behind.

Interlude |: Cm | Cm/B♭ | A♭ | A♭ G7 :| Cm | Cm ||

| D♭m | A♭ | Cm | D♭m ||
Ooh.— Ooh.— Ooh.— Ooh.—

Link 1 | Cm | Cm | Cm | Cm ||

Verse2

E♭
Oh, my mama said the time would come
Cm
When I would find myself in love with you
E♭
I didn't think, I never dreamed
Cm
That I would be around to see it all come true
A♭ Cm
Woah,— I,— oh,— I
(Cm)
Well, I just can't get enough of that sweet stuff
My little lady gets behind.

Interlude 2

| D♭m | A♭ | Cm | D♭m ||
Ooh.— Ooh.— Ooh.— Ooh.—

Link 2

| Cm | Cm | Cm | Cm |

Verse3

As Verse1

Outro

|: Cm | Cm/B♭ | A♭ | A♭ G7 :| *Play 11 times*

| N.C.(C5) | (C5) | C ||

Segue "Band on The Run" reprise to fade

No More Lonely Nights

Words & Music by
Paul McCartney

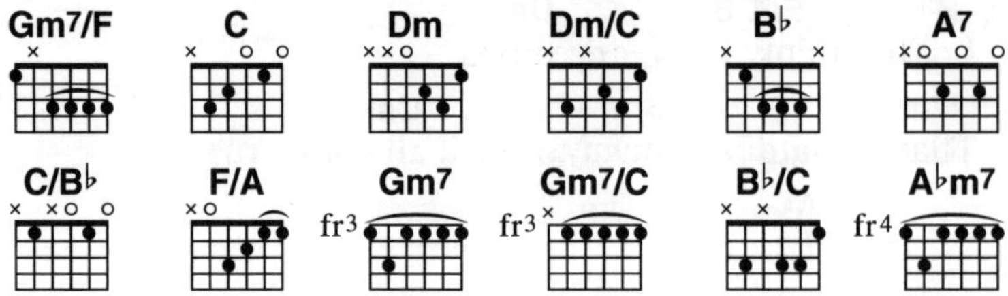

Verse 1

Gm7/F C Dm Dm/C
I can't wait another day— until I call you
B♭ C F A7 Dm Dm/C B♭
You've only got my heart on a string and every - thing a flutter.

Verse 2

C/B♭ Gm7/F C
But another lonley night (and another, and a - nother)
Dm Dm/C B♭
Might take for - ever(and another, 'nother)
C F A7
We've only got each other to blame
Dm Dm/C B♭
It's all the same to me love
C/B♭ F/A B♭
'Cause I know what I feel to be right.

Chorus 1

B♭ F/A B♭ C F
No more lone - ly nights
B♭ F/A B♭ C F
No more lone - ly nights
B♭ F/A B♭ C Dm
You're my guid - ing light
Gm7 Gm7/C C
Day or night I'm always there.

Verse 3

Gm7/F C Dm Dm/C
May I never miss the thrill— of being near you
B♭ C F A7
And if it takes a couple of years
Dm Dm/C B♭
To turn your tears to laughter
C/B♭ F/A B♭
I will do what I feel to be right.

Chorus 2

```
B♭    F/A   B♭     C F
   No more lone - ly nights, never be another
B♭    F/A   B♭     C F
   No more lone - ly nights
B♭        F/A B♭      C  Dm
   You're my guid - ing light
Gm7                 Gm7/C
Day or night I'm always there.
```

Bridge 1

```
         B♭/C                 C
And I won't go away until you tell me so
         B♭/C        C
No I'll never go away.
```

Solo

```
| Gm7/F | C | Dm  Dm/C | B♭  C | F  A7 | Dm Dm/C B♭ |
        C/B♭       F/A        B♭
Yes I know what I feel to be right.
```

Chorus 3

As Chorus 2

Bridge 2

```
         B♭/C                 C
And I won't go away until you tell me so
          B♭/C        C
No I'll never go away
         B♭/C                C
No, I won't go away until you tell me so
          B♭/C        C
No I'll never go away
                      B♭/C  C      B♭/C  C
No more lonely nights, no, no, ooh.—
```

Outro Solo

```
|: A♭m7 | A♭m7 | A♭m7 | A♭m7 :|
```
Repeat to fade

No Words (For My Love)

Words & Music by
Denny Laine & Paul McCartney

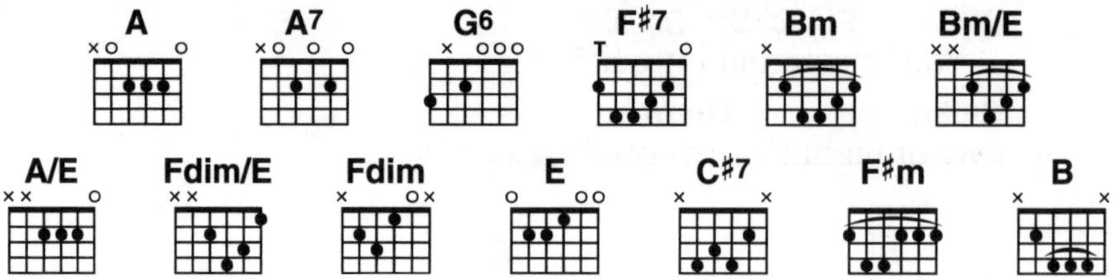

Intro | A | A7 | G6 | F♯7 |
| Bm | Bm/E A/E E7 | A | A

Verse 1
(A) A7
You want to give your love away
G6 F♯7
And end up giving no - thing
Bm Fdim/E A/E Fdim
I'm not surprised that your black eyes
A
Are gazing.

Verse 2
(A) A7
You say that love is everything
G6 F♯7
And what we need most of
Bm Fdim/E A/E Fdim
I wish you knew that's just how true
A
My love was.

Chorus 1 | E | E | C♯7 | F♯m |
B A E
No words for my love.
| (E) | E | C♯7 | F♯m ‖

Verse 3

```
A                    A7
   You're burning love, sweet burning love
G6
   It's deep inside
F#7                Bm                      Fdim/E  A/E
   You mustn't hide your burning love
Fdim                A7
Sweet burning love, your burning love.
```

Verse 4

```
A                          A7
   You want to turn your head away
    G6                      F#7
And someone's thinkning of you
 Bm                    Fdim/E  A/E  Fdim
I wish you'd see, it's on   -   ly   me
 A
I love you.
```

Chorus 2

As Chorus 1

Outro Solo

```
||: Bm   | E   :||
```
Repeat to fade

Nobody Knows

Words & Music by
Paul McCartney

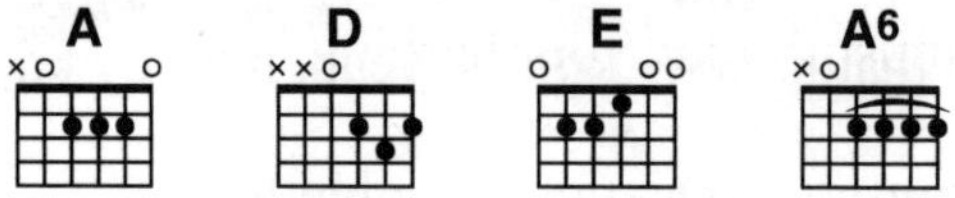

Intro
| A | A | A | A
| D | D | A | A |
Ooh.—

E
They're sayin' nobody knows, no nobody knows.
A

Verse 1
A
Which one of you can tell me what it is I'm looking at

Anyone who can has got to be a crazy cat
D
'Cause I believe that that nobody knows, no nobody knows
A
Yeah, nobody knows, no Lord I cannot tell you
E
Well that's the way I like it
D A
Yeah now, nobody knows.

| A | A | A | A |
Ooh,— ooh.—

Chorus 1
D A
Nobody knows, oh, nobody knows
E A
Well, Lord you know that nobody knows.

Verse 2

A
Samson and Delilah would have made a crazy pair

If that silly woman hadn't shaven off his hair

D A
I believe that nobody knows, yeah, nobody knows

E
But that's the way I like it

D A
Oh, now, nobody knows, no no, no no no.

Chorus 2

| A | A | A | A | A |

Nobody knows

| D | D | A | A |

Nobody knows

E A
That's the way I like it, nobody, nobody knows.

Verse 3

A
I may go hungry, maybe next week

Well, if I do then I'll still find something to eat

D A
And you know, nobody knows, no, nobody knows

E D A
Well, that's the way I like it, baby, nobody knows...

.......and that includes you.

Outro

A
Honey (nobody knows)

I'll pay your rent

I'll do you right (nobody knows)

Most every night

D
But still there's nobody knows

A
No now, nobody knows

E D
And that's the way I like to keep it

N.C A A6
Just so nobody knows.

Not Such A Bad Boy

Words & Music by
Paul McCartney

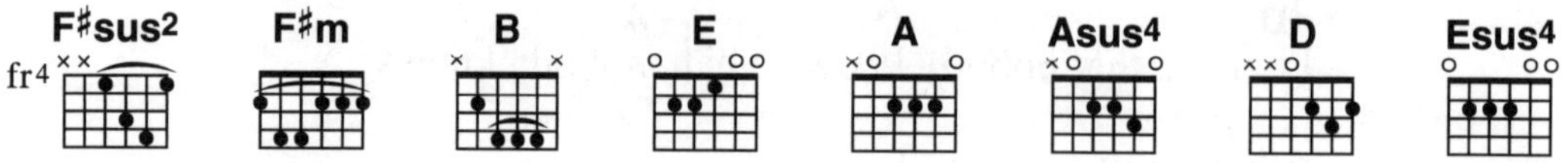

Intro ‖: F♯sus2 N.C. F♯sus2 N.C. :‖ F♯m | B | F♯m | B N.C. ‖

Verse 1

```
F♯m                 B
   I laughed at the teachers
F♯m                B
   Who taught in my school
F♯m                   B
   They kept one arm bandits
   F♯m           B
In the swimming pool.
```

Pre-chorus 1

```
E                A        Asus4  A
   They don't under - stand me
E              A   Asus4  A
   But they never will
E          A          D          B
   And if was there I'd be telling them still.
```

Chorus 1

```
    E        Esus4 E      Esus4 E  A                   Asus4 A    Asus4 A
So I'm not___       such a___      bad boy no more, no  more, no  more
E       Esus4 E      Esus4 E  A                   Asus4 A   Asus4 A
I'm not___     such a___      bad boy no more, no  more, no  more.
```

Verse 2

```
F♯m              B
   I followed the leader
F♯m        B
   Into her tent
F♯m            B
   But nobody told me
     F♯m          B
That she owed some rent.
```

Pre-chorus 2

```
E              A   Asus4 A
  She wanted to love me
E            A Asus4 A
  I wanted to go
E                    A        D       B
  But she taught me things that I needed to know.
```

Chorus 2 As Chorus 1

Solo

```
|: F#m  | B     | F#m  | B             :|
                        (2°) Ooh, yeah.
```

Pre-chorus 3 As Pre-chorus 2

Chorus 3 As Chorus 1

Verse 3

```
F#m          B
  I talked to my lawyer
F#m            B
  He picked up my bail
F#m              B
  Won't someone get me
F#m              B
Out of this lousy jail.
```

Pre-chorus 4

```
E                 A      Asus4 A
  We're both in a - greement
E                 A    Asus4 A
  That crime never pays
E                 A     D      B
  And I should be out in a couple of days.
```

Chorus 4

```
    E       Esus4 E        Esus4 E A
|:So I'm not—      such a—         bad boy no more,
              Asus4 A  Asus4 A
              no  more, no  more
E       Esus4 E        Esus4 E A
I'm not—      such a—        bad boy no more,
          Asus4 A      Asus4 A
          no    more, no    more. :| G (fermata) ||
```

The Note You Never Wrote

Words & Music by
Paul McCartney & Linda McCartney

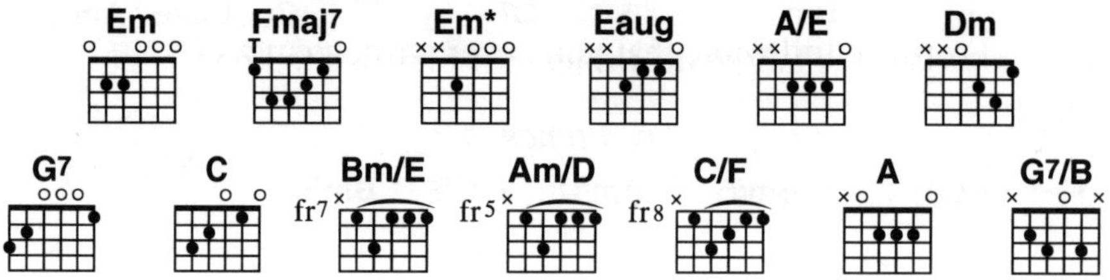

Intro | Em | Em |
Fade in ...

Verse 1
Em
Later on, the story goes
Fmaj7
A bottle floated out to sea
Em
After days, when it had found the perfect spot
Fmaj7 Em* Eaug | A/E
It opened up.

Chorus 1
Dm G7 C Bm/E | Am/D |
And I read the note that you never wrote to me.

Link 1 | C/F | Bm/E | Am/D ||

Verse 2
Em
After all, I'm sure you know
Fmaj7
The Mayor of Baltimore is here
Em
After days now he can finally appear
Fmaj7 Em* Eaug | A/E
Now at last he's here.

Chorus 2

```
        Dm           A
But he never is gonna get my vote,
           Dm          A
'Cause he never is gonna get a quote
          Dm                    G7                  C    Bm/E | Am/D   |
From the little note that you never wrote to me.
```

Play 4 times

Link 2

```
|: C/F   | Bm/E  | Am/D  :| C/F   Bm/E |
```

Solo

```
| Dm    | A     | Dm    | A     |
| Dm    | G7    | C   Bm/E | Am/D |
| C/F  Bm/E | Am/D    ||
```

Verse 3

```
Em
Further on, along the line
           Fmaj7
I was ar - rested on the shore
                     Em
Holding papers of governments galore
Fmaj7                   Em*  Eaug | A/E   |
  I was taken in.
```

Chorus 3

```
      Dm                   A
But I read the note that you never wrote
      Dm                   A
Yes, I read the note that you never wrote
      Dm                   G7         G7/B  C   Bm/E | Am/D  |
Oh, I read the note that you never wrote    to me.

  C/F  Bm/E | Fmaj7 (fermata) ||
To me.___
```

My Brave Face

Words & Music by
Paul McCartney & Declan MacManus

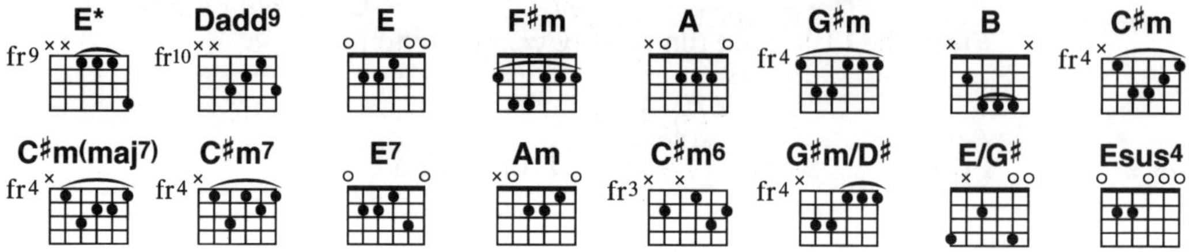

Intro

N.C E♯ Dadd9
My brave, my brave, my brave face.______

Verse 1

E
I've been living in style
F♯m E
Unaccustomed as I am to the luxury life
A G♯m F♯m B E
I've been hitting the town and it didn't hit back.

Verse 2

I've been doing the rounds
F♯m E
Unaccustomed as I am to the time on my hands
A G♯m F♯m B E
Now I don't have to tell any - body when I'm gonna get back.

Pre-chorus 1

C♯m C♯m(maj7) C♯m7 E7
Ever since you went away I've had this senti - mental
A Am E
Incli- nation not to change a single thing
C♯m C♯m(maj7) C♯m7 C♯m6 A
As I pull the sheets back on the bed I want to go bury my head
Am
In your pillow.

```
                E           B     E
*Chorus 1*      Now that I'm alone again

                  E          B           E
                I can't stop breaking down again

                     E          G♯m/D♯         C♯m
                The simplest things set me off again

                                  G♯m    F♯m
                And take me to that place

                F♯m      E/G♯       A            E
                Where I can't find my brave face

                A         E/G♯        F♯m        E
                Where I can't find my brave face

                A            E/G♯        F♯m    E
                My brave, my brave, my brave face.


                | A  E/G♯ | F♯m    | A  E/G♯ | F♯m      |
*Link*                                        My brave
                | E       | E      | E       | E        ||
                face. —


                E
*Verse 3*         I've been living a lie
                                  F♯m E
                Unaccustomed as I   am
                                     N.C.    E
                To the work of a house - wife
                A                           G♯m
                  I've been breaking up
                F♯m     B                     E
                  Dirty dishes and been throwing them away.
```

Pre-chorus 2

C#m C#m(maj7) C#m7
Ever since you left I have been trying to

E7 A Am E
Com - pose a "Baby, will you please come home" note meant for you

C#m C#m(maj7) C#m7 C#m6
As I clear a - way another untouched T.V. dinner

A Am
From the table I laid for two.

Chorus 2

E B E
Now that I'm alone again

E B E
I can't stop breaking down again

E G#m/D# C#m
The simplest things set me off again

G#m F#m
And take me to that place

F#m E/G# A E
Where I can't find my brave face

A E/G# F#m E
Where I can't find my brave face

A E/G# F#m A
My brave, my brave, my brave face.

Outro

| (A) E/G# | F#m | C#m B | A |
My brave

| E | E | Esus4 | E (fermata) ‖
face.—

The Other Me

Words & Music by
Paul McCartney

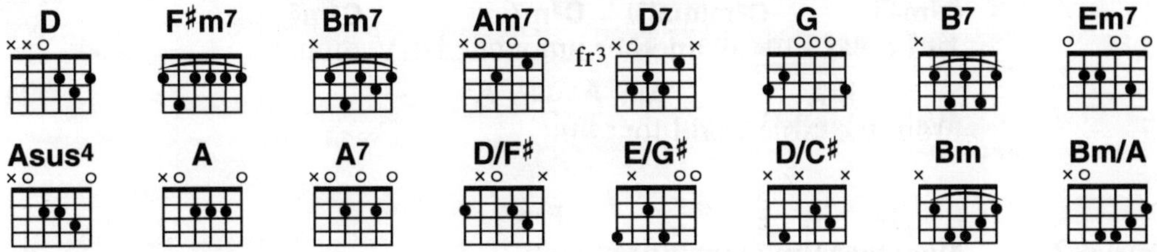

Verse 1

D F#m7
I know I was a crazy fool
Bm7 Am7 D7
For treating you the way I did
G B7
But something took hold of me
Em7 Asus4 A
And I acted like a dustbin lid.

Verse 2

D F#m7
I didn't give second thought
Bm7 Am7 D7
To what the consequence might be
G B7
I really wouldn't be surprised
Em7 A D
If you were trying to find another me.

Chorus 1

D D/F# G
The other me would rather be the glad one
D D/F# G
The other me would rather play the fool
D D/F#
I want to be the kind of me
G E/G# A
That doesn't let you down as a rule.

Verse 3

D F♯m7
I know it doesn't take a lot
Bm7 Am7 D7
To have a little self-con - trol
G B7
But every time that I for - got
Em7 Asus4 A
Well, I landed in another hole.

Verse 4

D F♯m7
But everytime you pull me out
Bm7 Am7 D7
I find it harder not to see —
G B7
That we can build a better life
Em7 A D
If I can try to find the other me, mm, ooh, ooh.

Chorus 2

As Chorus 1

Bridge

G D
But if I ever hurt you
G D D/C♯
Well you know that it's not real
Bm Bm/A G
It's no easy liv - ing by yourself
A N.C.
So imagine how I feel.

Verse 5

D F♯m7
I wish that I could take it back
Bm7 Am7 D7
I'd like to make a different mood
G B7
And if you let me try a - gain
Em7 A Asus4 A
I'll have a better atti - tude.

Verse 6

D F♯m7
Well I know that one and one make two
Bm7 Am7 D7
And that's what I want us to be —
G B7
I really would ap - preciate it
Em7 A D
If you'd help me find the other me, mm, yeah.

```
             D             D/F#          G
Chorus 3     The other me would rather be the glad one
             D             D/F#          G
             The other me would rather play the fool
               D           D/F#
             But I want to be the kind of me
                  G            E/G#     A       G   D
             That doesn't let you down as a rule, ooh.—

             | D      D/F#     | G       | D      D/F#     | G
Outro        Na na na, na na na, na na.  Na na na, na na na, na na na.
             | D        D/F#   | G       E/G#         | A       ||
             Na na na, na na na na na na na na, na na  na.
             D             D/F#          G
             The other me would rather be the glad one
             D             D/F#          G
             The other me would rather play the fool
               D           D/F#
             But I want to be the kind of me
                  G            E/G#     A         G   D
             That doesn't let you down as a rule, yeah.—
```

Off The Ground

Words & Music by
McCartney

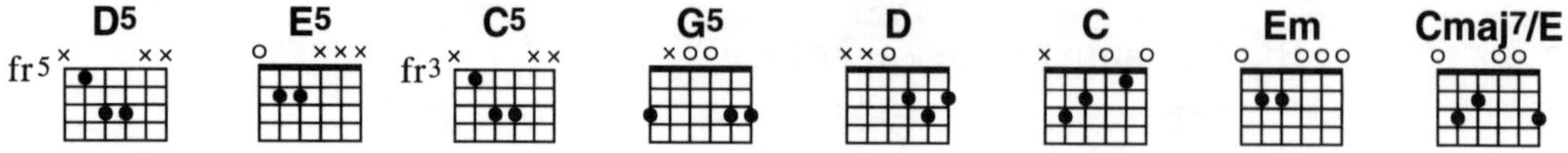

Intro | D5 | E5 | C5 | G5 | G5 ||

Verse 1

G5 D C
There must have been a lot of heart - ache
G5
For you to sink so low
D C
You must have had a ton of pres - sure
D Em
Only answer if the answer's no.

Pre-chorus 1

C D Cmaj7/E D
I need loving, you need loving too
C D
Doesn't take a lot to get off the ground.

Verse 2

G5 D C
There must have been a lot of ma - gic
G5
When the world was born
D C
Let me be the one you wish for
D Em
One you call for, when you're all a - lone.

Pre-chorus 2

C D Em D
I need loving, you need loving too
C D G5
Wouldn't take a lot to get off the ground.

Chorus 1

C D
Off the ground, la la, la la la la la
G5
Off the ground, la la, la la la la la
C D
Fly a - round, la la, la la la la la
G5
Fly a - round, la la, la la la la la
C G5
Hear the sound, hear the sound
C D
Off the ground, la la, la la la la la
G5
Off the ground, la la, la la la.—

Solo

| D | G5 | D | G5 | C | G5 | D | G5 ||

Verse 3

G5 D C
Though it takes a lot of pow - er
G5
To make a big tree grow
D C
It doesn't need a pot of know - ledge
D Em
For a seed knows what a seed must know.

Pre-chorus 3

C D Em D
You need loving, I need loving too
C D G5
Doesn't take a lot to get off the ground.

Chorus 2

As Chorus 1

Chorus 3

| D | G5 | D | G5 |
C G5
Hear the sound, hear the sound
C D
Off the ground, la la, la la la la la
G5
Off the ground, la la, la la la.—

Outro

| D | Em | C | G5 ||
Yeah,— off the ground.

Oh Woman, Oh Why

Words & Music by
Paul McCartney

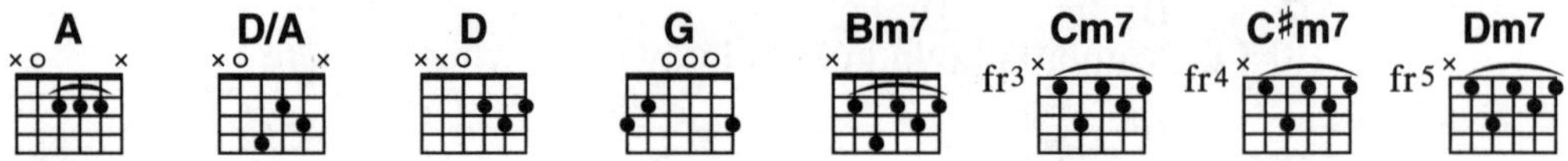

Intro
Drums
4

| A D/A | D/A A D/A | A D/A | D/A A D/A :|

Chorus 1
A D G
Woman, oh why, why, why, why, why
D A D/A
What have I done
A D G
Oh woman, oh where, where, where, where, where
D A
D'you get that gun
G D A
Oh, what have I done
G D A | A D/A |
Ooh, what have I done?

Link 1
| A D/A | D/A A D/A | A D/A | D/A A D/A ||

Verse1
A D/A A
Well I met her at the bottom of a well (of a well)
D/A A
Well I told here I was tryin' to break a spell (break a spell).

Pre-chorus 1
A
But I can't get by, my hands are tied
D G D A
Don't why I ever got her to try my - self
Bm7 Bm7 Cm7 C#m7 Dm7
'Cause I can't get by,——— my hands are tied.

```
            A                D              G
Chorus 2       Oh woman, oh why, why, why, why, why
               D     A
            What have I done
            A             D                   G
               Oh woman, oh where, where, where, where, where
               D     A
            D'you get that gun
            G       D       A
               Oh what have you done
            G            D          A     | A  D/A |
               Oh, woman what have you done?

Link 2      | A   D/A | D/A A   D/A | A   D/A | D/A A   D/A ||

                      A            D              A
Verse 2     Well I am fed up with you lying cheating ways (cheating ways)
                         D                A
            But I get up every morning and every day (every day).

Pre-chorus 2  As Pre-chorus 1

            A                D              G
Chorus 3       Oh woman, oh why, why, why, why, why
               D     A
            What have I done
            A             D                   G
               Oh woman, oh where, where, where, where, where
               D     A
            D'you get that gun
            G          D               A
            Woman, what have I done, what have I done
                       G    D                 A   | A   D/A |
            What have you done, woman what have I done?

Outro       ||: A   D/A | D/A A   D/A | A   D/A | D/A A   D/A :||
                                    Repeat to fade w/ad lib. vocal
```

Old Siam, Sir

Words & Music by
Paul McCartney

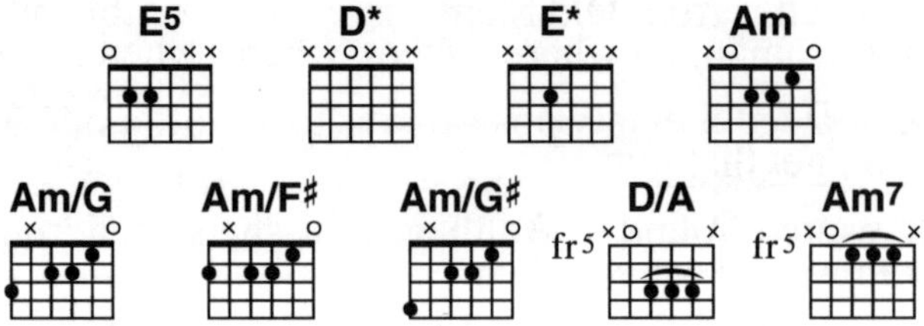

E5 riff

Intro ‖: E5 | E5 D* E* | E5 | E5 N.C. :‖ *Play 4 times*

E5 riff

Verse 1
In a village in Old Siam, sir, there's a lady who's lost her way
In an effort to find a man, sir, she found herself in the old UK
She waited 'round in Walthamstow, she skated 'round in Scarborough.
She waited 'round in Walthamstow, she skated 'round in Scarborough.

E5 riff

Verse 2
In a village in old East End, sir, she met a fellow who made her real
Took her rushes to show, this man, sir
He met her dad at the wedding meal.

Instr. 1
‖: Am | Am | Am/G | Am/G |
| Am/F♯ | Am/F♯ | Am/G | Am/G♯ :‖
‖: D/A Am7 | Am7 | D/A Am7 | Am7 :‖

Link 1 | E^5 | E^5 D* E* | E^5 | E^5 N.C. ||

Verse 3
E^5 riff
In a letter from Old Siam, sir, came a terrible tale of woe
She decided the only answer was to get off a pile of dough
She waited 'round in Walthamstow, she skated 'round in Scarborough
She waited 'round in Walthamstow, she skated 'round in Scarborough.

Verse 4
E^5 riff
When a relative told her man, sir, he directed her not to stay
In a village in Old Siam, sir, there's a lady who's lost her way.

Instr. 2 As Instr. 1

Link 2 As Link 1

Verse 5 As Verse 1

Link 3 ||: E^5 | E^5 D* E* | E^5 | E^5 N.C. :||

Outro As Verse 1 *to fade*

On The Way

Words & Music by
Paul McCartney

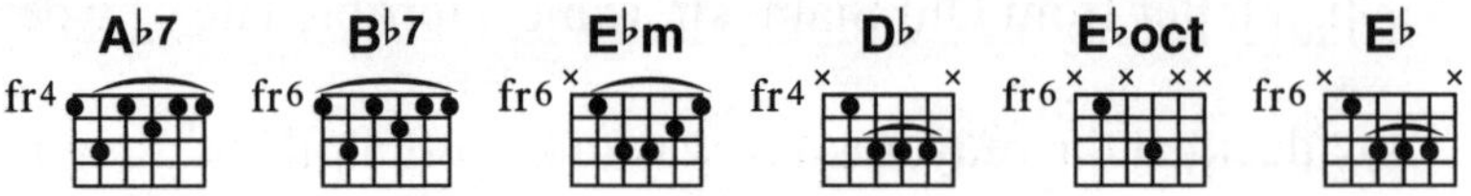

Intro | A♭7 | B♭7 | E♭m | E♭m ||

Verse 1

```
               E♭m
Well you know I'll always love you
          A♭7
But it would have been a lie
  B♭7
If I said that I could please you
        E♭m
Every moment that I try
                A♭7
Wouldn't want to see you crying
      E♭m
So I hope you don't mind
              B♭7
The things I say
           E♭m
On the way.
```

Link 1 | (E♭m) | B♭7 A♭7 | E♭m | E♭m B♭7 ||

```
                    E♭m
Verse 2    Well we've been travelling for a long time
                  A♭7
           And we finally finished here
                   B♭7
           Though I said some things to hurt you
                  E♭m
           Well it was only out of fear
                   A♭7
           Wouldn't want to see you crying
              E♭m
           So I hope you don't mind
                     B♭7
           The things I say
                  E♭m  | E♭m  | B♭7  | D♭  ||
           On the way.

Link 2     | E♭oct N.C | E♭oct N.C | B♭7 | B♭7 ||

Solo 1     | E♭m | E♭m | A♭7 | A♭7 |
           | E♭m | E♭m | B♭7 | B♭7 ||

                   E♭m
Verse 3    Well you know I'll always love you
           A♭7
           Everything will be alright
             E♭m
           If I know you don't mind
                     B♭7       E♭m
           The things I say on the way.

Solo 2     | E♭m | E♭m | A♭7 | A♭7 B♭7 |

             E♭m
           If I know you don't mind
                     B♭7       E♭m
           The things I say on the way.

Verse 4    As Verse 3

Outro      | B♭7 | B♭7 | E♭m | (E♭) ||
```

Once Upon A Long Ago...

Words & Music by
Paul McCartney

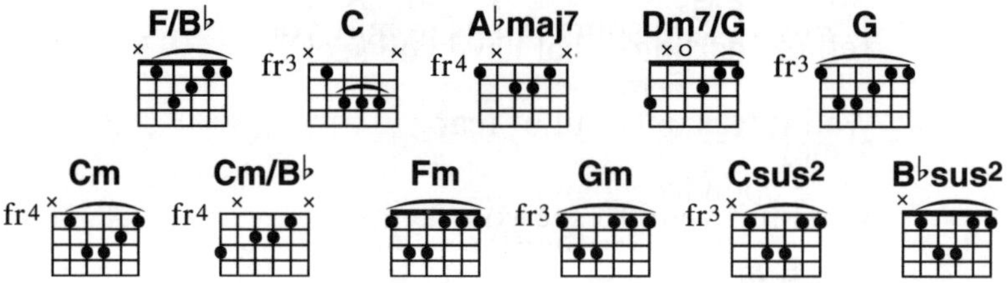

Intro | F/B♭ | C | F/B♭ | C ‖

Verse 1
F/B♭
Picking up scales and broken chords
C
Puppy dog tails in The House Of Lords
F/B♭ C
Tell me darling, what can it mean?

Verse 2
F/B♭
Making up moons in a minor key
C
What have those tunes got to do with me?
F/B♭ C
Tell me darling, where have you been?

Chorus 1
A♭maj7 Dm7/G G
Once upon along ago—
Cm Cm/B♭ A♭maj7
Children searched —— for treasure
Fm Gm G Cm
Nature's plan went hand in hand with pleasure
Csus2 C
Such pleasure.——

Sax Solo | F/B♭ | C | F/B♭ | C ‖

Verse 3

F/B♭
Blowing balloons on a windy day
C
Desolate dunes with a lot to say
F/B♭ C
Tell me darling, what have you seen?

Chorus 2

A♭maj7 Dm7/G G
Once upon along ago——
Cm Cm/B♭ A♭maj7
Children searched—— for treasure
Fm Gm G Cm
Nature's plan went hand in hand with pleasure
Csus2 C
My pleasure.——

Verse 4

F/B♭
Playing guitars on an empty stage
C
Counting the bars of an iron cage
F/B♭ C
Tell me darling, what can it mean?

Verse 5

F/B♭
Picking up scales and broken chords
C
Puppy dog tails in The House Of Lords
F/B♭ B♭sus2 C
Tell me darling,—— what does it mean?

Interlude 1

‖: A♭m7 | Gm G | Cm Cm/B♭ | A♭maj7 |
| Fm | Gm G | Cm | Csus2 C ‖

Solo

‖: F/B♭ | C | F/B♭ | C :‖ A♭maj7 | Gm G |
| Cm Cm/B♭ | A♭maj7 | Fm | Gm G | Cm | Csus2 C ‖

Verse 6

As Verse 4

Verse 7

As Verse 5

Outro

As Interlude 1 to fade

One More Kiss

Words & Music by
Paul McCartney

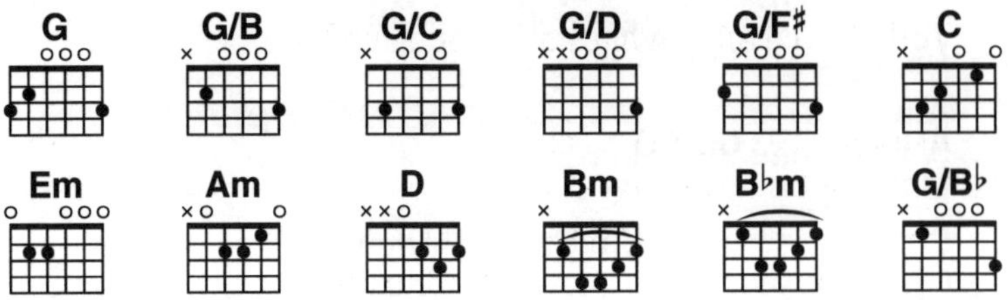

Intro One, two, three, four.

| G G/B G/C | G/D G/F♯ G | G G/B G/C | G/D G/F♯ G |

| C Em | Em Am | Am | D ||

Chorus 1

```
                 Bm
Only one more kiss
                  Em
I didn't mean to hurt you little girl
                         Bm        B♭m
Let's make it one to re - member
Am     D          G    G/B  G/C | G/D  G/F♯  G      ||
   Only one more kiss.
```

Verse 1

```
G          G/B    G/C G/D  G/F♯ G
   I said a fool - ish  thing last  night
          G/B   G/C   G/D G/F♯  G
I didn't think you'd take it     bad
C               Em              Am
   But now I'm on my way a - gain
                  D
And just before I go.
```

```
                  Bm
Chorus 2   Only one more kiss
                   Em
           I never mean to hurt you little girl
                        Bm        B♭m
           Let's make it one to re - member
           Am     D       G    G/B  G/C | G/D  G/F♯  G    ||
             Only one more kiss.


Solo       | G    G/B G/C | G/D G/F♯ G    | G    G/B G/C | G/D G/F♯ G    |

           | C  Em | Em  Am | Am    | D      ||


Chorus 3   As Chorus 1

           G              G/B  G/C  G/D    G/F♯  G
Verse 2      Somebody's built a    home for    us
                          G/B  G/C G/D     G/F♯  G
           Someday we'll see   it    stand - ing   there
           C              Em              Am
             But like the wind that has to blow
                            D
           I must be on my way.


                  Bm
Chorus 4   Only one more kiss
                   Em
           I never mean to hurt you little girl
                        Bm        B♭m
           Let's make it one to remember
           Am           D        G   G/B  G/C | D   G(fermata) ||
             Well, only one more kiss.
```

One Of These Days

Words & Music by
Paul McCartney

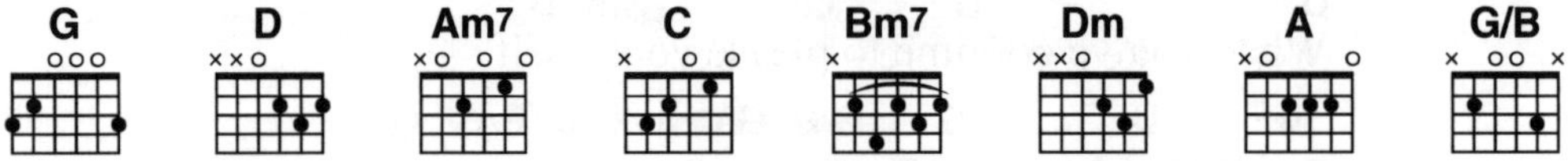

Capo first fret

Verse 1

```
G
One of these days
                D                 Am7
When my feet are on the ground
D           G          C              D
I'm gonna look a - round and see.
```

Chorus 1

```
G   Bm7   C     G   Bm7   C
See what's right, see what's there
     G          Bm7 C               G        G  Bm7 | C  | G
And breathe fresh air, ever af - ter.___
```

Verse 2

```
(G)
   One of these days
            D                   Am7
When a job just takes too long
D              G        C            D
I'm gonna sing my song and see.
```

Chorus 2 As Chorus 1

Bridge 1

```
G        Dm        Am7
   It's there, it's round
     G      Dm
It's to be found
     Am7     G
By you, by me
     A                    G/B  C   N.C.
It's all we ever wanted to     be.
```

```
             G
Verse 3      One of these days
                        D              Am7
             When we both are at our ease
             D               G     C          D
             When you've got time to please your - self

             G   Bm7  C      G  Bm7  C
Chorus 3     See what's right and see what's there
                G         Bm7 C          G       G Bm7 | C |
             And breathe fresh air ever af - ter.___

             G    Dm    Am7
Bridge 2       It's there, it's round
                G    Dm
             It's to be found
                Am7   G
             By you, by me
                A                    G/B  C  N.C.
             It's all we ever wanted to    see.

Verse 4      As Verse 1

             G   Bm7  C      G  Bm7  C
Chorus 4     See what's right and see what's there
                G         Bm7 C          G       G Bm7 | C        G
             And breathe fresh air, ever af - ter,___        ever af - ter
             G       Bm7 C       G
             Breathe fresh air, ever af  -  ter.
```

Only Love Remains

Words & Music by
Paul McCartney

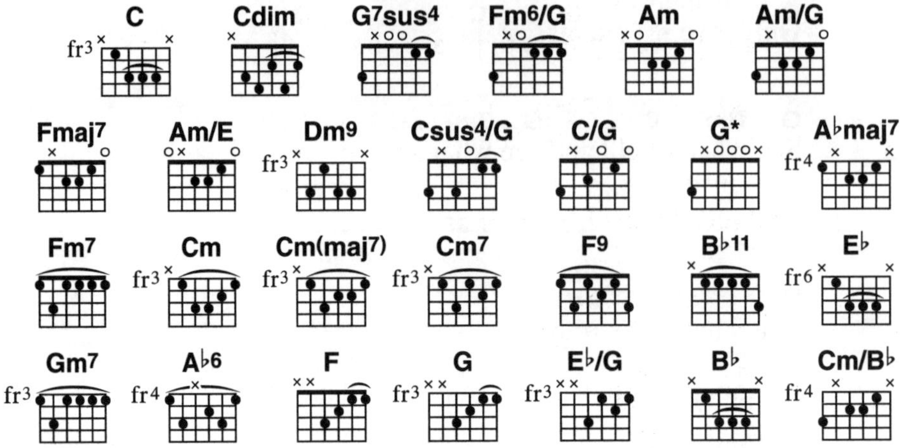

Verse 1

C Cdim G7sus4
And if you take your love away from me
Fm6/G
I'm only going to want it back
C Cdim G7sus4
I'll probably pre - tend I didn't see
Fm6/G Am Am/G Fmaj7
But knowing me, I'll want you back a - gain, and a - gain
Am/E Dm9 Csus4/G C/G
'Til the word has lost it's mean - ing
G* A♭maj7 C
And love is all that stays
A♭maj7 C
Only love re - mains.

Link 1

| A♭maj7 | C | A♭maj7 ‖

Verse 2

C Cdim G7sus4
If you should ever feel that something's wrong
Fm6/G
I'm going to want to put it right
C Cdim G7sus4
To bring a happy ending to our song
Fm6/G Am
I'll carry on believing in a love

cont.

Am/G Fmaj7 Am/E Dm9 Csus4/G C/G
If your love was to trickle through my fin - gers

G* A♭maj7 C
What would it leave me with?

A♭maj7 C
Only love re - mains.

Link 2

A♭maj7 C
Only love, love remains

A♭maj7 Fm7
Only love—— re - mains.

Bridge

Cm Cm(maj7) Cm7 F9 B♭11 E♭
Old e - nough and strong enough to stretch across the world

Gm7 A♭6 E♭ Fm7
Taking the sand in - side an oyster, changing it into a pearl

Gm7 A♭6
Making another magic transformation

E♭ F G | E♭/G |
Find the right boy for the right girl.

Verse 3

C Cdim G7sus4
When all our friends have gone away and we're a - lone

Fm6/G
There's nothing left to shout about

C Cdim G7sus4
Together we'll ex - plore the great un - known

Fm6/G Am
I'd say we won't be going out to - night

Am/G Fmaj7 Am/E Dm9 Csus4/G C/G
Let to - night be the one that we re - mem - ber

G* A♭maj7 C
When love is all that stays

A♭maj7 C
Only love re - mains.

Outro

A♭maj7 C
When love is all that stays

A♭maj7 C
Only love re - mains

A♭maj7 B♭ C | Cm/B♭ | A♭maj7 | C (fermata) ||
Only love ——— re - mains.

Oo You

Words & Music by
Paul McCartney

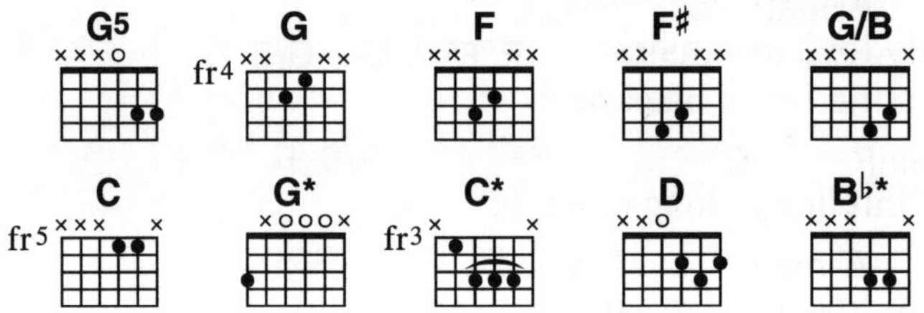


```
        | N.C.(G5) | (G5)              | (G5)       | (G5)   F  F♯ ||
Intro          Spoken: 'More guitar'.

          G                            F  F♯ | G   G/B  C    F  F♯ |
Verse 1     Look like a woman
          G                         F  F♯ | G   G/B  C    F  F♯ |
            Dress like a lady
          G                        F  F♯ | G   G/B  C    F  F♯ |
            Talk like a baby
          G                            F  F♯ | G   G/B  C      ||
            Love like a woman.

          G*       | G*       | C*       | C*       |
Chorus 1    Oo,      oo you
          G*       | G*         | C*       | D        ||
          Oo——— you.
```

Link 1 | N.C.(G5) | (G5) | (G5) | (G5) F F# ||

```
      G                               F F# | G  G/B C  F F# |
*Verse 2*  Walk like a woman
      G                                  F F# | G  G/B C  F F# |
           Sing like a blackbird
      G                            F F# | G  G/B C  F F# |
           Eat like a hunger
      G                               F F# | G  G/B C    ||
           Cook like a woman.
```

```
           G*     | G*          | C*    | C*  |
*Chorus 2* Oo,       woman, oo    oo!
           G*     | G*      | C*   | D   ||
           Oo,——     oo you.
```

Link 2 | N.C.(G5) | (G5) | (G5) | (G5) F F# ||

Verse 3 As Verse 1

```
           G*     | G*          | C*    | C*  |
*Outro*    Oo,       oo you
           G*     | G*      | B♭ (fermata) ||
           Oo.
```

Pipes Of Peace

Words & Music by
Paul McCartney

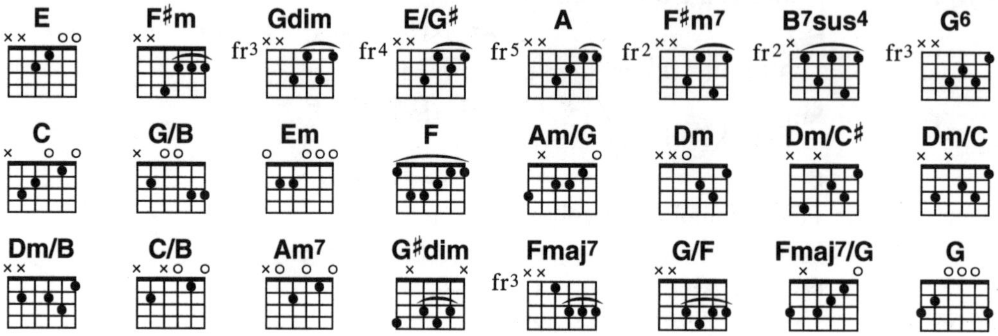

Intro

E F♯m Gdim E/G♯
I light a candle to our love
A E/G♯ F♯m7 B7sus4
In love our problems disap - pear
E F♯m Gdim E/G♯
But all in all we soon dis - cover
A E/G♯ G6 B7sus4 C
That one and one is all we long to hear.

Verse 1

C
All 'round the world
G/B Em
Little children being born to the world
F Am Am/G F
Got to give them all we can 'til the war is won
C G/B
Then will the work be done.

Chorus 1

Dm Dm/C♯ Dm/C
Help them to learn (help them to learn)
Dm/B C C/B Am7
Songs of joy instead of burn, baby, burn (burn, baby burn)
G♯dim Am Am/G F
Let us show them how to play the pipes of peace
Am Am/G Fmaj7 G/F | Fmaj7/G G ||
Play the pipes of peace.———

Link 1 | Am Am/G | F | C | Em | Am Am/G | F (F/E) ||

Chorus 2

Dm Dm/C♯
Help me to learn
Dm/C Dm/B C C/B
Songs of joy instead of burn, baby, burn
Am7 G♯dim Am
Won't you show me how to play (how to play)
Am/G F
The pipes of peace(pipes of peace)
Am Am/G Fmaj7 G/F | Fmaj7/G G |
Play the pipes of peace.———
| Fmaj7 G/F | Fmaj7/G G ||
Ooh.———

Verse 2

C
What do you say?(What do you say)
G/B Em
Will the human race be run in a day? (In a day)
F Am Am/G F
Or will someone save this planet we're play - ing on?
C G/B
Is it the only one? (What are we going to do?)

Chorus 3

Dm Dm/C♯ Dm/C
Help them to see (help them to see)
Dm/B C C/B Am7
That the people here are like you and me (you and me)
G♯dim Am
Let us show them how to play (how to play)
Am/G F
The pipes of peace (pipes of peace)
Am Am/G Fmaj7 G/F | Fmaj7/G G ||
Play the pipes of peace
| Fmaj7 G/F | Fmaj7/G G ||
Ooh.———

Outro As Intro

| (C) G/B | Am | E (fermata) ||

The Pound Is Sinking

Words & Music by
Paul McCartney

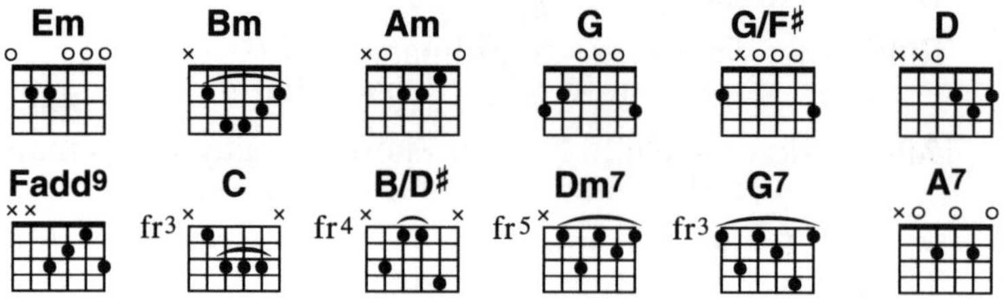

Intro | Em | Em | Em | Em ||

Verse 1
Em Bm Em
The pound is sinking
(Em) Bm Em
The peso's falling
(Em)
The lira's reeling
Am
And feeling quite appalling.

Pre-chorus 1
G G/F♯
The mark is holding
Em
The franc is fading
Am
The drachma's very weak
D
But everyone's still trading.

Chorus 1
G Fadd9 G
The market's bottom has fallen right out
Fadd9 G | Fadd9 | G | Fadd9 ||
And only the strong are sur - vivors.——

Link 1 | Em | Em | Em | Em ||

Verse 2

```
              Em
Well I fear, my dear that it's eminently clear
           C                          Em
That you can't see the trees for the forest
                              Am
Your father was an ex - traordinary man
      D                                   G       C          Em
But you don't seem to have in - herited many of his mannerisms

| C      | Em     | Em     |

        C         Em
Oh, any of his mannerisms.
```

Pre-chorus 2

```
G                          G/F#
   The dollar's moving
Em
   The rouble's rising
Am
   The yen is keeping up
         D
Which hardly seems surprising.
```

Chorus 2 As Chorus 1

Bridge

```
Em              B/D#
Hear me my love
  Dm7                        G7
I can't be held responsible now
     D                         A7
For something that didn't happen
  D            C    Bm
I knew you for a minute
G            Em       C        Bm
Oh, it didn't happen only for a minute
        Em               Bm        C
Your heart just wasn't in it any - more.
```

Verse 3

```
      N.C(Em)            Bm  Em
The pound is sinking
      (Em)           Bm  Em
The peso's falling
      (Em)
The lira's reeling
      Am
And feeling quite appalling.
```

Put It There

Words & Music by
Paul James McCartney

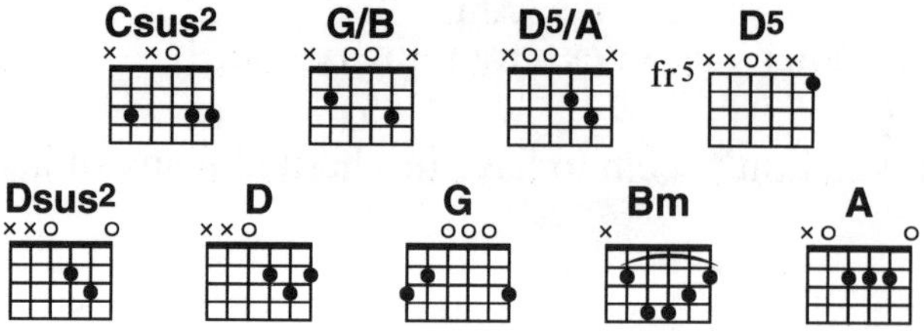

Intro

| Csus2 G/B | D5/A D5 | Csus2 G/B | D5/A Dsus2 D |
| Csus2 G/B | D5/A D5 | Csus2 G/B | D | D ||

Verse 1

G   D
Give me your hand, I'd like to shake it
G   D
I want to show you I'm your friend
G   D
You'll understand if I can make it clear
G   D
It's all that matters in the end.

Chorus 1

Bm   A   G
Put it there — if it weighs a ton
                        D   A   G
That's what the father said to his younger son
Bm   A   G
I don't care — if it weighs a ton
          D   A   Bm   G
As long as you and I are here, put it there
          D   A   D
Long as you and I are here, put it there.

```
Link 1      | Csus2  G/B | D5/A  D5 | Csus2  G/B | D5/A  Dsus2 D |

            | Csus2  G/B | D5/A  D5 | Csus2  G/B | D        | D        ||


               G                 D
Verse 2          If there's a fight, I'd like to fix it
               G                         D
                 I hate to see things go so wrong
               G                  D
                 The darkest night  and all it's mixed emotions
               G                         D
                 Is getting lighter, sing a - long.


                    Bm    A               G
Chorus 2       Put it there — if it weighs a ton
                             D     A       G
               That's what the father said to his younger son
                      Bm   A                G
               I don't care — if it weighs a ton
                         D          A           Bm   G
               As long as you and I are here, put it there
                       D          A           G     D
               Long as you and I are here, put it there.
```

Picasso's Last Words

Words & Music by
Paul McCartney & Linda McCartney

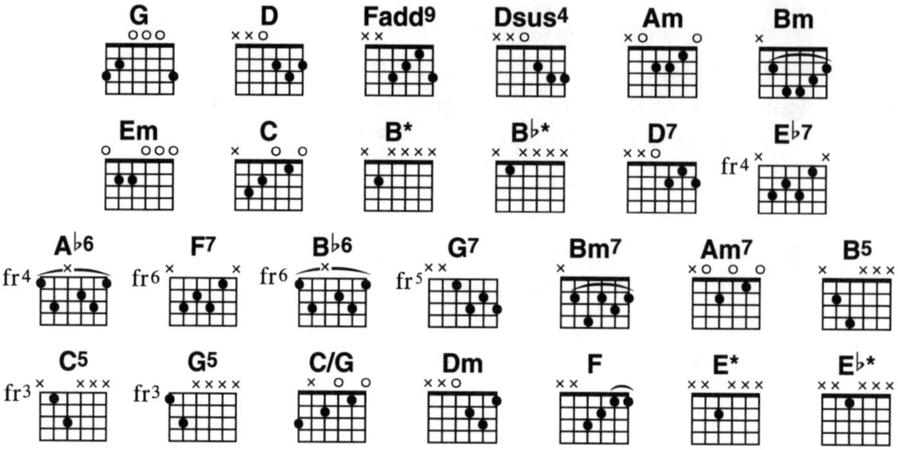

Verse 1

G D Fadd9 G
The grand old painter died last night

G D Dsus4 D
His paintings on the wall

Am
Be - fore he went he bade us well

D G
And said goodnight to us all.

Chorus 1

G Bm Em Am
Drink to me, drink to my health

G D G D
You know I can't drink any more

G Bm Em Am
Drink to me, drink to my health

G D C G
You know I can't drink any more.

```
              Bm                  Em
Bridge 1        Three o'clock in the morning
              Bm                   Em
                I'm getting ready for bed
              Am                 G
                It came without a warning
                       Bm
              But I'll be waiting for you baby
                   Am          D
              I'll be waiting for you there.

              G              Bm Em         Am
Chorus 2        So drink to me, drink to my health
                 G           D        G    D
              You know I can't drink any more
              G           Bm Em       Am
                Drink to me, drink to my health
                 G           D        C      B*  B♭*  | Am7  D7 ||
              You know I can't drink any more.

Interlude 1   | E♭7    | A♭6    | E♭7    | A♭6    |

              | F7     | B♭6    | F7     | B♭6  G7 ||

Link 1        | N.C.   | N.C.   ||
(double tempo)
              |: Bm7   | Bm7    | Am7   B5 C5 | C5   |

              | G5     | G5   C5 G5 | G5     | G5   ||
                  Jet, ooh.—          Jet, ooh.—

              G              Bm Em         Am
Chorus 3        So drink to me, drink to my health
                 G           D        G    D
              You know I can't drink any more
              G           Bm Em       Am
                Drink to me, drink to my health
                 G           D        C/G   G
              You know I can't drink any more.
```

Bass solo | Bm7 | Em | Bm7 | Em |

| Am7 | G | Bm7 | Bm7 |

```
        Am7                           D
I'll be waiting for you baby, yeah.
```

Link 2 | Em | D G ||
(original tempo)

Chorus 4

```
C               Em  Am          Dm
   So drink to me, drink to my health
     C          G          C    G
You know I can't drink any more
C            Em  Am          Dm
   Drink to me, drink to my health
     C          G          F     E* E♭* | Dm   G ||
You know I can't drink any more.
```

Interlude 2 As Interlude 1

Link 3
(double tempo)

```
                                      1.            2.
||: F       | F        | B♭6       | B♭6      :|| G        ||
Ooh.________
```

Outro

```
C            Em  Am          Dm
   Drink to me, drink to my health
     C       N.C. (C)          (G)
You know I.......  hey ho, hey ho
    (Dm)     (C)       (G)
||: Ho, hey ho, hey ho. :||  Repeat to fade
```

Ram On

Words & Music by
Paul McCartney

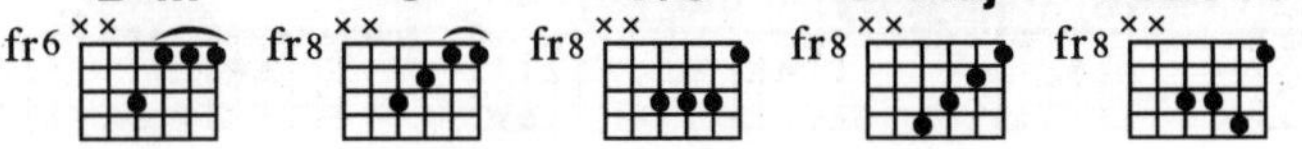

Intro

| B♭m ‖ C F/C | C F/C | C F/C | C F/C C ‖
Fade in...

Verse 1

D♭maj7 B♭m
Ram on give your heart to somebody
D♭maj7 B♭m C F/C | C F/C | C F/C | C F/C C ‖
Soon right a - way, right a - way.

Outro

| C | Fsus4/C F/C | C | Fsus4/C F/C |
Who's that comin' round?—
| C | Fsus4/C F/C | C ‖
They're gonna leave. Who's that comin' round?
Fade out...

Rinse The Raindrops

Words & Music by
Paul McCartney

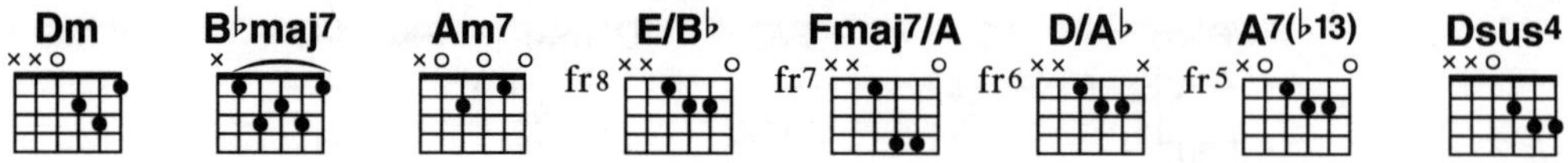

Intro

| Dm | Dm | B♭maj7 | B♭maj7 |

| Am7 | Am7 | Dm | Dm :| *Play 3 times*

|: E/B♭ | Fmaj7/A | D/A♭ | D/A♭ :| A7(♭13) | A7(♭13) ||

Verse 1

Dm
Rinse the raindrops from your head
B♭maj7
Wipe your eyes go back to bed
Am7
In the morning, skies'll clear
Dm Dsus4
And I'll be here
Dm
See the sunlight break the ice
B♭maj7
For the birds of paradise
Am7
Listen to the song they sing
Dm
A - wakening.

Link 1 ‖: E/B♭ | Fmaj7/A | D/A♭ | D/A♭ :‖ A7(♭13) | A7(♭13) ‖

Verse 2 As Verse 1

Link 2 As Link 1

Verse 3 As Verse 1

Link 3

‖: E/B♭ | Fmaj7/A | D/A♭ | D/A♭ :‖
Awakening, awakening.

| A7(♭13) | A7(♭13) ‖ N.C.(Dm) ‖
Bass solo... "two, three, four"

Interlude 1 ‖: Dm | Dm | Dm | Dm :‖ *Repeat ad lib.*

‖: Dm | Dm |
Do do do do do do do do— do do do,

| Dm | Dm :‖
do do do do do do do do.—

Verse 4 ‖: As Verse 1 :‖

Link 4

‖: E/B♭ | Fmaj7/A | D/A♭ | D/A♭ :‖ *Play 3 times*
And I'll be here.

| E/B♭ | Fmaj7/A | D/A♭ | D/A♭ ‖

Verse 5

```
Dm
   Rinse the raindrops from your head
B♭maj7
   Wipe your eyes go back to bed
Am7
   In the morning, skies'll clear
    Dm          Dsus4
And I'll be here
Dm
   See the sunlight break the ice
B♭maj7
   For the birds of paradise
Am7
   Listen to the song they sing
   Dm
Awakening.
Dm
   Rinse the raindrops from your head
B♭maj7
   Wipe your eyes go back to bed
Am7
   In the morning, skies'll clear
    Dm
And I'll be here.
```

Link 5 As Link 1

Interlude 2 ‖: As Interlude 1 :‖ *Repeat ad lib.*

Link 6 As Link 3

Outro ‖: As Verse 1 :‖ *w/ad lib. vocal*

‖: E/B♭ | Fmaj7/A | D/A♭ | D/A♭ :‖ A7(♭13) | A7(♭13) (fermata) ‖

Rockestra Theme

Words & Music by
Paul McCartney

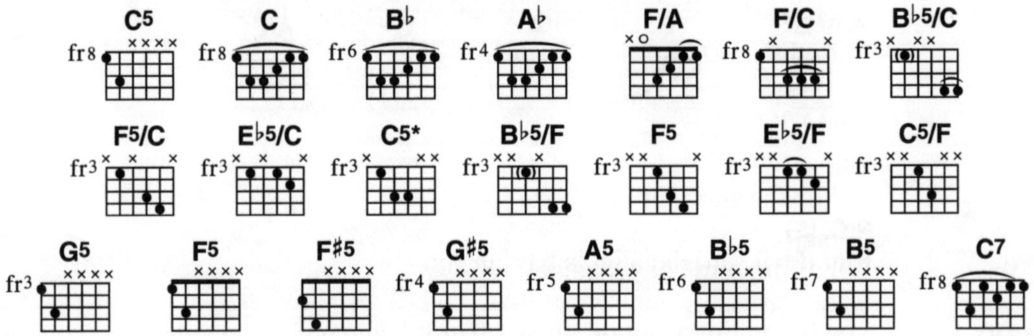

Intro | C5 | C5 | C5 | C5 ||

Verse 1 ||: C | B♭ | A♭ | F/A | F/C C | C | F/C C | C :||

Bridge 1 | B♭5/C F5/C | E♭5/C C5* | B♭5/C F5/C | E♭5/C C5* |

| B♭5/C F5 | E♭5/F C5/F | B♭5/C F5/C | E♭5/C C5* |

| G5 N.C. | F5 | C5 | C5 ||

Verse 2 As Verse 1

Bridge 2 As Bridge 1

Verse 3 As Verse 1

Tag | N.C. G5 F♯5 G5 G♯5 A5 | N.C. G5 F♯5 G5 G♯5 A5 |

| N.C. A5 G♯5 A5 B♭5 B5 |

C5 C7
Wow, wow, wow, no no no no, no no no.—

Run Devil Run

Words & Music by
Paul McCartney

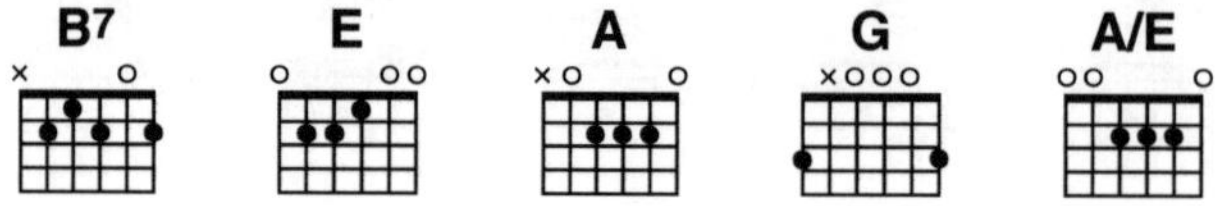

N.C. (E)
Intro Run devil run, the angels having fun

Chorus 1 Making winners out of sinners better leave before he's done
B7
When he gets through, he'll be coming after you
E **A** **G** **A/E** **E**
Listen what I'm saying to you run, —— run devil run.

E
Verse 1 By a swamp in Alabama in the cold, in the damp

Sittin' reading by the light of a kerosene lamp
A
Lives a holly roller with a mission on her mind
E
Got to spread the word to anybody she can find,
B7
You can hear her screaming any time of night or day
E
This is what she says to keep her demons away.

Chorus 2 As Chorus 1

```
                E
Verse 2     Her brother and her sister said that she brought them down

            Steppin' on the bus that was heading for town.
            A
            There they started drinking, they got into a fight
                E
            The sheriff introduced them to the jailhouse for a night,
            B7
            When the holy roller came to town to pay the bail
            E
            This is what she sang as she was leaving the jail.


Chorus 3    As Chorus 1


Solo        |: A      | A      | E      | E      |

            | A       | A      | B7     | B7     :|

            | B7      | B7


            (B7)          E
Verse 3     Well by the middle of the summer they were back at the shack

            Picking cotton for a livin' keepin' on the right track,
            A
            Visiting the neighbours trying to spread the good news
            E
            Singing gospel music with a hint of the blues
            B7
            All of them determined to deliver the goods
            E
            Mmm, you hear the music comin' out of the woods.


Chorus 4    As Chorus 1


                               A    G  A/E         E
Outro       Ah, you better run,_____    run devil run
                          A   G  A/E          (E)
            You better run,_____    run devil run.
            | E      | E      | E      | E      ||
```

Rockshow

Words & Music by
Paul McCartney & Linda McCartney

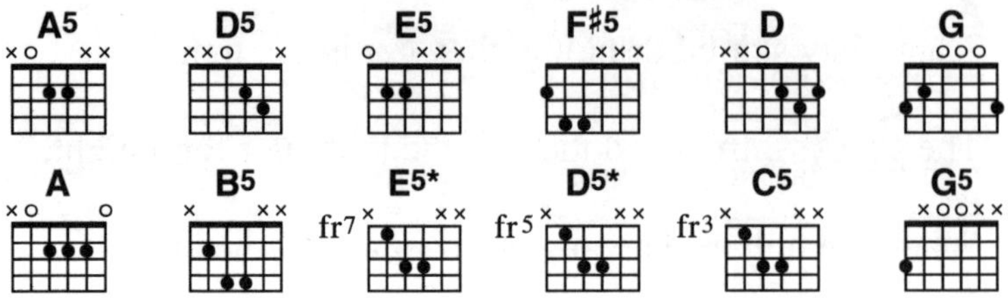

Intro | A5 | A5 D5 | A5 | A5 D5 A5 |
| E5 | N.C.(E5) ||

A5
Verse 1 What's that man holding in his hand?

He looks a lot like a guy I knew way back when
E5
It's Silly Willy with that Philly band
A5
Could be,— ooh-ee. Tell me...

A5
Verse 2 What's that man movin' cross the stage?

It looks a lot like the one used by Jimmy Page
E5
It's like a relic from a different age
A5
Could be,— ooh-ee.

Chorus 1

D5
If there's a rock show
A5
At the Concertgebow
D5
They've got long hair
A5
At the Madison Square
D5
You've got rock and roll
A5 F♯5
At the Hollywood Bowl
E5
We'll be there, — oh yeah.—

Link 1

| A5 | A5 D5 | A5 | A5 D5 A5 |
| D | (D) | D | (D) ||

Bridge 1

D
The lights go down, they're back in town O.K.
G A
Behind the stacks you glimpse an axe
D
The tension mounts you score an ounce, ole!
B5 N.C. B5 N.C. E5 N.C.
Tem - peratures rise as you see the white of their eyes.

Chorus 2

D5
If there's a rock show
A5
At the Concertgebow
D5
You've got long hair
A5
At the Madison Square
D5
They've got rock and roll
A5 F♯5
At the Hollywood Bowl
E5
We'll be there,— oh yeah.—

Link 2 | A5 N.C | A5 N.C | A5 N.C | A5 N.C ||

Bridge 2

A5
In my green metal suit, I'm preparing to shoot up the city
B♭5
And the ring at the end of my nose makes me look rather pretty
B5
Its a pity there's nobody here to witness the end
E5* D5* C5
Save for my dear old friend and confidante
B5 A5 G5
Madamoiselle Kitty, Kitty, Kitty, Kitty!

Link 3 | E5 G5 D5 | C5 D5 | A5 | A5 G5 |

| E5 G5 D5 | C5 D5 | A5 | A5 ||

Verse 3

A5
What's that man movin' to and fro?

That decibel meter doesn't seem to be reading low
E5
But they was louder at The Rainbow
A5
Could be, ooh-ee.—

Chorus 3 As Chorus 1

Outro

D5
||: If there's rock show
A5
At the Concertgebow
D5
They've got long hair
A5
Oh, out at the Madison
D5
Rock and Roll

1, 2, 3.
A5
At the Hollywood Bowl. :||

4.
| A (fermata) ||

Sally G

Words & Music by
Paul McCartney & Linda McCartney

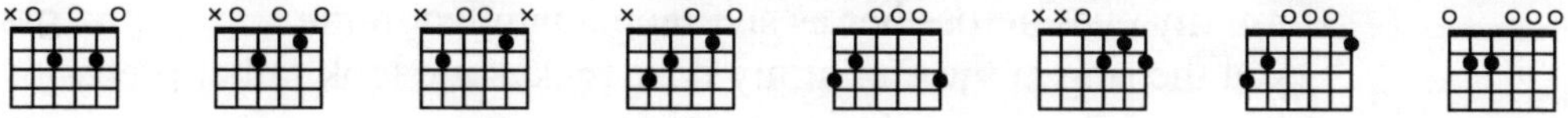

Intro | A7 | Am7 | Am7 G/B | C |
| G C | G C | G C | G C ‖

Verse 1

```
G                                          A7
Somewhere to the south of New York City
Am7                                     G
   Lies the friendly state of Tennes - see
                                       A7
Down in Nashville town I met a pretty
Am7                    C           G
Who made a pretty big fool out of me.
```

Chorus 1

```
                          C      G
And they call her  Sal - ly
C          G  A7                              D7    G7
   Sally G, why d'you wanna do the things you do to me?
                C    G C      G
You're my Sal - ly, Sally G
     A7                    Am7             Am7 G/B C     G
You took the part that was the heart of me,          Sally G.
```

Link 1 | (G) C | G C | G C | G C ‖

Verse 2

```
   G                                       A7
The night life took me down to Printers Alley
        Am7                    G
Where Sally sang a song behind a bar
                                   A7
I ran my eyes across her as she sang a tangled mime
Am7              C                    G
I used to love to hear her sweet gui - tar.
```

Chorus 2 As Chorus 1

Link 2 As Link 1

Bridge

```
Am
  Me and Sally took up
Em
  Things began to look up
G                       D
  Me and her were going strong
Am
  Then she started lyin'
G                        Am
  I could see our love was dyin'
                            Em              C
I heard a voice say "Move along, move a - long".____
```

Link 2

```
| G   C | G   C | G   C | G   C ||
```

Verse 3

```
    G
Well now. I'm on my own again
 A7     Am7                      G
I wonder    if she ever really under - stood
                                          A7
I never thought to ask her what the letter "G" stood for
Am7               C        G
  But I know for sure it wasn't good.
```

Chorus 3 As Chorus 1

Link 3 | G C | G C | G C | G C ||

Take it chaps.

Outro | A7 | Am7 | Am7 G/B | C ||

Sally

| G C | G C | G C | G C G ||

G.___

San Ferry Anne

Words & Music by
Paul McCartney & Linda McCartney

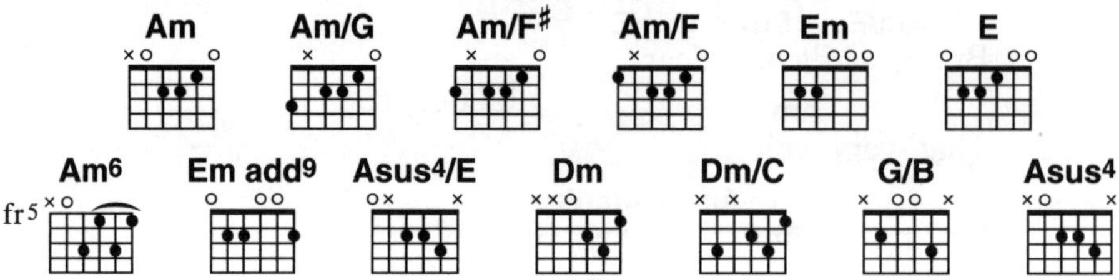

Verse 1

```
N.C.            Am
You've got a lot
                        Am/G
And from what you've got
   Am/F♯      Am/F  Em       E
I'd say you're doing well, dear
              Am
Dressed like a dream
                 Am/G      Am/F♯
And if things are what they seem
       Am/F   Em          E
You're looking swell, dear.
```

Link 1

| Am6 | Am6 | Am6 | Am6 |

| Am6 | Am6 | Em add9 | Em add9 |

| Em | E

Verse 2

```
(E)       Am
Your little man
                                Am/G     Am/F#
Brings you trinkets when he can
    Am/F     Em        E
But he can't stay, dear
                  Am
That' very well
                          Am/G Am/F#
But inside your shiny shell
     Am/F      Em          E
You dance all day, dear.
```

Link 2 As Link 1

Verse 3

```
(E)          Am
So go, be gay
                            Am/G   Am/F#
Let your feelings leap     away
    Am/F Em        E
In - to the laughter
             Am
San Ferry Anne
                                  Am/G   Am/F  Asus4/E Dm
And the world keeps turning happy ever       after.
```

Repeat to fade

Outro

```
|: (Dm)  Dm/C | G/B  Asus4 | Dm   Dm/C | G/B  Asus4    :|
                Do da do.___               Do da do.___
```

Say Say Say

Words & Music by
Paul McCartney & Michael Jackson

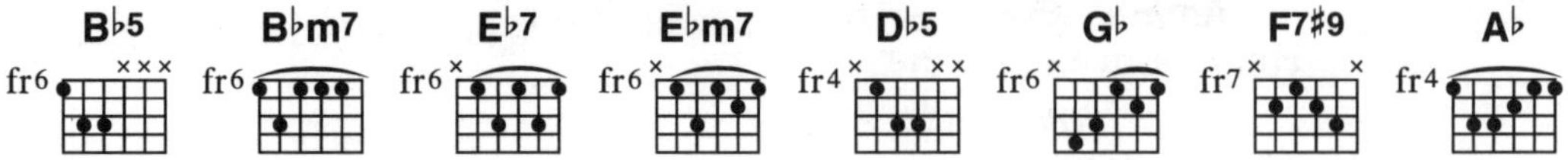

Intro | B♭5 B♭m7 | B♭m7 E♭7 | E♭m7 | E♭m7 D♭5 B♭5 ‖
| B♭5 B♭m7 | B♭m7 E♭7 | E♭m7 | E♭m7 D♭5 B♭5 N.C. ‖

Chorus 1
B♭5 B♭m7 E♭7
Say, say, say what you want
E♭m7 D♭5 B♭5
But don't play games with my affection
B♭m7 E♭7
Take, take take what you need
E♭m7 D♭5 B♭5
But don't leave me with no direction.

Verse 1
E♭m7 G♭
All alone, I sit home by the phone
B♭m7
Waiting for you, baby
E♭m7
Through the years
G♭
How can you stand to hear
F7♯9
My pleading for you dear?
(F7♯9) N.C.
You know I'm crying ooh, ooh, ooh, ooh.

Line 1 | B♭ B♭m7 | B♭m7 E♭7 | E♭m7 | E♭m7 D♭5 B♭5 N.C. ‖

Chorus 2

Bb5 Bbm7 Eb7
Go, go, go where you want
Ebm7 Db5 Bb5
But don't leave me here forever
Bbm7 Eb7
You, you, you stay away
Ebm7 Db5 Bb5
So long girl, I see you never.

Verse 2

Ebm7
What can I do
Gb
Girl to get through to you?
Bbm7
'Cause I love you baby
Ebm7 Gb
Standing here, baptisted in all my tears
F7#9
Baby through the years
(F7#9) N.C.
You know I'm crying ooh, ooh, ooh, ooh.

Brass Instrumental

‖: Bb Bbm7 | Bbm7 Eb7 | Ebm7 | Ebm7 Db5 Bb5 :‖
Say, say, say.

Bridge

Ab Bbm7
You never ever worry
Ab Bbm7
And you never shed a tear
Ab Bbm7
You saying that my love ain't real
F7#9 N.C.
Just look at my face
F7#9 N.C.
These tears ain't drying.

Chorus 3

```
Bb5  Bbm7              Eb7
You, you, you can never say
      Ebm7                    Db5   Bb5
That I'm not the one who really loves you
        Bbm7            Eb7
I pray, pray, pray every day
      Ebm7                  Db5   Bb5
That you'll see things, girl like I do.
```

Verse 3 As Verse 2

Outro

```
| Bb5  Bbm7 | Bbm7  Eb7 | Ebm7    | Ebm7 Db5   Bb5     ||
                                    ooh,  ooh,  ooh,  ooh.
                                             Play 3 times
||: Bb5  Bbm7 | Bbm7  Eb7 | Ebm7   | Ebm7 Db5   Bb5   :||
(1° & 2°) Say, say, say.            Ooh,  ooh,  ooh,  ooh.
                                                Repeat to fade
||: Bb5    Bbm7 | Bbm7  Eb7 | Ebm7          | Ebm7  Db5  Bb5  :||
  Ooh, ooh, ooh,  say, say, say. Ooh, ooh, ooh,  say,  say,  say.
```

She's My Baby

Words & Music by
Paul McCartney & Linda McCartney

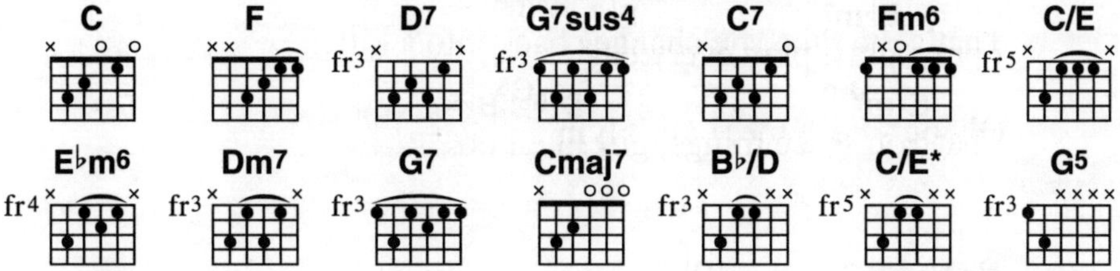

Chours 1

N.C. (C) F
My baby, she comes out at night
D7 G7sus4
She's takin' me by surpri - ise
C G7sus4
She's my baby
C F
Like gravy, down to the last drop
D7
I keep mopping her up
G7sus4 C C7
Yeah, yeah, she's my baby.

Verse 1

F Fm6
She's the baby in the morning time
C/E
When the sleep is in her eyes
E♭m6
And the world is waking up she has arisen
Dm7 G7sus4 G7
Oh be - lieve me, I ain't lyin'
Cmaj7 | C7 B♭/D C/E* ‖
She's a woman.

Verse 2

F Fm6
She's a lady in the evening time
C/E
When the stars are in the sky
E♭m6
That's the time she changes back into a kitten
Dm7 G5
Oh, be - lieve me, I ain't lyin'.

Chorus 2

N.C. (C) F
She's my baby, she comes out at night
D7 G7sus4
She's takin' me by surpri - ise
C G7sus4
She's my baby.
C F
Like gravy, down to the last drop
D7
I keep mopping her up
G7sus4 C C7
Yeah, oh yeah, she's my baby.

Verse 3

F Fm6
Well, she's the baby in the morning time
C/E
When the sleep is in her eyes
E♭m6
And the world is waking up, she has a - risen
Dm7 G7sus4 G7
Oh, be - lieve me, I ain't lyin'
Cmaj7 | C7 B♭/D C/E* ||
She's a woman.

Verse 4

F Fm6
She's the lady of the evening time
C/E
When the stars are in the sky
E♭m6
That's the time she changes back into a kitten
Dm7 G5
Oh be - lieve me, I ain't lyin'.

Chorus 3

```
N.C.                (C)            F
My baby, she comes out at night
                     D7           G7sus4
She's takin' me by surpri - ise
             C        G7sus4
She's my baby
            C                   F
Oh, like gravy down to the last drop
                        D7              G7sus4
I keep moppin' it up, moppin' it up, yeah
             C
She's my baby.
```

Link 1

```
| (C)      | F  G7sus4 | C        | F  G7sus4  |
                                      𝄐
| C        | F  G7sus4 | C        | F  G7sus4  ||
```

Outro

```
| C      | F       | D7    G7sus4 | C   G7sus4 |

||:          C                        F
Ooh, like gravy, down to the last drop
                        D7              G7sus4
I keep moppin' it up, moppin' it up, yeah
             C        G7sus4  :||  Repeat to fade
She's my baby.
```

Smile Away

Words & Music by
Paul McCartney

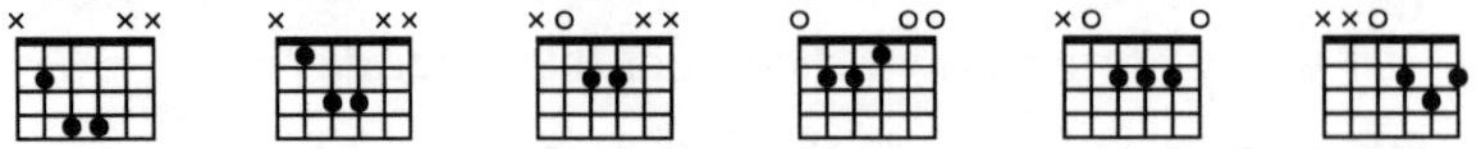

Intro One, two, three, four…

| B5 | B5 B5 B♭5 | A5 | A5 A5 B♭5 |

| B5 | B5 B5 B♭5 | A5 | A5 N.C. ‖

1. / 2.

‖: E | E | A | A :‖ A D ‖

Dum, da da da doo da…

Verse 1

B5 … B5 B♭5
I was walking down the street the other day
A5 … A5 B♭5
Who did I meet?
B5 … B5 B♭5
I met a friend of mine and he did say
A5
"Man, I can smell your feet a mile away."

Chorus 1

E … A
Smile a - way, smile away, smile away, yeah smile a - way
E … A
Smile a - way, smile away, smile away, yeah smile a - way.

Intrumental | B5 | B5 B5 B♭5 | A5 | A5 A5 B♭5 |

| B5 | B5 B5 B♭5 | A5 | A5 ‖

Chorus 2

```
              E                                              A
Smile a - way, smile away, smile away, yeah smile a - way
              E                                              A         D
Smile a - way, smile away, smile away, yeah smile a - way, uh oh.
```

Verse 2

```
B5                                                        B5 B♭5
   I was walking down the street the other day
A5                     A5 B♭5
   Ah, who did I meet?
B5                                           B5 B♭5
   I met a friend of mine and he did say
A5
   "Man, I can smell your breath a mile away."
```

Chorus 3

```
              E                                              A
Smile a - way, smile away, smile away, yeah smile a - way
              E                                              A
Smile a - way, smile away, smile away, yeah smile a - way,

Ah smile away sweetly now.
```

Breakdown

```
‖: E
                              Come on now
(Da - oo da da day do da, da - oo da da day do da
        A                                                 x5
ooh, ____ sweetly, smile away.                            :‖
Da - oo da da day do da, da - oo da da day do do.)
              E               A     | A   D ‖
Smile a - way, ah, ooh. ____
```

Verse 3

```
B5             | B5     B5 B♭5 |
A5                     A5 B♭5
   Ah, who did I meet?
B5                                           B5 B♭5
   I met a friend of mine and he did say
A5
   "Well, I can smell your teeth a mile away."
```

Outro

```
‖:
              E                                A
Smile a - way, ooh, ooh, ooh, ooh, smile a - way, ooh, ooh, ooh
              E                                A                      :‖ Repeat
Smile a - way, ooh, ooh, ooh, ooh, smile a - way, ooh, ooh, ooh.         to fade
```

Silly Love Songs

Words & Music by
Paul & Linda McCartney

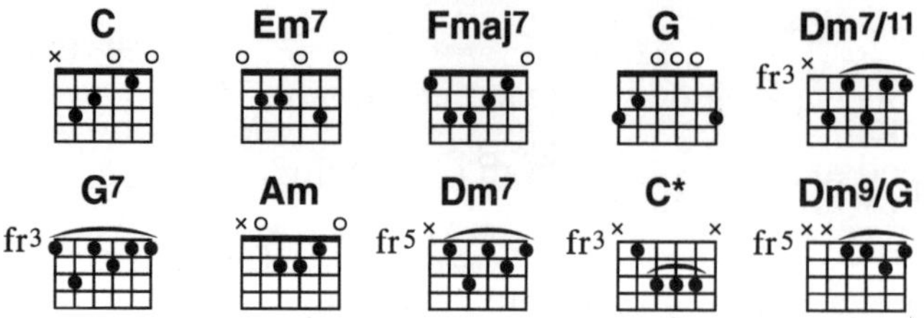

Intro ‖: C | Em7 | Fmaj7 | Fmaj7 :‖

| C | Em7 | Fmaj7 | Fmaj7 N.C. ‖

Verse 1

```
C                                   Em7                      Fmaj7
   You'd think that people would have had enough of silly love songs
C                                 Em7        Fmaj7
   But I look around me and I see it isn't so
C                                 Em7            Fmaj7
   Some people wanna fill the world with silly love songs
          Em7
And what's wrong with that?
   Fmaj7                  G                N.C. (Dm7/11  G7 )
I'd like to know, 'cause here I go again. ___
```

Chorus 1

```
C      Em7       Fmaj7
I ___  love ___  you ___
C      Em7       Fmaj7
I ___  love ___  you ___
C      Em7       Fmaj7
I ___  love ___  you ___
C      Em7       Fmaj7
I ___  love ___  you. ___
```

Verse 2

```
C             Em7                Fmaj7
I can't ex - plain the feeling's plain to me, now can't you see?
C                    Em7                  Fmaj7
Ah, she gave me more, she gave it all to me, now can't you see
      Em7
What's wrong with that
 Fmaj7                Em7                 N.C. (Dm7/11 G7 )
I need to know, 'cause here I go again. ——
```

Chorus 2

```
C       Em7       Fmaj7
I——   love——    you ——
C       Em7       Fmaj7
I——   love——    you. ——
```

Bridge 1

```
Em7 N.C.                       Am
    Love doesn't come in a minute
Dm7 N.C.                              C
    Sometimes it doesn't come at all
Em7 N.C.                       Am
    I only know that when I'm in it
Dm7              C* Dm7                C* Dm7                 Dm7/G
  It isn't silly,     no it isn't silly,     love isn't silly at all. __
```

Instrumental 1 𝄆 C | Em7 | Fmaj7 | Fmaj7 𝄇 *x4*

Bridge2

```
         𝄆 C         Em7          Fmaj7                               𝄇 x4
            How—     can I tell ——  you about ____   my loved one?
3 & 4°  (I          love          you.) ——
```

Instrumental 2 As Instrumental 1

Chorus 3

```
     𝄆 C          Em7                      Fmaj7
        I           love                     you,
  1° (I can't ex - plain the feel - ing's plain to me, say, can't you see?)
        C            Em7                  Fmaj7                     𝄇 x4
        I            love                   you.
      (Ah, he gave me more, he gave it all to me, say, can't you see?)
```

Link | C | Em7 | Fmaj7 | Fmaj7 N.C. ‖

Verse 3

```
C                                  Em7                        Fmaj7
 You'd think that people would have had enough of silly love songs
C                                  Em7     Fmaj7
 But I look around me and I see it isn't so, oh no
C                               Em7          Fmaj7
 Some people wanna fill the world with silly love songs
           Em7
And what's wrong with that.
```

So Glad To See You

Words & Music by
Paul McCartney

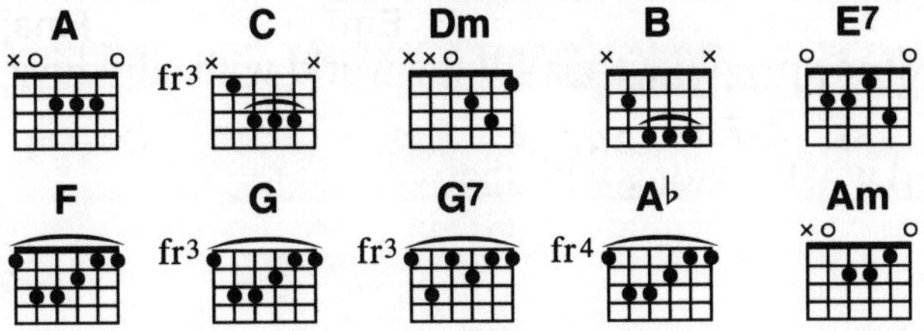

Intro | A | C | A | C ‖

Verse 1

A C
Someone's got a home to - night
A C
Someone's got a road to - night
Dm C
Someone's got a wad, action will be red
B
Why'd you you wanna worry?
E7 F A
Oh, you're gonna knock 'em dead,—— oh yeah.

Verse 2

A C
Someone's got a show to - night
A C
Someone's gotta go to - night
Dm C
Someone's doing rhyme, someone turn your mind
B
Someone to lift your eyes up
E7 F G A
Leanin' toward the light,—— ooh.——

```
             G7         F
Chorus 1     So glad to see you here
             G7                  F
             So glad you could come, yeah!
             G7         F
             So glad to see you here
                  G   A♭        Am   A
             Carry on,    carry on,___ yeah, yeah!


             A                      C
Verse 3      Oh, we're going up to - night
             A                     C
             Well in time to make a flight
             Dm                         C
               The airplane's standing on the runway
             B                     E7                          F          G    A
               Engine nervously waiting for something to bite,___ yeah, yeah. yeah


             A                C
Verse 4        Got to roll to - night
             A                   C
               You got to roll to - night
                  Dm                        C
             Well, some have got it bad, some have got to do it
             B                         E7                F        G  A
               You got it better, and there's nothing to it,___     no, no, no, no.


             G7         F
Chorus 2     So glad to see you here
             G7                  F
             So glad you could come, yeah!
             G7         F
             So glad to see you here
                  G   A♭        Am   A
             Carry on, carry on,___ yeah!
```

Verse 5 Someone's got a home to - night

Someone's got a road to - night

Someone's got a wad, action will be red

Why'd you you wanna worry?

Oh, you're gonna knock 'em dead, oh yeah.

```
       F                                G
Link   Oh, no no no no no no, no no no,  woah ___

Outro  | A      | A      | A      | A      |

       ||: F              G        A        :||  Play 4 times
           We're open to - night for fun
```

So Bad

Words & Music by
Paul McCartney

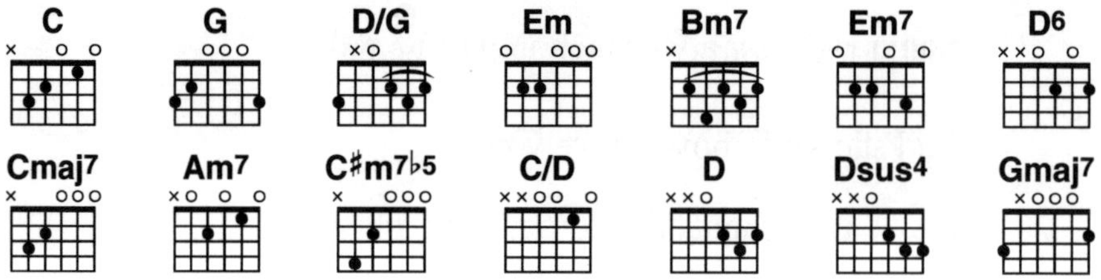

Intro | C | C | G | G ||

Verse 1

G D/G G Em Bm7
There is a pain inside my heart

C
You mean so much to me

G
Girl, I love you, girl, I love you so bad.

Verse 2

G D/G G Em Bm7
And if you leave, my pain will go

C
But that's no good to me

G
Girl, I love you, yes, I love you so bad.

Bridge

Bm7 Em7 Bm7 Em7
Well it feels so good, sometimes it feels so bad

D6 Cmaj7 Bm7 Am7 C♯m7♭5 C/D | D Dsus4 D ||
This is worse than any - thing I've ever had. _____

Verse 3

```
G      D/G G Em                Bm7
 There was a  pain, but now you're here
              C
And I don't fear a thing
                                    G
Girl, I love you, yes I love you so bad
               C
And she said  boy, I love you
                  G
Boy, I love you so bad.
```

Verse 4

```
| G  D/G  G | Em     | Bm7    | C      |
(C)                                G
Girl, I love you, girl, I love you so bad.
```

Bridge 2

As Bridge 1

Verse 3

```
G      D/G  G  Em                 Bm7
There was   a  pain, but now you're near
              C
And I don't fear a thing
                                    G
Girl, I love you, girl, I love you so bad
                C
And she said, boy, I love you
                  G
Boy, I love you so bad
C
Girl, I love you
                  Gmaj7
Girl, I love you. ___
```

Some People Never Know

Words & Music by
Paul McCartney & Linda McCartney

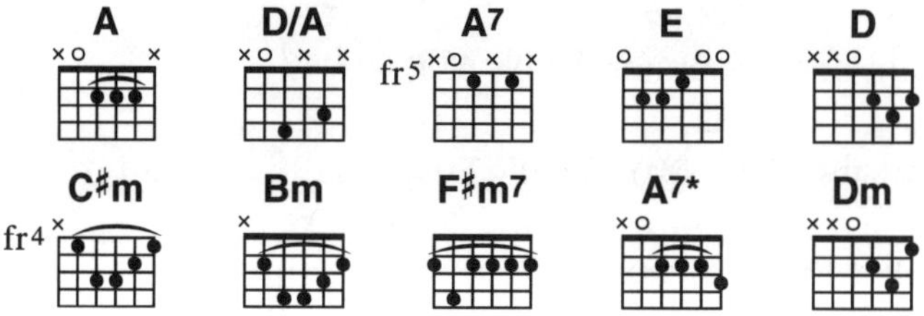

Intro ‖: A D/A A | A D/A A7 D/A :‖

Verse 1
G D
No one else will ever see
C#m Bm
How much faith you have in me
A E D
Only fools would disagree that it's so
C#m Bm (A)
Some people never know.

Link 1 ‖: A D/A A | A D/A A7 D/A :‖

Verse 2
E D
Like a fool I'm faraway
C#m Bm
Ev'ry night I hope and pray
A E D
I'll be coming home to stay and it's so
C#m Bm (A)
Some people never know.

Link 2 ‖: A D/A A | A D/A A7 D/A :‖ *Play 3 times*

Bridge 1

```
C♯m                     F♯m7
   Some people can sleep at night-time
      C♯m                 F♯m7
Be - lieving that love is a lie
C♯m             F♯m7
   I'm only a person like you, love
      A7*                        D          Dm
And who in the world can be right all the right time
C♯m             F♯m7              Bm    D
I know I was wrong, make me right, right. ——
```

Instrumental

```
| E        | D        | C♯m      | Bm       |

| A        | E        | D        | C♯m  Bm  ||
```

Link 3

```
|: A      D/A   A   | A   D/A   A7   D/A  :|   Play 4 times
```

Bridge 2

As Bridge 1

Verse 3

```
E              D
Only love can stand the test
C♯m              Bm
Only you out - shine the rest
A               E                    D
Only fools take second best, but it's so
C♯m           Bm    (A)
Some people never know.
```

Link 4

```
|: A      D/A   A   | A   D/A   A7   D/A  :|   Play 6 times
```

Bridge 3

```
C♯m        F♯m7
Ooh, ——    ooh ——
C♯m        F♯m7
Ooh, ——    ooh ——
C♯m        F♯m7
Ooh, ——    ooh ——
A7*        D    Dm
Ooh, ——    ooh ——
C♯m  F♯m7  Bm         D
Ooh, ——    ooh, ——    right. ——
```

Verse 4

```
E                  D
Only love can stand the test
C#m                Bm
Only you out - shine the rest
A              E                  D
Only fools take second best, but it's so
C#m            Bm    (A)
Some people never know.
```

Outro ‖: A D/A A | A D/A A7 D/A :‖ *Repeat to fade*

Somedays

Words & Music by
Paul McCartney

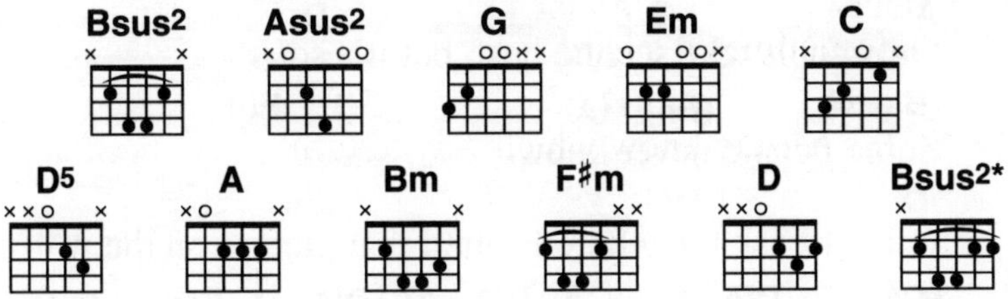

Intro | Bsus2 Asus2 | Bsus2 Asus2 ||

Verse 1

Bsus2 Asus2
Somedays I look
Bsus2 Asus2 G Em
I look at you with eyes that shine
Bsus2 Asus2
Somedays I don't,
Bsus2 Asus2 G Em
I don't be - lieve that you are mine.
C Em
It's no good asking me what time of day it is,
C Em
Who won the match or scored the goal
Bsus2 Asus2
Somedays I look
Bsus2 Asus2 Bsus2 Asus2 | Bsus2 ||
Somedays I look into your soul. ——

Verse 2

```
Bsus2        Asus2
   Sometimes I laugh
Bsus2       Asus2                     G     Em
  I laugh to think how young we were
Bsus2               Asus2
  Sometimes it's hard
Bsus2        Asus2                     G    Em
  It's hard to know which way to turn
C                                       Em
  Don't ask me where I found that picture on the wall
C                                    Em
  How much it cost or what it's worth
Bsus2              Asus2
  Sometimes I laugh
Bsus2       Asus2                     Bsus2 Asus2 | Bsus2  Asus2  ||
  I laugh to think how young we were.
```

Bridge 1

```
D5    A          Bm        F#m
   We don't need anybody else
G     A            D5
   To tell us what is real
   A        Bm         F#m
In - side each one of us is love
G       A            D
   And we know how it feels.
```

Verse 3

```
Bsus2          Asus2
   Somedays I cry,
Bsus2       Asus2              G      Em
   I cry for those who live in fear
Bsus2             Asus2
   Somedays I don't
Bsus2          Asus2             G     Em
   I don't re - member why I'm here.——
C                                Em
   No use reminding me, it's just the way it is
C                                   Em
   Who ran the race or came in first
Bsus2            Asus2
   Somedays I cry
Bsus2       Asus2               Bsus2 Asus2 | Bsus2   Asus2  ||
   I cry for those who fear the worst.
```

Instrumental ‖: Bsus2 Asus2 | Bsus2 Asus2 :‖

| Bsus2 Asus2 |

Bridge 2 As Bridge 1

Verse 4

```
Bsus2          Asus2
  Somedays I look
Bsus2      Asus2                 G     Em
  I look at you with eyes that shine
Bsus2          Asus2
  Somedays I don't
Bsus2          Asus2                G     Em
  I don't be - lieve that you are mine.
C                                 Em
  It's no good asking me what time of day it is,
C                                      Em
  Who won the match or scored the goal
Bsus2        Asus2
Somedays I look
Bsus2          Asus2           Bsus2 Asus2 | Bsus2  Asus2  ‖
  Somedays I look into your soul.
```

Outro ‖: Bsus2 Asus2 | Bsus2 Asus2 :‖

| Bsus2 Bsus2* (fermata) ‖

Somebody Who Cares

Words & Music by
Paul McCartney

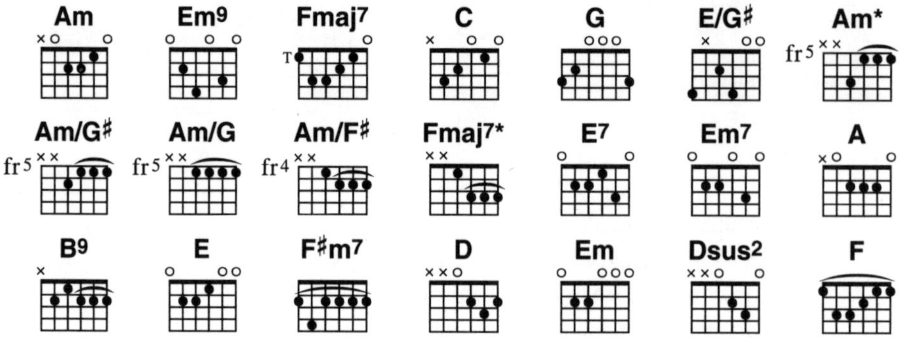

Intro | N.C. (Am) | Am | N.C. (Am) | Am |
| N.C. (Am) | Am | N.C. (Am) ‖

Verse 1

Am Em9 Fmaj7
When your body is coming a - part at the seams
C G
And the whole thing's feeling low
E/G♯ Am* Am/G♯ Am/G Am/F♯ Fmaj7*
You're con - vincing your - self that there's nobody there, I know
E7
I know now you feel.

Verse 2

Am Em7 Fmaj7
Like sombody has taken the wheels off your car
C G
When you had somewhere to go
E/G♯ Am* Am/G♯ Am/G Am/F♯ Fmaj7*
Well it's an - noying not going to get very far I know
E7
But somebody cares.

Chorus 1
A B9
There's always someone, somewhere
E F♯m7
You should know by now
D A
Always somebody who cares
B9
It's happening day in, day out
E F♯m7
Well you know by now
D A
Always somebody who cares.

Bridge 1
Em Dsus2
And if you don't know it how will it find you?
Em F
How will we know your whereabouts?

| Em | Dsus2 | Em | F |

F E7
But I know how you feel.

Solo
| Am | Em7 Fmaj7 | C | G E/G♯ |

| Am* Am/G♯ | Am/G Am | Fmaj7* | Fmaj7* E7
I know how you feel.

Verse 3
N.C. Am Em7 Fmaj7
Like somebody has taken the wheels off your car
C G
When you had somewhere to go
E/G♯ Am* Am/G♯ Am/G Am/F♯ Fmaj7*
Well it's frus - trating not going to get very far I know
E7
But somebody cares.

Chorus 2
As Chorus 1

Bridge 2
As Bridge 1

The Song We Were Singing

Words & Music by
Paul McCartney

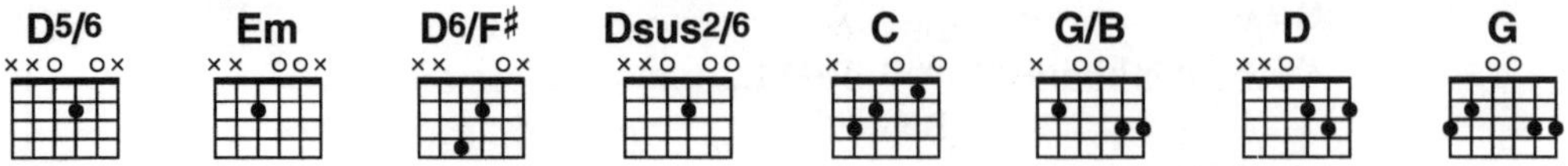

Intro ‖: D5/6 Em | D6/F♯ Em :‖

Verse 1

D5/6 Em D6/F♯
For a while,—— we could sit, smoke a pipe
Em D5/6 Em D6/F♯ Em
And discuss all the vast intricacies of life
D5/6 Em
We could jaw,—— through the night
D6/F♯ Em D5/6 Em
Talk about a range of subjects, anything you like
D6/F♯ Em Dsus2/6
Oh yeah.

Chorus 1

C G/B D
But we always came back to the song we were singing
C G/B D
At any par - ticular time
C G/B D
Yeah, we always came back to the song we were singing
C G/B G D
At any par - ticular time.

Verse 2

D5/6 Em D6/F#
Take a sip, see the world through a glass
Em D5/6 Em D6/F# Em
And speculate a - bout the cosmic solu - tion
D5/6 Em
To the sound, —— blue guitars
D6/F# Em D5/6 Em
Caught up in a philosophical dis - cussion
D6/F# Em D
Oh yeah.

Chorus 2

C G/B D
But we always came back to the song we were singing
C G/B D
At any par - ticular time
C G/B D
Yeah, we always came back to the song we were singing
C G/B G D
At any par - ticular time
C G/B | G D
Ah. ——

Link 1

| D5/6 Em | D6/F# Em ||

Verse 3

D5/6 Em D6/F#
For a while, —— we could sit, smoke a pipe
Em D5/6 Em D6/F# Em
And discuss all the vast intricacies of life
D5/6 Em
We could jaw, —— through the night
D6/F# Em D5/6 D6/F# Em D5/6
Talk about a range of subjects, anything you like.

Chorus 3

C G/B D
But we always came back to the song we were singing
C G/B D
At any par - ticular time
C G/B D
Yeah, we always came back to the song we were singing
C G/B G D
At any par - ticular time.

Link 1

```
| C  G/B | G   D |
          C            G/B           G   D   N.C
Yeah, we always came back.
```

Verse 4

As Verse 2

Link 2

```
| D5/6     | D5      |
```

Chorus 4

```
          C               G/B           D
But we always came back to the song we were singing
     C         G/B    D
At any par - ticular time
            C               G/B            D
Yeah, we always came back to the song we were singing
     C         G/B    D
At any par - ticular time
         C    G/B | D      | G    D   |
Yeah.________________

| C  G/B | G   D |

     C               G/B   G    D
We always came back
          C                 G/B    G  D
To the songs we were singing.
```

Souvenir

Words & Music by
Paul McCartney

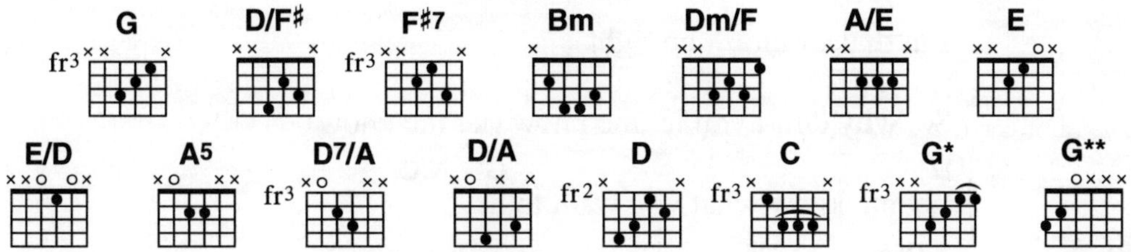

Tune Guitar down a semitone

Verse 1

G D/F♯
When you're fed up shedding too many tears
F♯7 Bm
And your memory seems like just so many souvenirs
Dm/F A/E E E/D
I will come to you to ease the pain.

Chorus 1

A5 D7/A A5 D/A
If you want me, tell me now
A5 D7/A A5 D/A
If I can be of any help, tell me how
A5 D7/A A5 D/A
Let me love you like a friend
A5 D7/A A5 D/A
Everything is gonna come right in the end.

Verse 2

G D/F♯
When you're crying like a poor little child
F♯7 Bm
And you feel like you never could be reconciled
Dm/F A/E E E/D
Don't forget a word of what I'm saying, oh.

Chorus 2 As Chorus 1

Bridge 1

```
        D     G
Well, I can hold you too tight
      D
I could never let you go
    G
But that wouldn't be right
D   N.C.         C
So, why don't you let me know (let me know)
D                                G*  N.C.
Let me know what you want to do.
```

Verse 3

```
G                        D/F♯
   Everybody's got a handful of fear
F♯7                          Bm
   But tomorrow it may only be a souvenir
Dm/F            A/E        E          E/D
   Of the way it was 'til it went away.——
```

Chorus 3 As Chorus 1

Link | G** | D7/A | G** | G N.C. |

Bridge 2

```
        D     G
Well, I can hold you too tight
      D
I could never let you go
    G
But that wouldn't be right
D   N.C.         C
So, why don't you let me know
                  A5
What you want to do.
```

Chorus 4

```
(A5)          D7/A      A5                    D/A
If you want me, you won't tell me now.
A5                         D7/A  A5            G  D
   If I can be of any help, tell me how
A5            D7/A      A5             D/A
   Let me love you like a friend
A5                D7/A                    A5             D/A
   Ev'ry little thing is gonna come right in the end.
```

Outro

```
| G**    | D7/A     | G**    | D7/A            |
                             Souvenir.
|: G**   | D7/A     | G**    | D7/A           :|  Repeat ad lib.
           Souven  -  ir.      No, not another...  to fade
```

Spin It On

Words & Music by
Paul McCartney

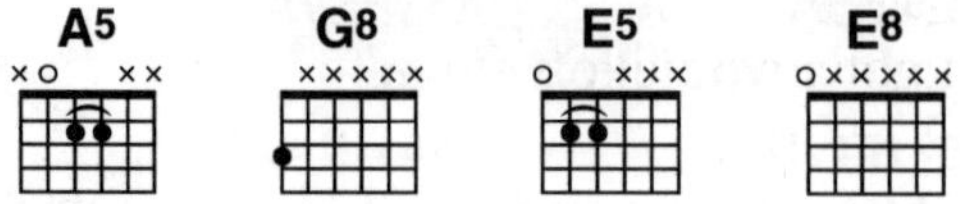

Intro

```
          A5 N.C.
This is it

                     Play 4 times
┌ A5 riff ─────────────────────┐   ┌ E5 riff ──────────────────────┐
‖: A5 G8 A5 G8 A5 G8 A5 G8 :‖  { | E5 G8 E8 G8 E8 G8 E8 G8 | }
```

Chorus 1

```
          A5 riff
Spin it on, don't stop

Take it back to the top
          E5 riff            A5 riff
'Cause I got a whole lotta love for you
E5 riff            A5 riff
   I wanna spin it on. Spin it on!
```

Link 1

| A5 riff | A5 riff | E5 riff | A5 riff ‖

Verse 1

```
A5 riff
Off to the flicks with the piddle in her nicks

To the fair with her hair in curlers.
E5 riff                                        A5 riff
   Their cousins didn't get all down to the pleasure dome
E5 riff                                        A5   N.C.  A5    N.C.
   Their cousins didn't spend their night in an air - craft han - ger
A5    N.C.
Me - mories!
```

Chorus 2

A5 riff
Spin it on, don't stop

Take it back to the top

E5 riff **A5 riff**
'Cause I got a whole lotta love for you

E5 riff **A5 riff**
That's why I wanna spin it on. Spin it on! Spin it on!

Link 2

| A5 riff | A5 riff | E5 riff | A5 riff |

| A5 riff | A5 riff | E5 riff | A5 riff ||

Spin it on!

Chorus 3

A5 riff
Spin it on, don't stop

Take it back to the top

E5 riff **A5 riff**
'Cause I got a whole lotta love for you

E5 riff **A5 riff**
That's why I wanna spin it on.

Verse 2

A5 riff
Off to the fields with a missionary's zeal

With the life of the wife of the farmer

E5 riff **A5 riff**
Their cousins didn't get on down to the village hall

E5 riff **A5 N.C. A5 N.C.**
Their cousins didn't spend the night on a pin - ball ta - ble

A5 N.C.
Me - mories!

Chorus 4

As Chorus 2

Outro

A5 riff
Spin it on! Spin it on!

E5 riff A5 riff
I wanna spin it on! Spin it on!

| A5 riff | A5 riff | E5 riff | A5 riff |

I wanna spin it on. Spin it on!

A5 riff
Spin it on, don't stop,

Take it back to the top

E5 riff A5 riff A5
'Cause I got a whole lotta love for you!

Stranglehold

Words & Music by
Paul McCartney & Eric Stewart

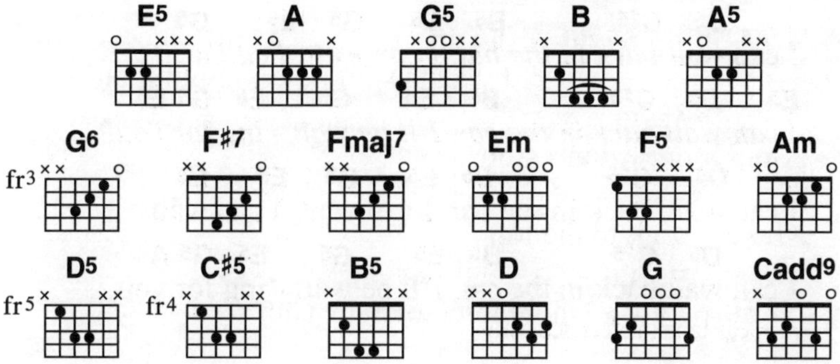

Intro ‖: E5 | E5 | E5 | E5 :‖

Verse 1
E5 A G5
Can I get you to give me a minute of your time?
E5 A B A5
Can I get you to slip me the an - swer?
E5 A
Can I get you to slow me a little of your mime?
G6 F#7 Fmaj7 Em G6 F#7 A
You were always a very good dan - cer

Link 1 | E5 | E5 | E5 | E5 G5 F5 ‖

Verse 2
E5 A G5
I'd be happy to show you a bit of what I found
E5 A B A5
I'd be happy to share in its beau - ty
E5 A
I'd be happy to lay low inevitably bound
G6 F#7 Fmaj7 Em G6 F#7 A
I would only be doing my du - ty.

Pre-Chorus 1

A
I wait, (I wait, I wait, I wait…)

Am
I wait, (I wait, I wait, I wait…)

D5 C#5 B5 E5 G5 E5 G5
I can wait *back in the bar, I can wait, I can wait*

E5 D5 C#5 B5 E5 G5 E5 G5 E5
*I can wait back in the car, I'll be wait - ing for you**

D5 C#5 B5 E5 G5 E5 G5
I can wait, back in the bar, I can wait, I can wait

D5 C#5 B5 E5 G5 E5 G5 A
I can wait back in the car, I'll be wait - ing for you.

* vocal tacet, reference only

Chorus 1

D A
Stranglehold, you know you've got one on me

D A
I don't want to go with - out you.

D A
Stranglehold, you've got me where you want me

G A
But I want to know more a - bout you

G Cadd9
I want to know more a - bout you.

Link 2

| E5 | E5 | E5 | E5 ||

Verse 3

E5 A
Are you willing to wager a little of your life?

E5 A B A5 G5
Are you willing to take such a gam - ble?

E5 A
Are you ready to walk on the edge of the knife?

G6 F#7 Fmaj7 Em G6 F#7 A
Then I think we can skip the pre - am - ble.

Pre-Chorus 2

A
I wait, (I wait, I wait, I wait…)
Am
I wait, (I wait, I wait, I wait…)
D5 C#5 B5 E5 G5 E5 G5
I can wait *back in the bar, I can wait, I can wait*
E5 D5 C#5 B5 E5 G5 E5 G5 E5
*I can wait back in the car, I'll be wait - ing for you**
D5 C#5 B5 E5 G5 E5 G5
I can wait, back in the bar, I can wait, I can wait
D5 C#5 B5 E5 G5 E5 G5 A
I can wait back in the car, I'll be wait - ing for you.

I'll be waiting…

* vocal tacet, reference only

Chorus 2

D A
Stranglehold, you know, you've got one on me
D A
I don't want to go with - out you
D A
Stranglehold, you've got me where you want me
G A
And I want to know more a - bout you
G Cadd9
I want to know more a - bout you.

Outro

‖: D5 C#5 B5 E5 G5 E5 G5
I can wait back in the bar, I can wait, I can wait
E5 D5 C#5 B5 E5 G5 E5 G5 E5 :‖
I can wait back in the car, I'll be wait - ing for you.

Sweetest Little Show

Words & Music by
Paul McCartney

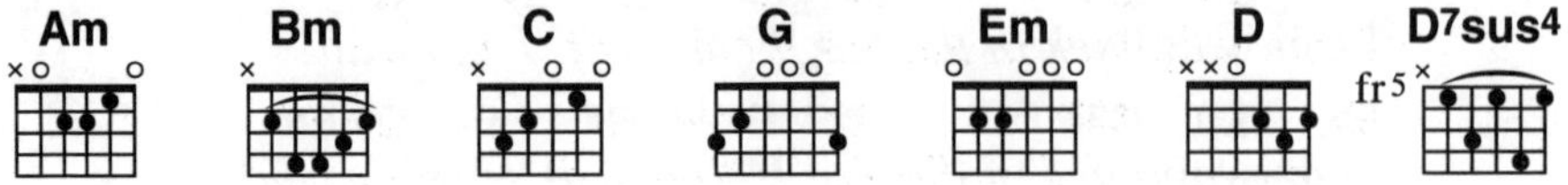


```
Intro      | N.C. (G)  | (G)  (D7)  ||

           ||: Am Bm C N.C. | Am Bm C N.C. | Am Bm C | G :||


                          G     D    C     G
Verse 1    Well they can treat you like a brother
                                 D    C      Em
           Yeah, they can treat you like a clown
                       G     D    C      G
           But if they treat you like a lover
                              Am         Bm  C           G
           They've got the sweetest little show in town.


                        Am         Bm   C
Chorus 1   You got the sweetest little show
           Am        Bm  C
           Sweetest little show
           Am        Bm  C         G
           Sweetest little show in town.


           Em                            Am
Bridge        You've been around a long time
           C                               G
              But you're still good for a while
           Em                                 Am
              And if they try to cristi - cise you
                                               D
           Make them smile, make them smile.
```

Verse 2

```
           G    D          C     G
And if they treat you like a brother
                                C          Em
Well, you will never never let 'em down
                   G     D   C       Em
But if they treat you like a lover
                              Am        Bm   C        G
They've got the sweetest little show in town.
```

Chorus 2

```
                         Am         Bm   C
They got the sweetest little show
Am          Bm  C
Sweetest little show,
Am          Bm  C         G
Sweetest little show in town
                         Am        Bm   C
You got the sweetest little show
Am          Bm  C
Sweetest little show,
Am          Bm  C         G
Sweetest little show in town.
```

Guitar solo

```
||: G    | G    | G    | G    |
| G      | G    | G    | G    |
| G      | G    | G    | G    :||
| G      | G    | G    | G    | G (fermata) ||
```

Outro

```
| Am Bm C N.C. | Am Bm C N.C. | Am Bm C | G
                        Am        Bm   C
You got the sweetest little show
Am          Bm  C
Sweetest little show…
Am           Bm            C     N.C.  D7sus4
Bah, ___ bah, ___ dap,         bah. ___
```

Summer's Day Song

Words & Music by
Paul McCartney

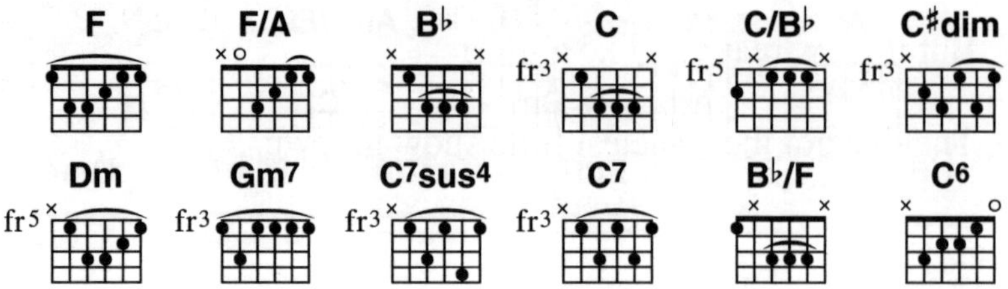

Intro | F | F | C | B♭ F (fermata) ||

Verse 1

F
Someone's sleeping
F/A B♭ C
Through a bad dream ___
C/B♭ F/A B♭
Tomorrow it will be over ___
C C♯dim Dm Gm7
For the world will soon be waking ___
C7sus4 C7 F
To a sum - mers day.

Instrumental | F | F | F B♭/F | B♭/F | F C | B♭ || F |

| F F/A B♭ | C | C C/B♭ | F/A B♭ | C C♯dim |

| Dm Gm7 | C7sus4 C7 F ||

| F | F | C | B♭/F F | B♭ C | F | F ||

| F | B♭ | C6 | B♭ ||
Solo flute __________

Verse 2 As Verse 1

Outro | F | F | F | F F/A B♭ | C | C C/B♭ | F/A B♭ | C F (fermata) ||

Take It Away

Words & Music by
Paul McCartney

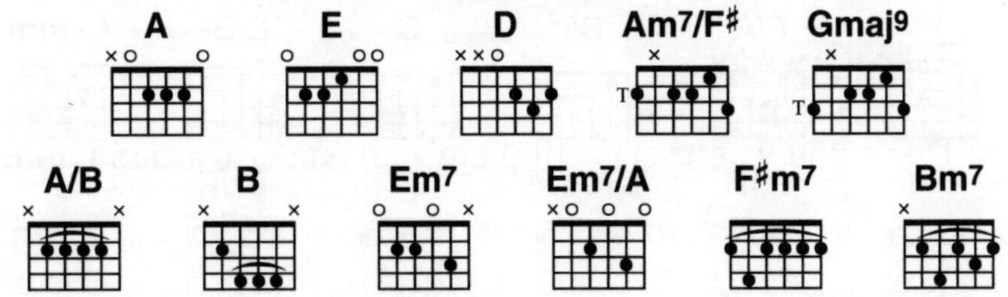

Intro | Drums ‖ A E | A D | A E | A D ‖

Chorus 1

```
A        E    A
    Take it a - way
            D          A              E          A     D
Wanna hear you play 'til the lights go down
A        E    A
    Take it a - way
                D         A               E         D
Don't you wanna stay 'til there's no one else around.
```

Chorus 2

```
A        E    A
    Take it a - way
            D          A              E          A     D
Wanna hear you play 'til the lights go down
A        E    A
    Take it a - way
                D         A               E         D                       Am7/F♯
Don't you wanna stay 'til there's no one else around.
```

Verse 1

```
Gmaj9           A/B           B
Lonely driver    out on the road
Em7            Em7/A             D   Am7/F♯
    With a hundred miles to go
Gmaj9              A/B                B
    Sole survivor,    carrying the load
Em7                Em7/A  D
    Switches on  his  radio.
```

Chorus 3

```
A       E   A
   Take it a - way
           D             A                  E            A       D       A
Wanna hear you play 'til the lights go down (down, down)
        E   A
Take it a - way
                    D         A                     E          D
Don't you wanna stay 'til there's no one else around, mm.——
```

Chorus 4

```
A       E   A
   Take it a - way
           D             A                  E            A       D       A
Wanna hear you play 'til the lights go down (down, down)
     E      A
Take it a - way
                    D         A                     E          D                Am7/F#
Don't you wanna stay 'til there's no one else around.
```

Verse 2

```
Gmaj9                 A/B                B
   In the audience,    watching the show
Em7    Em7/A        D                                    Am7/F#
With a paper in his hand (in his hand, in his hand——)
Gmaj9                     A/B          B
   Some important, impresario
Em7       Em7/A                 D       E
   Has a message for the band, oh oh.
```

Chorus 5

```
A       E   A
   Take it a - way
           D             A                  E            A       D       A
Wanna hear you play 'til the lights go down (down, down)
     E      A
Take it a - way
                    D         A                     E          D
Don't you wanna stay 'til there's no one else around.
```

```
            F♯m7                          Bm
Bridge      You never know who may be listening to you
             F♯m7                          Bm
            (You never know who may be listening to you)
            F♯m7                          Bm
            You never know who may be listening to you
            F♯m7  Bm
            Ah.___
                 N.C.  A N.C.          D  Am7/F♯
            Take it away,   take it away.


            Gmaj9         A/B         B
Verse 3       After hours,   late in the bar
            Em7   Em7/A           D    Am7/F♯
              By a darkened corner seat
            Gmaj9            A/B          B
              Faded flowers,   wait in the jar
            Em7       Em7/A            D     Am7/F♯
              'Til the evening is com - plete.

                                                                   Repeat to fade
Outro       |: Gmaj9 | Gmaj9 | A/B | B    | Em7 | Em7/A | D | D  Am7/F♯ :|
               Ah,________________________  oh,________________________
```

Teddy Boy

Words & Music by
Paul McCartney

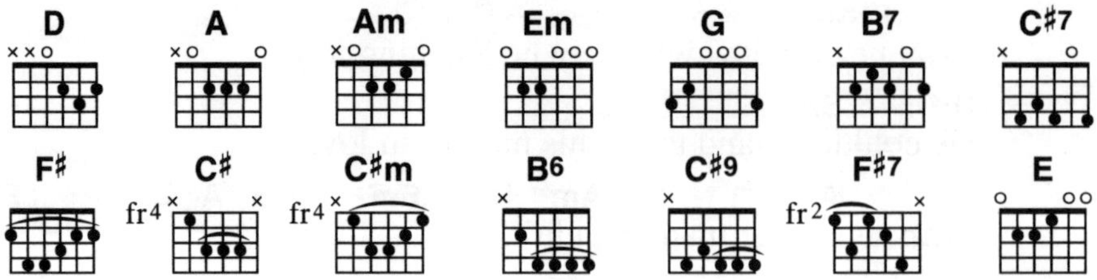

Intro | D A | D A | D A | D A ||

Verse 1
D
This is the story of a boy named Ted
A Am Em G A | D |
If his mother said Ted be good, he would.

Verse 2
D
She told him tales about his soldier Dad
A Am Em G A | B7 C♯7 | F♯
But it made her sad, and she'd cry, oh my.

Pre-Chorus 1
F♯
Ted used to tell her he could be twice as good
C♯ C♯m B6 B7 C♯7
And he knew he could 'cause in his head he said.

Chorus
F♯7 B7
Mummy don't worry now Teddy Boy's here
E A
Taking good care of you
F♯7 B7
Mummy don't worry, your Teddy Boy's here
E A D A | D A |
Teddy's gonna see you through.

Verse 3

D
Then came the day she found herself a man
A Am Em G A | D
Teddy turned and ran far away, ok.

Verse 4

D
He couldn't stand to see his mother in love
A Am Em G A | B7 C#7 | F#
With a - nother man he didn't know, oh no.

Pre-Chorus 2

F#
He found a place where he could settle down
C# C#m B6 B7 C#9
And from time to time, in his head, he said.

Chorus 2

F#7 B7
Mummy don't worry now Teddy Boy's here
E A
Taking good care of you
F#7 B7
Mummy don't worry, your Teddy Boy's here
E A D
Teddy's gonna see you through.

Chorus 3

F#7 B7
She said, "Teddy don't worry now Mummy is here
E A
Taking good care of you
F#7 B7
Teddy don't worry, your Mummy is here
E A D A | D A |
Mummy's gonna see you through."

Outro

D
This is a story of a boy named Ted
A Am Em G A | B7 C#7 | F# ||
If his mother said Ted be good, he would.

That Would Be Something

Words & Music by
Paul McCartney

(Tune Guitar slightly sharp)

Intro

E5 riff
| E5 E4 E3 E4 E N.C. | E5 E4 E3 E4 E N.C. | A E7 | A E7 | E5/7 ||

Verse 1

E5 riff
That would be something
E5 riff
It really would be something
E5 riff
That would be something
A E7
To meet you in the fallin' rain momma
A E7
Meet you in the fallin' rain.

Verse 2

E riff | E riff | E riff |
Ooh, ___ ooh, ___ ooh ___
A E7
Meet you in the fallin' rain momma
A E7
Meet you in the fallin' rain.

Verse 3

As Verse 1

Verse 4

| E5 riff | E5 riff | E5 riff |
w/ad lib. vocal fx.
||: A E7
Meet you in the fallin' rain momma
A E7 :||
Meet you in the fallin' rain.

Verse 5

E5 riff
That would be something
E5 riff
It really would be something
E5 riff
That would be something
A E7
To meet you in the fallin' rain momma
A E7
Meet you in the fallin' rain
A E7
Meet you in the fallin' rain momma
A E7
Meet you in the fallin' rain.

Verse 6 As Verse 4

Verse 7 As Verse 4

Outro

‖: **A E7**
Meet you in the fallin' rain momma
A E7 :‖ **E7** ‖
Meet you in the fallin' rain.

That Day Is Done

Words & Music by
Paul McCartney & Declan MacManus

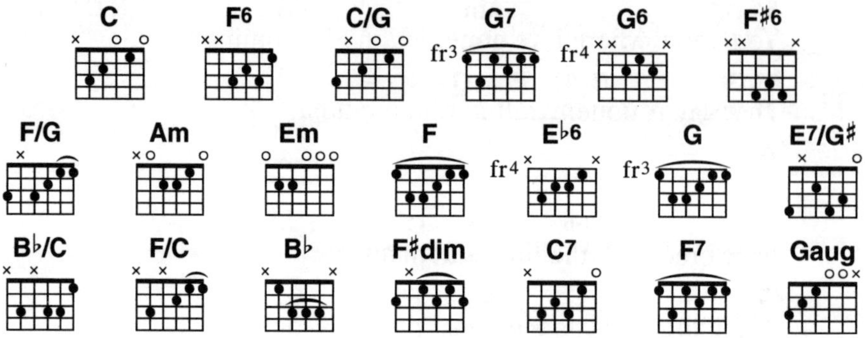

Verse 1

C
I feel such sorrow
F6 C
I feel such shame
C/G F6 C F6 C
I know I won't ar - rive on time
G7 G6 F♯6 G7
Before what - ever out there is gone
F6 C F6 C
What can I do, that day is done.

Verse 2

G6 F♯6 G7 C F6 C
It's just a promise, that I made
C/G F6 C F6 C
I said I'd walk in her pa - rade
G7 G6 F♯6 G7
Hot scalding tears I thought would flow
F/G C F6 C
Still in my heart they'll never show.

Chorus 1

```
                Am    Em
That day is done___
                F     E♭6  C
That day is done___
                                 Am              G                N.C.
You know where I've gone, I won't be coming back
E7/G♯              B♭/C   F/A  C
That day is done.___
```

Verse 3

```
                C     F6                C
Well I re - call, the time and place
C/G              F6   C              F6        C
When they an - nounced her precious face
                 G7    G6               G7
I thought at once my heart would burst
F/G              C      F6              C
Still, every time is like the first.
```

Verse 4

```
G6       F♯7  G7   C         F6                   C
There was ap - plause when she stepped up
G6 F♯6       G7   C          F6        C
I    wished that I could inter - rupt
                  G7      G6        F♯6  G7
I made no sign, I made no   sound
F/G                    C     F6        C
I know I must stay under - ground.
```

Chorus 2 As Chorus 1

Link

```
| E♭6   B♭ | C
```

Bridge

```
(C)                   F                      F♯dim
That's why she walks, or so they say
                C/G                  C7
She always knew just what I needed
                F7                      F♯dim
Now if she would, just look my way
       G                           Gaug
One time before they pro - ceed.
```

Verse 5

```
                C    F6      C
She sprinkles flowers  in the dirt
C/G          F6 C    F6         C
That's when a  thrill becomes a hurt
          G7    G6 F♯6 G7
I know I'll never see her face
F/G             C        F6        C
She walks a - way from my resting place.
```

Chorus 3

```
            Am     Em
That day is done___
            F    E♭6 C
That day is done___
                          Am            G          N.C.
You know where I've gone, I won't be coming back
E7/G♯         B♭/C   F/C  C
That day is done.___
                                Am             G          N.C.
Well, you know where I've gone, I won't be coming back
E7/G♯         B♭/C   F/C  C
Their day is done.___

| E♭6  B♭ | C     ‖
```

This One

Words & Music by
Paul McCartney

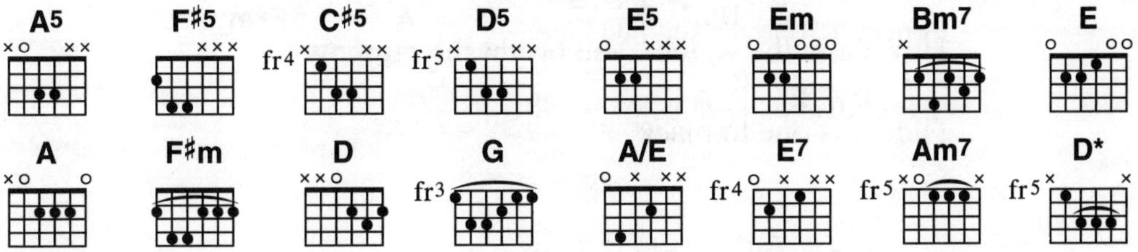

Intro | (E5) | (E5) | (E) | (Esus2) | (Esus4) (A5) |
Keyboard cue This one… + *echo repeats*

Verse 1

A5 F♯5
Did I ever take you in my arms
C♯5 D5
Look you in the eye, tell you that I do?
A5 E5
Did I ever open up my heart
Em A5
And let you look in - side?

Chorus 1

Bm7 E A F♯m
If I never did it, I was only waiting
Bm7 E A
For a better moment that didn't come
Bm7 E A F♯m
There never could be a better moment
D E A
Than this one, this one.

```
Chorus 2   Bm7 E          A      F♯m
           This swan is gliding  above the ocean
                Bm7 E        A
           A god is riding  upon his back
                     Bm7 E            A       F♯m
           How calm the water   and bright the rainbow
              D  E   A
           Fade this one to black.

              A5                    F♯5
Verse 2    Did I ever touch you on the cheek
                              C♯5              D5
           Say that you were mine, thank you for the smile
              A5                   E5
           Did I ever knock upon your door
             Em           A5
           And try to get in - side?

Chorus 3   As Chorus 1

Chorus 4   As Chorus 2

           D                E          A          F♯m
Bridge        What oppor - tunities did we allow to flow by
           G                    Em          A
           Feeling like like the timing wasn't quite right?
           D               E                   A              F♯m
              What kind of magic might have worked if we had stayed calm
           G                                E  A/E E7 | E     | E N.C.
           Couldn't I have given you a bet - ter   life?

                  A5                  F♯5
Verse 3    Did you ever take me in your arms
                            C♯5          D5
           Look me in the eye, tell me that you do?
              A5               E5
           Did I ever open up my heart
           Em             A5
           Let you look in - side?
```

Chours 5 As Chorus 1

Chorus 6 As Chorus 2

Outro

```
                     Am7        | Am7     D* | Am7      | Am7
This swan is riding, ——             oh ——
     D*        Am7           | Am7       D* | Am7      | Am7
The god is riding, ——            oh ——
      D*              Am7                               | Am7     D* |
How calm the water (how calm the water ——)                  and
Am7                  D*
Bright the rainbow.
```

Repeat w/ad lib. vocal to fade

```
||: Am7  | Am7   D* | Am7   | Am7   D* :||
```

3 Legs

Words & Music by
Paul McCartney

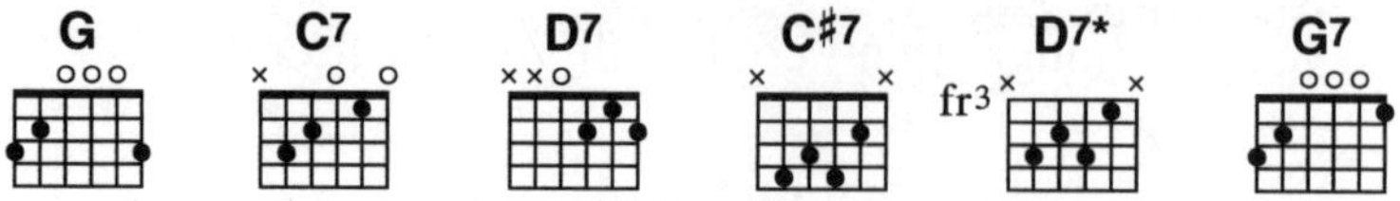

Capo second fret

Verse 1

G
Well when I walk, when I walk
C7 G
On my horse upon the hill (when I walk the horse upon a hill)
C7
Well when I walk, walk, walk, walk
G
Walk my horse upon the hill (when I walk the horse upon a hill)
D7
And I lay me down
N.C. G C7 C#7 D7*
Will my lover love me still.

Verse 2

N.C. G
A dog is here, (a dog is here)

A dog is there (a dog is there)

My dog he got three leg
N.C. G
But he can't run.

Verse 2 (cont.)

```
            C7
Well when I thought, well I thought
                           G
When I thought you was my friend

(When I thought that I could call you my friend)
        C7
When I thought, when I thought
                           G
When I thought you was my friend

(When I thought that I could call you my friend)
          D7
But you laid me down
N.C.                       G       C7  C#7  D7*
Put my heart around the bend.
```

Verse 3

```
          G7
A fly flies in (a fly flies in), a fly flies out (a fly flies out)
                           N.C.              G7
Most flies they got three leg,   but mine got one
            C7                                          G
Well when I fly when I fly when I fly, when I fly above the cloud

(When I fly above the man in the crowd)
            C7                                          G
Well when I fly when I fly when I fly, when I fly above the crowd

(When I fly above the man in the crowd)
        D7                     C7
You can knock me down with a feather, yes you could
N.C.                         G               C7        C#7      D7*     N.C.
But you know it's not al - lowed (but you know it's not al - lowed).
```

Chorus

```
         G
A dog is here, (a dog is here)

A dog is there (a dog is there)

My dog he got three leg
N.C.         G
  But he can't run.
```

Outro

G
My dog he got three leg
C7
Your dog he got none
G
My dog he got three leg
C7
Your dog he got none
G
My dog he got three leg
C7 G
Your dog he got none.

Through Our Love

Words & Music by
Paul McCartney

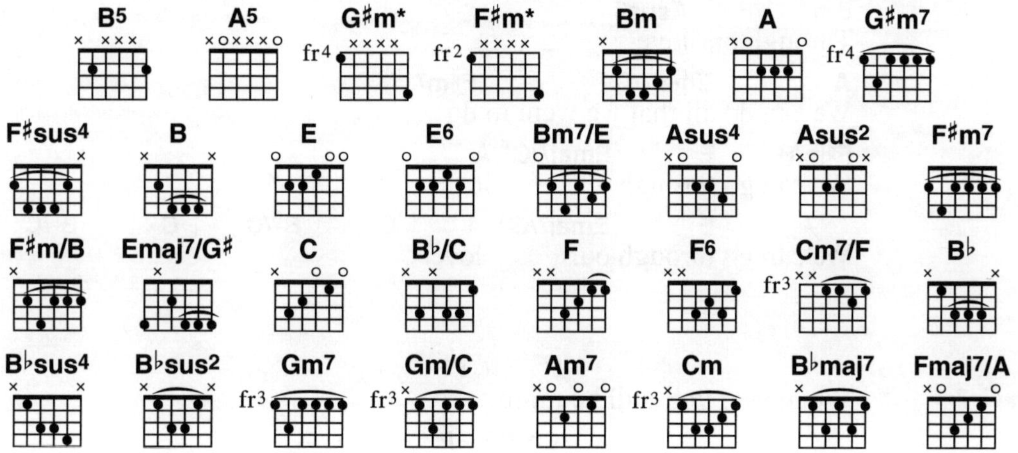

Intro

```
B5             A5                  G♯m*
We wasted time and again on things
F♯m*                A
Things we already knew
Bm        A          G♯m7   F♯sus4   B
Born to do, I give my love to you.
```

Verse 1

```
                                 E       E6
When ever you get some time
                                 Bm7/E    E
When ever you get some time
                A         Asus4  A          Asus2
I'd like to roll it all       up in a ball
            E
And spend it with you
                       F♯m7
You've got the power of love
                                   F♯m/B                  B
And love has the power to make it come true.
```

```
                E               G♯m7
Chorus 1     We can go through our love
             A                              B
             We can do things that they said were impossible
             Bm             Asus2
             Through our love
             A          Emaj7/G♯             F♯m7
             We can do all that we went to do
             F♯m/B      E          Emaj7/G♯ A
             We can go through our         love
                        E          Emaj7/G♯  A  | C    | B♭/C  | C    | B♭/C
             We can go through our          love.


                                      F       F6
Verse 2      When ever you will be more
                                      Cm7/F   F
             When ever you will be more
                       B♭            B♭sus4
             I wanna be with you
               B♭        B♭sus2    F                  B♭  F
             I just wanna do what - ever feels right
                              Gm7
             You've got the power of love
                                          Gm/C           C
             And love has the power to turn on the light.


                        F          Am7
Chorus 2     Here we go through our love
             B♭                            C
             We can see things that they said were invisible
             Cm             B♭maj7
             Though our love
                        Am7                 Gm7
             We can see where we are going to
             Gm/C       F           Am7
             Were going through our love, through our love
```

```
                  B♭                           C
(cont.)   We can learn to do things that they said were impossible
          Cm            B♭maj7
          Though our love
                 Am7                      Gm7
          We can be blessed with a better view
          Gm7/C    F         Fmaj7/A  B♭
          We can go through our       love
                   F         Fmaj7/A  B♭
          We can go through our       love
                   F         Fmaj7/A  B♭
          We can go through our       love.
```

Tomorrow

Words & Music by
Paul & Linda McCartney

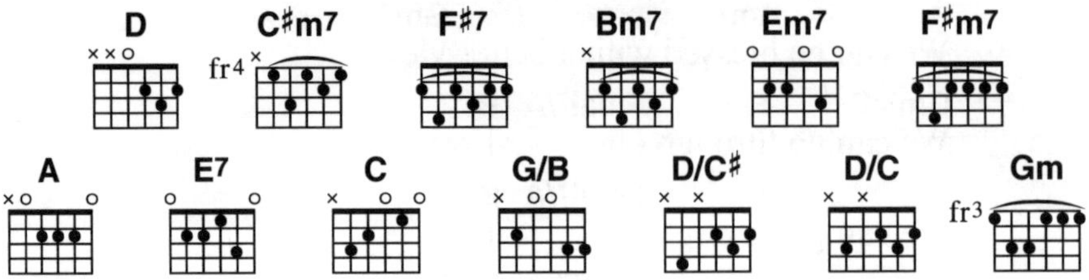

Intro | D |

Verse 1

D C♯m7 F♯7 Bm7
Oh, baby, don't you let me down to - morrow
Em7 D
Holding hands we both abandon sorrow
F♯m7 Em7 A D
Oh, ___ for a chance to get a - way tomorrow.

Verse 2

D C♯m7 F♯7 Bm7
Hey, baby's got a lazy day on Sunday
Em7 D
Here's a pound, we hang around 'til Monday
F♯m7 Em7 A D F♯7
Oh, ___ baby don't you let me down on Sun - day.

Pre-Chorus 1

Bm7 E7
Bring a bag of bread and cheese and find a shady spot
Bm7 E7
Beneath the trees
Bm7 E7
Catch a breath of country air and run your pretty fingers
Bm7 E7
Through my hair.

Chorus 1

C G/B A
To - morrow, when we both abandon sorrow

```
             D   C♯m7           F♯7            Bm7
Verse 3      Oh, baby, don't you let me down to - morrow
             Em7                                    D
             Through the week we beg and steal and borrow
                F♯m7          Em7        A      D             F♯7
             Oh,___ for a chance to get a - way to - morrow.

             Bm7                                 E7
Pre-Chorus 2 Honey, pray for sunny skies so I can speak to rainbows
                       Bm7  E7
             In your eyes
             Bm7                                  E7
             Let's just hope the weather man is feeling fine
                                Bm7  E7
             And doesn't spoil our plan.

                C                 G/B          A
Chorus 2     To - morrow, when we both abandon sorrow.

             D         C♯m7          F♯7            Bm7
Verse 4      Oh, babe, baby, don't you let me down to - morrow
             Em7                          D
             Holding hands we both abandon sorrow
                F♯m7                       Em7  A      D
             Oh,___ baby, don't you let me down to - morrow
             F♯m7       Em7               A      D        D/C♯  D/C
               Oh, for a chance to get a - way to - morrow.

             (D/C)       G/B    Gm       D
Chorus 3       Baby, don't let me down to - morrow
             |: (D)      G/B    Gm       D      :|  Play 3 times
               Baby, don't let me down to - morrow.

             G/B      Gm         D
Outro        Oh,___ don't let me down
                       G/B   Gm       D
             Baby, don't let me down to - morrow
                       G/B         Gm       D
             Baby, don't let, let me down to - morrow
                       G/B   Gm       D
             Baby, don't let me down to - morrow.
```

Too Many People

Words & Music by
Paul McCartney

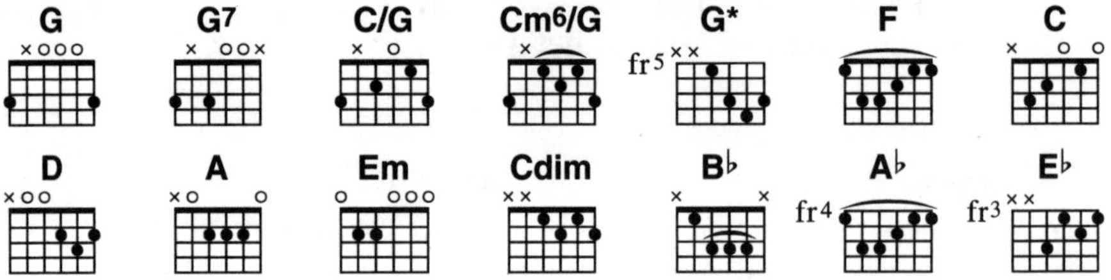

Intro

| G G7 | C/G Cm6/G | G G7 | C/G Cm6/G |

| G | Cm6/G | G | Cm6/G |

| G* | G* ||

Verse 1

F C D G
Too many people going underground
F C D G
Too many reaching for a piece of cake
F C D G
Too many people pulled and pushed around
F C D G
Too many waiting for that lucky break.

Chorus 1

G G7 C/G Cm6/G
That was your first mis - take
G G7 C/G Cm6/G G
You took your lucky break and broke it in two
Cm6/G C Cm6/G
Now what can be done for you?
G* | G* ||
You broke it in two.

Verse 2

```
F               C      D       G
  Too many people sharing party lines
F               C             D       G
  Too many people never sleeping late
F               C      D        G
  Too many people paying parking fines
F               C              D      G
  Too many hungry people losing weight.
```

Chorus 2 As Chorus 1

Solo

```
||: A    | Em    | G    | D    :|| G    ||
```

Verse 3

```
F               C       D         G
  Too many people breaching practices
F                C                   D      G
  Don't let 'em tell you what you wanna be
F               C       D    G
  Too many people holding back
       F          C          D      G
This is crazy and maybe it's not like me.
```

Chorus 3

```
G                    G7         C/G     Cm6/G
  That was your last mis - take,
G                G7       C/G         Cm6/G           G
  I find my love a - wake and waiting to be
Cdim                G
  Now what can be done for you?
Cdim              G
She's waiting for me, yeah.
```

Outro

```
| A      | Em     | G      | D      |
| B♭     | F      | A♭     | E♭     |
| C      | G      | B♭     | F      |
                    𝄐
| C  G   | F  C   | C      ||
```

To You

Words & Music by
Paul McCartney

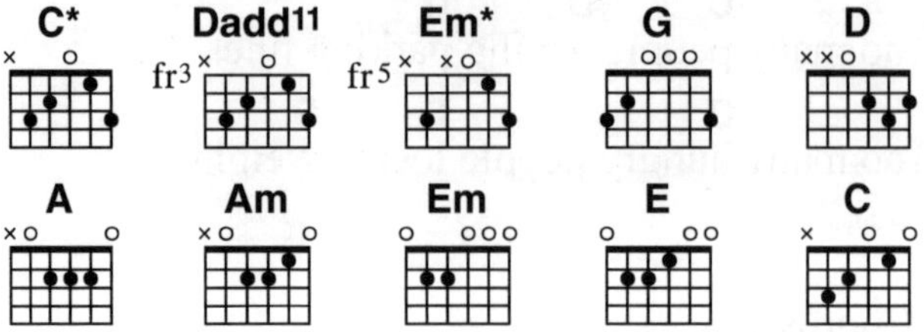

Intro

| C* | Dadd11 | C* | Dadd11 Em* Dadd11 |

| C* | Dadd11 | C* | G

Verse 1

D A
Well if the same thing happened to you
Am Em E
Would you still put me through what you put me through?

Chorus 1

C E
If it happened to you
C E
What if it happened to you?

Verse 2

A D A
What if it happened and a man kept shaking you down
Am Em E
But you can't get a ride to his side of town?

Chorus 2

C E
If it happened to you
C E
What if it happened to you?
C D
What if happened to you?
C D
Keep it out of my shoes.
C D
And if you're stepping on toes
C G
Keep it outta my nose.

Verse 3

N.C. (D) A
'Cause if the same thing happened to me
Am Em E
Well, it won't be as bad as it used to be.

Chorus 3

C E
If it happened to you
C E
What if it happened to you?
C E
What if it happened to you?
C E
What if it happened to you?
C
What if it happened to you, too?

Solo

𝄆 (C) | E | C | E 𝄇

Chorus 4

C E
What if it happens to you?
C E
What if it happens to you?
C D
What if it happens to you?
C D
Keep it out of my shoes
C D
And if you're stepping on toes
C G
Well, keep it outta my nose.

Verse 4

N.C. (D) A
'Cause if the same thing happened to me

Am Em E
Well, it won't be as bad as it used to be.

Chorus 5

C E
If it happened to you

C E
What if it happened to you?

C E
What am I going to do?

C E
If it happened to you?

C
Well, what if happened to you?

Outro

‖: (C) | E | C | E :‖

‖:
C E
If it happened to you____

C E :‖ *Repeat to fade*
What if it happened to you?____

Tough On A Tightrope

Words & Music by
Paul McCartney

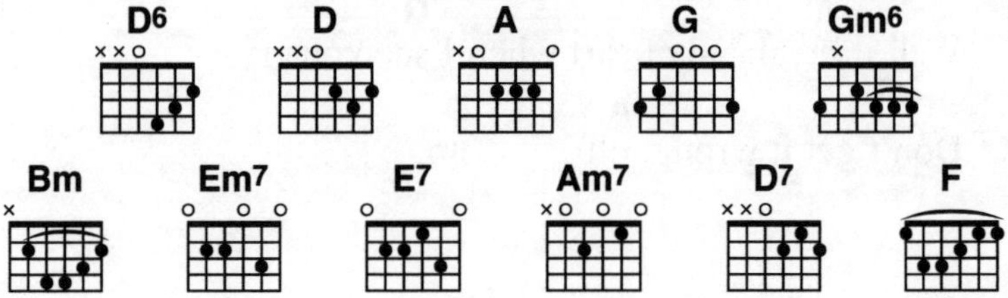

Intro ‖: D6 D | D6 D :‖

Verse 1
A G
You don't feel right when I come on strong
D A G | D |
Don't get it wrong
A G
I wait all night but you won't be long
D A G | D |
Don't get it wrong.

Chorus 1
D
Hear me right
Gm6 Bm
I love you from the bottom of my heart
Em7 A Bm
You make the answer bright
G Gm6 D E7
You touch me in a way that no-one else could ever do
A D G Em7 A D
If you'll only love me, I'll love you.

Verse 2

```
       A                     G
And if you're tempted to tell a lie
        D                A  G | D    |
Don't get it wrong
          A                      G
Well it breaks my heart when I see you cry
        D                A     G   D
Don't get it wrong, oh           no.
```

Chorus 2

```
        D
Get it right
     Gm6                                 Bm
The brightest light that's shining in the skies
Em7          A          Bm
  Is shining from your eyes
  G           Gm6              D              E7
I love you in a way that no-one else could ever do
  A      D        G    Em7 A    D
If you'll only love me, I'll love you.
```

Bridge

```
     Am7               D7
I'm often accused of giving too little
   G                      E7
It's got me confused I'm split down the middle
      Am7                       F
Con - flicting reviews of our life coming in
    D6            D
It's tough on a tight - rope
        D6              D      D6  D
Yes, it's tough on a tight - rope.
```

Solo

```
|: A    | G    | D   A G | D    :|
```

```
                        D
Chorus 3      Hear me right
                Gm6                          Bm
              I love you from the bottom of my heart
              Em7              A       Bm
                You make the picture bright
                  G            Gm6            D              E7
              You love me in a way that no-one else could ever do
                A      D           G    Em7 A    D
              If you'll only love me, I'll   love you
                  G             Gm6            D              E7
              You touch me in a way that no-one else could ever do
                A      D           G    Em7 A    D6
              If you'll only love me, I'll   love you.

                                                                    Repeat to fade
Outro         ||: (D6)                 D     | D6        D      :||   w/ad lib. vocal
                Tough on a tight - rope . ___________
```

Treat Her Gently (Lonely Old People)

Words & Music by
Paul & Linda McCartney

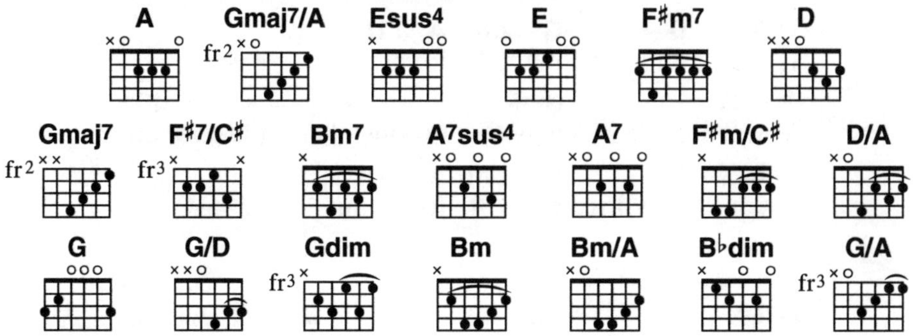

Verse 1

A
Treat her gently
Gmaj7/A
Treat her kind
Esus4 E A F♯m7
She doesn't even know her own mind
D Gmaj7
Treat her simply
D Gmaj7
Take it slow
D Gmaj7
Make it easy
D F♯7/C♯ Bm7
And let her know
Esus4 E A7sus4 A7
You'll never find another way.

```
            D          F♯m/C♯
Chorus 1    Here we sit
                Bm7          D/A
            Two lonely old people
            G                   D     G/D  D
            Eaking our lives a - way
            D      F♯m/C♯
            Bit by bit
                Bm7          D/A
            Two lonely old people
            G                   D     G/D  D
            Keeping the time of day.


            Gmaj7   Gdim
Bridge      Here we sit
            F♯m7  Bm    Bm/A
            Out of breath
                G                      D     G/D   D
            And nobody asked us to play
            A               B♭dim         Bm         Bm/A       G
            Old people's home for the day, yeah, yeah, yeah____
                    G/A         D
            Nobody asked us to play.


            A
Verse 2       So, treat her gently
            Gmaj7/A
              Treat her kind
            Esus4           E              A     F♯m7
              She doesn't even know her own mind
            D            Gmaj7
              Treat her simply
            D          Gmaj7
              Make it slow
            D          Gmaj7
              Take it easy
               D   F♯7/C♯ Bm7
            And let her    know
                 Esus4 E            A7sus4    A
            You'll never find another way.____


Chorus 2    As Chorus 1

Outro       As Bridge 1
```

Tug Of War

Words & Music by
Paul McCartney

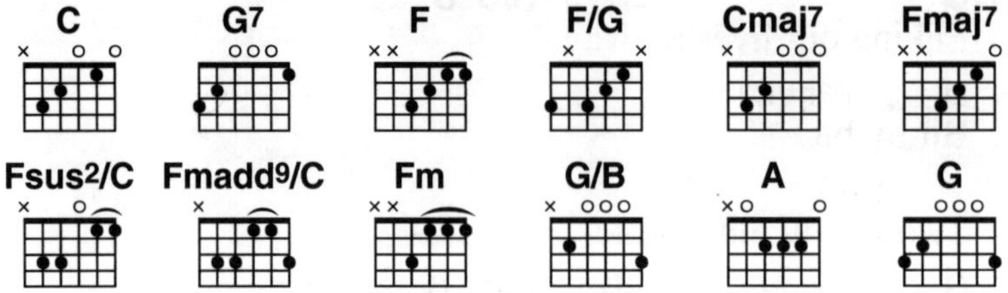

Chorus 1

N.C. C
It's a tug of war

What with one thing and another

G7
It's a tug of war

We expected more

But with one thing and another

We were trying to outdo each other

C
In a tug of war.

Verse 1

F
In another world

In another world we could

Stand on top of the mountain

C
With our flag un - furled

F
In a time to come

In a time to come we will be

Dancing to the beat played

F/G C
On a different drum.

Chorus 2

N.C. C
It's a tug of war

Though I know I mustn't grumble

G7
It's a tug of war

But I can't let go

If I do you'll take a tumble

And the whole thing is going to crumble

C
It's a tug of war.

Link 1

(C) Cmaj7
Pushing pushing, pulling and pulling

F Fmaj7 C
Pushing and pull - ing.——

Bridge

N.C. C Fsus2/C
In years to come they may dis - cover

Fmadd9/C C
What the air we breathe and the life we lead are all a - bout

F Fm
But it won't be soon enough (soon enough)

C
Soon enough for me

F Fsus2/C
No, it won't be soon enough (it won't be soon enough)

Fmadd9/C C | C | F |
Soon enough for me.

Verse 2

```
                F
In another world we could

Stand on top of the mountain
                        C         F
With our flag un - furled
                F
In a time to come we will be

Dancing to the beat played
      F/G        C
On a different drum
          F
We will be dancing to the beat
                F/G       C
Played on a different drum
          F
We will be dancing to the beat
                F/G       C
Played on a different drum.
```

Chorus 3

```
N.C.         C
It's a tug of war

What with one thing and another
             G7
It's a tug of war

We expected more

But with one thing and another

We were trying to outscore each other
            C
In a tug of war.
```

Link 2

```
(C)                Cmaj7
Pushing pushing, pulling and pulling
F                 Fmaj7
Pushing and pulling.——
```

Outro

```
| C    | C  G/B | A    | A    G | Fmaj7  | Fmaj7 G | A (fermata) ||
```

Uncle Albert/Admiral Halsey

Words & Music by
Paul & Linda McCartney

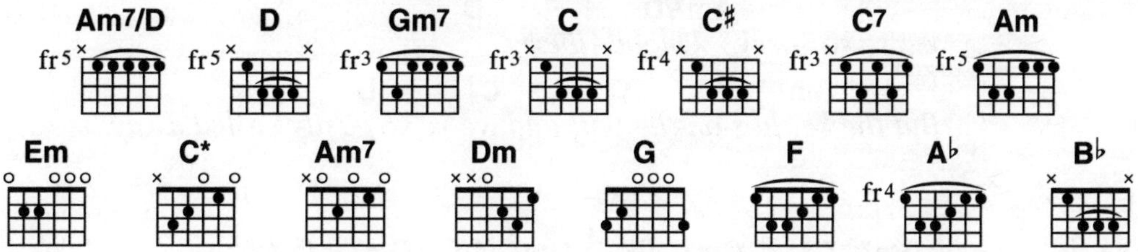

Verse 1

Am7/D **D**
We're so sorry, Uncle Albert
Am7/D **D**
We're so sorry if we caused you any pain
Am7/D **D**
We're so sorry, Uncle Albert
Gm7 **C**
But there's no one left at home
C♯ **D**
And I be - lieve I'm gonna rain.

Link 1

| **Gm7** | **C** | **Gm7** | **C** |
| **Gm7** | **C** | **Gm7** | **C** **C♯** |
| **D** ‖ **Am7/D** | **D**

Verse 2

Am7/D **D**
We're so sorry but we haven't heard a thing all day
Am7/D **D**
We're so sorry, Uncle Albert
Gm7 **C** **C♯** **D**
But if anything should happen we'll be sure to give a ring.

Link 2

| **Gm7** **C7** | **Gm7** **C7** | **Gm7** **C7** | **Gm7** **C** **C♯** |
w/ad lib. vocal fx.
| **D** | **C** **D** ‖

Verse 3 (spoken)

Am7/D **D**
We're so sorry, Uncle Albert
Am7/D **D**
But we haven't done a bloody thing all day
Am7/D **D**
We're so sorry, Uncle Albert
Gm7 **C** **C♯** **D**
But the kettle's on the boil and we're so easily called away.

Link 3

| Gm7 C7 | Gm7 C7 | Gm7 C7 | Gm7 C C♯ |
w/ad lib. vocal fx.
| D | C | Gm7 ||

Trumpet Solo 1

| Am C | Am C | Am C | Em | Em ||

Chorus 1

C* **Am7** **Dm**
Hands a - cross the water (water)
G **F** **A♭** **B♭** **C***
Heads across the sky______
C* **Am7** **Dm**
Hands a - cross the water (water)
G **C*** **N.C.**
Heads across the sky.

Verse 3

Am **C**
Admiral Halsey notified me
Am **C**
He had to have a berth or he couldn't get to sea
Am **C** **Em**
I had another look and I had a cup of tea and butter pie

(The butter wouldn't melt so I put it in the pie, alright).

Chorus 2

C* **Am7** **Dm**
Hands a - cross the water (water)
G **F** **A♭** **B♭** **C***
Heads across the sky______
C* **Am7** **Dm**
Hands a - cross the water (water)
G **C***
Heads across the sky.

Bridge

𝄆 C*
Live a little, be a gypsy, get around (get around)

G
Get your feet up off the ground

C 𝄇 N.C.
Live a little, get around.

Trumpet Solo 2 As Solo 1

Chorus 3 As Chorus 2

Repeat ad lib. to fade

Outro

𝄆 C* | C* | C* | C* 𝄇
Ooh.___ Ooh.___

Vanilla Sky

Words & Music by
Paul McCartney

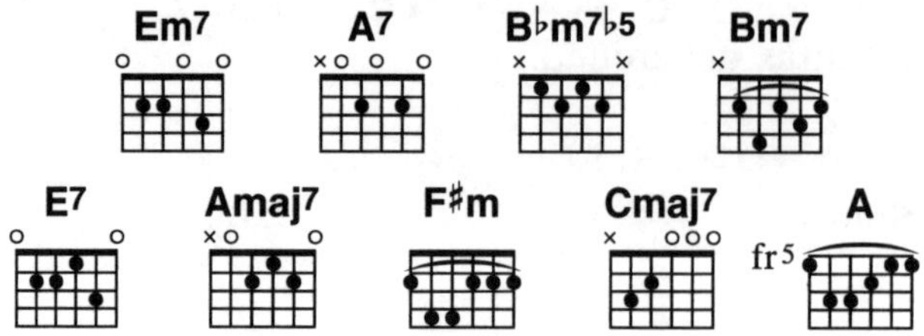

Intro

N.C. ‖: Em7 | A7 | Em7 | A7 :‖

Verse 1

Em7 A7 Em7 A
The chef prepares a special menu for your delight, oh my,
Em7 A7 Em7 A
Tonight you fly so high up in the vanilla sky.

Verse 2

Em7 A7
Your life is fine, it's sweet and sour
Em7 A7
Unbearable or great
Em7 A7 Em7 A7
You gotta love every hour, you must appre - ciate.

Chorus 1

B♭m7♭5 Bm7
This is your time,
Em7 Amaj7
This is your day,
B♭m7♭5 Bm7
You've got it all
E7 F♯m
Don't blow it a - way.

Link

| Cmaj7 | Cmaj7 ‖: Em7 | A7 | Em7 | A7 :‖
(2°) Do, do, do…

Verse 3
Em7 A7 Em7 A7
The chef prepares a special menu for your delight, oh my,
Em7 A7 Em7 A7
Tonight you fly so high up in the vanilla sky.

Verse 4
Em7 A7 Em7 A7
Melted tin beads cast your fortune in a glass of wine
Em7 A7 Em7 A7
Snail or fish, balloon or dolphin, see silver shine.

Chorus 2 As Chorus 1

Link 2 As Link 1

Verse 5
Em7 A7 Em7 A7
The chef prepares a special menu for your delight, oh my,
Em7 A7 Em7 A7
Tonight you fly so high up in the vanilla sky
Em7 A7 Em7 A7
In the vanilla, in the vanilla, in the vanilla sky
Em7 A7 Em7 A7
In the vanilla, in the vanilla, in the vanilla sky.

Coda
B♭m7♭5 Bm7
Mm ____ mm
E7 A
In the vanilla sky.

Venus And Mars

Words & Music by
Paul McCartney & Linda McCartney

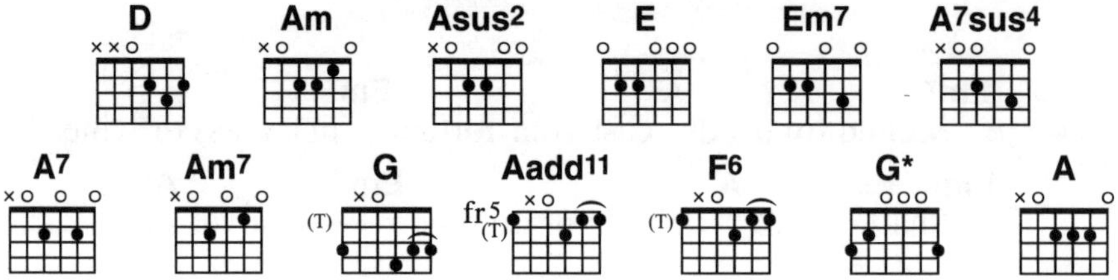

Intro

| D | D | D | D |

| D | Am Asus2 | Em | Em7 |

| A7sus4 | A7 ||

Verse 1

D Am Am7
Sitting in the stand of the sports a - rena
D
Waiting for the show to be - gin
Am Asus2
Red lights, green lights, strawberry wi - ne
Em Em7
A good friend of mine, follows the stars
A7sus4 A7
Venus And Mars are al - right tonight.

Outro

| G Aadd11 | F6 D | G Aadd11 | F6 D |

| G Aadd11 | F6 G* D || A *segue "Rockshow"*

We're Open Tonight

Words & Music by
Paul McCartney

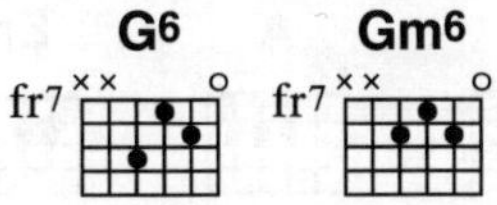

Intro | G6 | Gm6 | G6 | Gm6 ||

Verse 1

```
G6                    Gm6
   We're open to - night for fun
G6                      Gm6
   So bring all your friends, come on
G6                    Gm6          G6              Gm6
   We're open to - night, come one, come all.
```

Verse 2

```
G6                  Gm6   G6
   We're opening all our doors
                            Gm6
We're clearing back all the floors
G6                    Gm6          G6                   Gm6
   We're open to - night, come one, come all, ooh. ___
```

Outro

```
G6                Gm6
Ooh, ___ ay, ___ ooh ___
G6     Gm6
Ooh, ___ ooh, ___
G6     Gm6          G6            Gm6
Ooh, ___ come one, come all
G6                    Gm6
   We're open to - night.
```

Wanderlust

Words & Music by
Paul McCartney

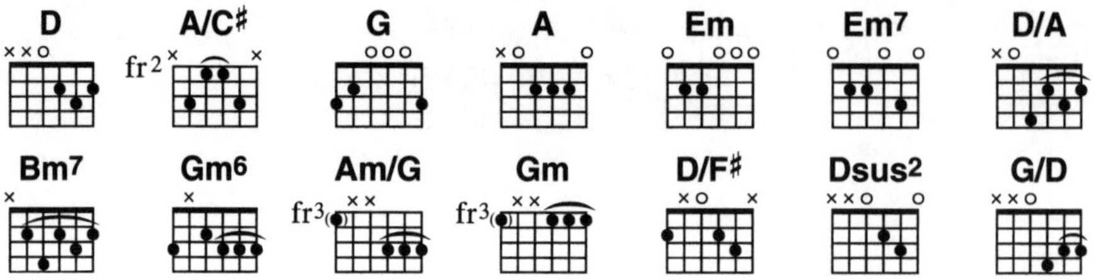

Intro

| D A/C♯ D G | D | D A/C♯ D G | A |

| Em Em7 | Em7 | A D/A | D ||

Verse 1

D A/C♯ D G D
Light out wan - der - lust
D A/C♯ D G A
Head us out to sea
Em Em7
Captain says there'll be a bust
A D/A D
This one's not for me.

Verse 2

D A/C♯ D G D
Take us from the dark
D A/C♯ D G A
Out where we can see
Em Em7
Captain's out to make his mark
A D/A D
This one's not to be.

Chorus 1

```
G                    A    D
Light out wan - der - lust
G              A  D
Help us to be free
G                    A    D    Bm7
Light out wan - der - lust____
Em7             Gm6
Do it just for me
Am/G     Gm
Wander - lust
```

Instrumental As Intro

Verse 3

```
D      A/C#D        D  G  D
   Oh, where did I_____ go wrong my love?
D         A/C# D       G    A
   What petty crime was I found guilty of?
Em                     Em7                   A      D/A  D
   What better time to find a brand new day?_____
    D          G
Oh, wanderlust away.
```

Chorus 2 As Chorus 1

Verse 4

```
| D A/C# D G | D     | D A/C# D G | A     |

Em                Em7
Captain's out to make his mark
A            D/A   D
This one's not to be.
```

Chorus 3 As Chorus 1

Verse 5 As Verse 3

Outro

```
(A)
Dropping a line
D            D/F#
Maybe this time
    G          A       D   Dsus2 D G/D D(fermata)
It's wander - lust for me._____
```

Warm & Beautiful

Words & Music by
Paul McCartney

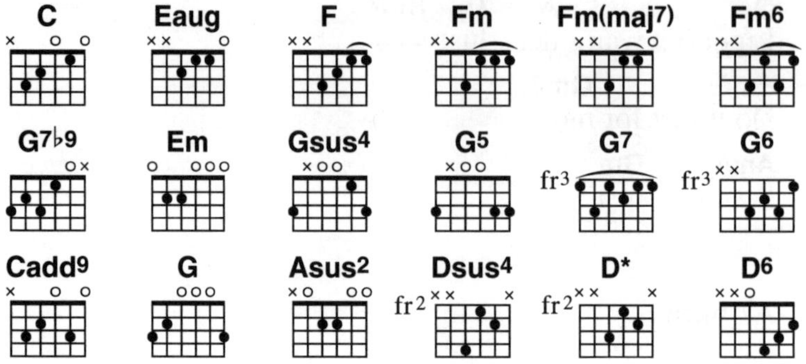

Intro | C Eaug | F Fm Fm(maj7) Fm6 | C G7♭9 | C G7♭9 |

Verse 1

C Eaug F Fm Fm(maj7) Fm6
A love so warm and beau - ti - ful
C Em F Gsus4 G5
Stands when time it - self is fall - ing,
C Eaug F Fm Fm(maj7) Fm6
A love so warm and beau - ti - ful
C G7♭9 C G7♭9 G7
Never fades a - way.

Verse 2

C Eaug F Fm Fm(maj7) Fm6
Love, faith and hope are beau - ti - ful
C Em F Gsus4 G5
When your world is touched by sad - ness,
C Eaug F Fm Fm(maj7) Fm6
To each his own is won - der - ful,
C G7♭9 C
Love will never die.

Bridge 1

```
F              G6        Cadd9  C
Sunlight's morning glo  -  ry
        Eaug F     G        C
Tells the    story of our love
Fm             G6      Cadd9   C
Moonlight on the wa    -   ter
Asus2       Dsus4 D*   D6  D   Gsus4 G G6 G5
Brings me in   -  spi - ra - tion ev  -  er af - ter.
```

Instrumental

```
| C  Eaug | F  Fm  Fm(maj7)  Fm6 | C    Em | F      G |

| C  Eaug | F  Fm  Fm(maj7)  Fm6 | C   G7♭9 | C       ||
```

Bridge 2 As Bridge 1

Verse 3 As Verse 1

Coda

```
C      G7♭9     C
Never fades a - way.
```

Waterfalls

Words & Music by
Paul McCartney

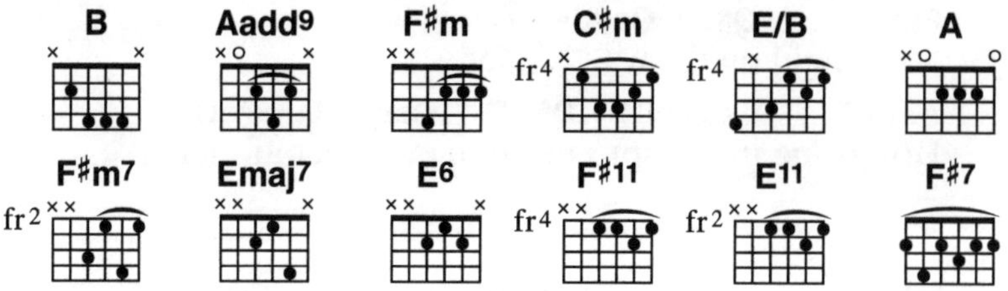

Verse 1

B Aadd9 F♯m
Don't go jumping waterfalls
C♯m Aadd9 B
Please keep to the lake
B Aadd9 F♯m
People who jump waterfalls
C♯m E/B A
Sometimes can make mis - takes.

Chorus 1

F♯m F♯m7 Emaj7 E6 F♯m F♯m7 Emaj7 E6
And I need love, yeah, I need love
F♯m F♯m7 Emaj7 E6
Like a second needs an hour,
F♯m F♯m7 Emaj7 E6
Like a rain - drop needs a shower,
F♯m F♯m7 Emaj7 E6 F♯11
Yeah, I need love every minute of the day
E11
And it wouldn't be the same
F♯11 F♯7
If you ever should decide to go a - way.

Solo

| B Aadd9 | F♯m | C♯m Aadd9 | B |
| B Aadd9 | F♯m | C♯m E/B | A ||

Chorus 2

F♯m F♯m7 Emaj7 E6   F♯m F♯m7   Emaj7 E6
And I   need love,   yeah, I   need   love

F♯m   F♯m7   Emaj7 E6
Like a castle needs a tower,

F♯m   F♯m7   Emaj7 E6
Like a gar - den needs a flower,

F♯m F♯m7 Emaj7 E6   F♯11
Yeah, I   need   love every minute of the day

E11
And it wouldn't be the same

F♯11   F♯7
If you ever should decide to go a - way.

Verse 2

B   Aadd9   F♯m
Don't go chasing polar bears

C♯m Aadd9   B
In the great un - known

B   Aadd9 F♯m
Some big friendly polar bear

C♯m   E/B   A
Might want to take you home.

Chorus 3

As Chorus 1

Verse 3

B   Aadd9 F♯m
Don't run after   motor cars

C♯m   Aadd9 B
Please stay on the side

B   Aadd9 F♯m
Someone's glossy motor car

C♯m   E/B A
Might take you for a ride.

Chorus 4

F♯m F♯m7 Emaj7 E6 F♯m F♯m7 Emaj7 E6
And I need love, yeah, I need love

F♯m F♯m7 Emaj7 E6
Like a castle needs a tower,

F♯m F♯m7 Emaj7 E6
Like a gar - den needs a flower,

F♯m F♯m7 Emaj7 E6 F♯m F♯m7 Emaj7 E6
Yeah, I need love, said I need love

F♯m F♯m7 Emaj7 E6
Like a raindrop needs a shower,

F♯m F♯m7 Emaj7 E6
Like a se - cond needs an hour

F♯11
Every minute of the day

E11
And it wouldn't be the same

F♯11 F♯7
If you ever should decide to go a - way.

Outro

B Aadd9 F♯m
Don't go jumping waterfalls

C♯m Aadd9 B
Please keep to the lake.

We Got Married

Words & Music by
Paul McCartney

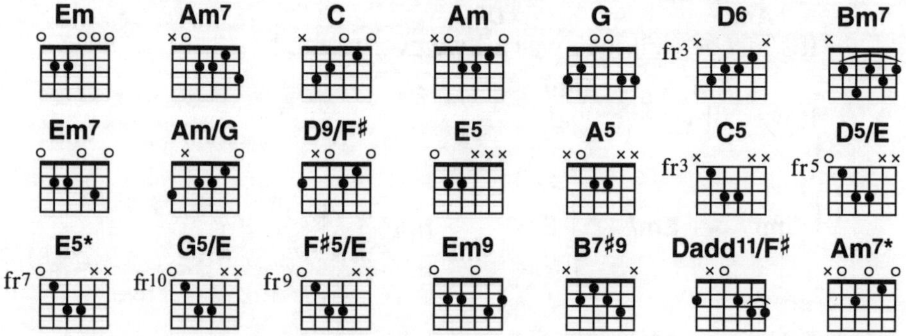

Intro | Em | Em | Em | Em ||

Verse 1

```
Em              Am7
Going fast, coming soon
                C           Em
We made love in the afternoon
                  Am7
Found a flat, after that
C                  Em
We got married.
```

Verse 2

```
Em                 Am7
Working hard for the dream
C                      Em
Scoring goals for the other team
                      Am7
Times were bad, we were glad
C                  Em
We got married.
```

Middle

C Am Em C
Like the way you open up your hearts to each other
C Am G
When you find a meeting of the minds
Am D6
It's just as well love was all we ever wanted
Am Bm7
It was all we ever had.

Link

| Em7 | Em7 | Em7 | Em7 ||

Verse 3

Em Am7
Further on in the game
C Em
Waiting up till the children came
Am7
Place your bets and no regrets
C Em
We got married,
C Em
We got married,
Am Am/G D9/F♯ Bm7
We got married, yeah.____

Interlude

| E5 | E5 | E5 A5 | C5 D5/E E5* D5/E |

| E5* A5 | C5 E5 | G5/E F♯5/E E5* D5 E5* |

Verse 4

(E5*) A5 C5
Nowadays every night flashes by
E5*
At the speed of light
D5 A5
Living life, loving wife
C5 E5
We got married.

Bridge 1

```
C
I love the things that happen
                Em7
When we start to discover
C                        Am7*                    G
Who we are and what we're living for
C                             Em9
Just because love was all we ever wanted
         C           B7#9
It was all we ever had.
```

Link 2

```
| Em  Dadd11/F# | G  Am7* | Bm7    |
```

Interlude 2

```
|: E5  A5 | C5  D5/E  E5*  D5/E | E5*  A5 | C5  E5 |

 1.                                          2.
| G5/E  F#5/E  E5*  D5/E  E5*  :|  E5   |

| C       | Em7     | C   Am7*  | G     |

| C       | Em9     | C         | B7#9  ||
```

Outro

```
|: Em             Dadd11/F#              G
It's not just a loving machine, it doesn't work out
          Am7*                | Bm7                          :|  Repeat to fade
If you don't work at it.
```

What It Is

Words & Music by
Paul McCartney

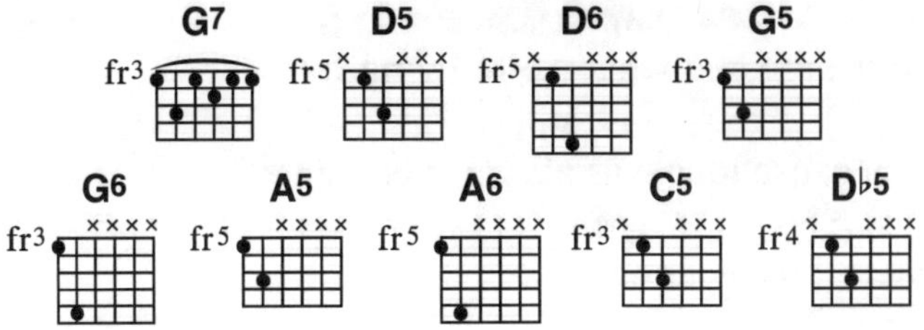

Chorus 1

```
    G7 N.C.           G7 N.C.
You ———  are what it is
                   D5      D6 D5      D6 G5 G6 G5 G6
That makes the world go around for me
G7
You are what I need
                 A5  A6        A5  A6    D5 D6 D5 D6
You make me feel good a - bout my - self.
```

Verse 1

```
C5
   You see, I love you so much
D5             G6
I can never do without your touch
C5              G5             D5  D5 D♭5 C5
   I'm like a busy honey bee
(C5)              G5
   I'm always hungry for it
D5
How could anyone ignore it?
C5                 G5             D5 D6 D5 D6
Surely ev'ry - body will a - gree.
```

Chorus 2

```
     G7
That you are what it is
                    D5     D6       D5     D6 G5 G6 G5 G6
That makes the cloud roll a - round the sky
           G7
Oh yeah, you got what it takes
                 A5     A6    A5    A6 D5 D6 D5 D6
You make me proud to be who I    am.
```

```
            C5          G5
Verse 2       You see, I love you so much
            D5
            I can never be without your touch
            C5          G5            D5 D♭5 C5
              I'm like a busy honey bee
            (C5)       G5
            I'm always hungry for it
            D5
            How could any - one ignore it
            C5          G5               D5 D♭5 C5
            Surely ev'ry - body must a - gree.


                G7
Chorus 3    That you are what it is
                                  D5   D6    D5    D6 G5  G6 G5 G6
            That makes the world go a - round for me
                G7
            Yeah, you got what I need
                                 A5  A6    A5   A6  D5 D6 D5 D6
            You make me feel good a - bout my - self,   ooh.


Solo        | C5  G5 | D5  G5 | C5  G5 | D5  D5 D♭5 |

            | C5  G5 | D5  G5 | C5     G5      | D5     ||
                                Yeah, yeah, yeah, yeah. __


                G5  G7  N.C.               G7  N.C.
Chorus 3    Well, you ___   are what it is
                                  D5   D6 D5     D6 G5 G6 G5 G6
            That makes the world go around for me
                G7
            Yeah, you got what I need
                                 A5  A6   A5 A6  D5 D6 D5 D6
            You make me feel good to be my - self.
```

Verse 3

C5 G5
You see, I love you so much
D5
I can never do without your touch
C5 G5 D5 D5 D♭5 C5
I'm like a busy honey bee
(C5) G5
I'm always hungry for it
D5
How could anyone ignore it
C5 G5 D5 D6 D5 D6
Surely ev'ry - body must a - gree.

Outro

G7
That you are what it is
D5 D6 D5 D6 G5
That makes the world go a - round for me,
D5 D6 D5 D6 G5
You make the world go a - round for me,
D5 D6 D5 D6 D5 D6 D5 D6
Yeah, you make the world go a - round, world go a - round,
D5 D6 D5 D6 G5
World go a - round for me
G7 N.C.
You're what it is!

When The Night

Words & Music by
Paul McCartney & Linda McCartney

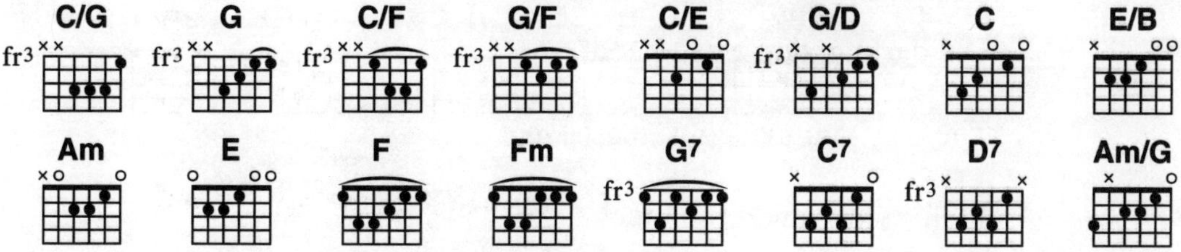

Intro | C/G G | C/F G/F | C/E G/D C | E/B |
| Am | E | Am | E ||

Verse 1
Am E
Well, the night (well the night ——)
F Fm
Was beautiful and mellow (mel - low, mel - low)
C G7
And the light (and the light) of the night (of the night)
C G7
Fell on me (fell on me).

Verse 2
Am E
You said right (you said right ——)
F Fm
Made me a happy fellow (fel - low, fel - low)
C G7
And the light (and the light) of the night (of the night)
C G7
Fell on me (fell on me).

Bridge 1

```
  F
I never will forget the night
  Fm
I held you close, I held you tight
     C                          C7
Oh, darling, don't you know
     F
The way you made my senses reel
  Fm
I fell in love and now I feel
      C           Am
Like I will never go
          D7                  G7
Oh, little darling don't you know.
```

Verse 3

```
          Am                        E
That the night (that the night ____ )
                               F               Fm
Was marvellous and yellow (yel - low, yel - low)
         C                            G7
And the light (and the light) of the night (of the night)
        C                G7
Fell on me (fell on me).
```

Instrumental

```
| Am | E | F | Fm |

C               G7            C              C7
   And the light   of the night   fell on me.
```

Bridge 2

```
  F
I never will forget the way
     Fm
You taught me how to swing and sway
     C                          C7
Oh, darling don't you know
     F
That ever since that special day
     Fm
My mind can only contemplate
      C               Am
The magic that you show
          D7                  G7
Oh, little darling don't you know.
```

Verse 5

```
           Am                  E
That the night (that the night ___)
                        F           Fm
Is beautiful and yellow (yel - low, yel - low)
       C                            G7
And the light (and the light) of the night (of the night)
      Am                  Am/G    F
Fell on me (fell on me),   fell on me (fell on me)
       C                              G7
Oh, the li, li li li li li li li li li li light (of the night)
      C
Fell on me (fell on me), ooh ___(fell on me)
```

𝄆 Yes the light fell on me (fell on me___) (fell on me.) 𝄇 *Repeat to fade w/ad lib. vocals*

Wild Life

Words & Music by
Paul McCartney & Linda McCartney

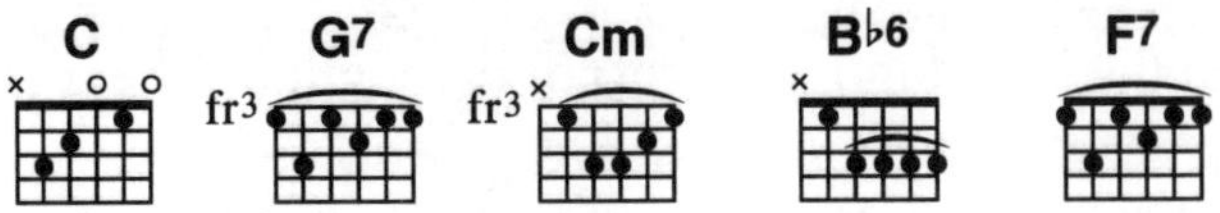

Intro

C G7 Cm
The world "wild" ap - plies to the words "you" and "me".

‖: Cm | B♭6 | F7 | F7 :‖ *Play 3 times*

Verse 1

Cm B♭6 F7
While takin' a walk ___ through an African park one day
Cm B♭6 F7
I saw a sign say, "The animals have the right of way".

Chorus 1

Cm B♭6 F7
Wild life, ___ whatever happened to
Cm B♭6 F7
Wild life, ___ the animals in the zoo?

Verse 2

Cm B♭6
You're breathing so hot ___
(B♭6) F7
A lot of political nonsense in the air
Cm B♭6 F7
You're making it hard ___ for the people who live in there
Cm B♭6 F7
You're moving so fast, ___ but baby, you know not where.

Chorus 2

Cm B♭6 F7
Wild life, (wild life), what's gonna happen to
Cm B♭6 F7
Wild life, (wild life), the animals in the zoo? Oh! ___

Solo 1 |: Cm | B♭6 | F7 | F7 :|

Verse 3

Cm N.C. B♭6 F7
You'd better stop, ___ there's animals ev' - rywhere
Cm B♭6
And man is the top, an animal too
F7
And, man, you just got to care.

Chorus 3 As Chorus 2

Solo 2 |: Cm | B♭6 | F7 | F7 :|

Verse 4

Cm B♭ F7
You're breathing a lot ___ of political non - sense in the air.
Cm B♭6 F7
You're making it hard ___ for the people who live in there.

Chorus 4

Cm B♭6 F7
Wild life, (wild life), what's gonna happen to

(Whatever happened to, whatever happened to)
Cm B♭6 F7
Wild life, (wild life), the animals in the zoo?

(Whatever happened to, whatever happened to)

Repeat w/ad lib. vocals to fade

Outro

|: Cm B♭6 F7 :|
Wild life, ___ (whatever happened to, whatever happened to...)

Winter Rose/Love Awake

Words & Music by
Paul McCartney

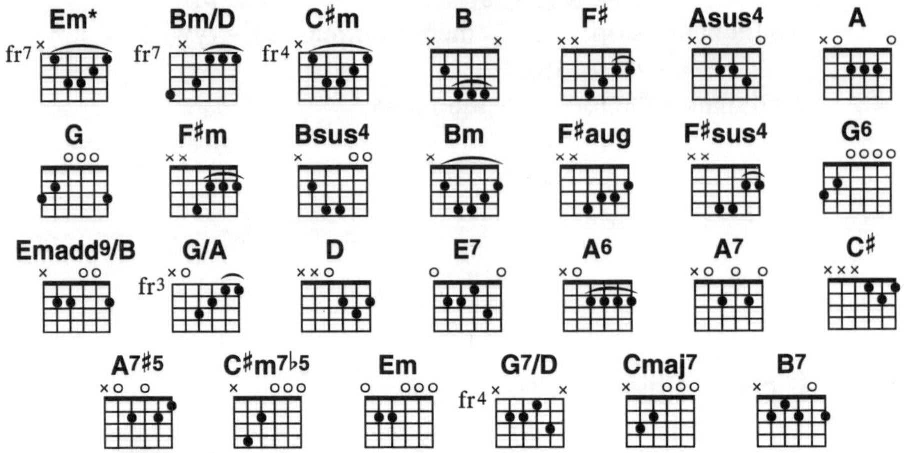

Intro | Em* | Bm/D | C#m | B |
| Em* | Bm/D | C#m | B ||

Verse 1

Asus4 A G F#m F#
All through the summer I have followed you a - round
Bsus4 Bm G Asus4 A G
Bring - ing a rose for the winter that's coming
F#m F# F#aug
Now the snow is on the ground.

Chorus 1

Bsus4 Bm F#sus4 G6 G Emadd9/B
Win - ter rose, win - ter rose,
Asus4 A G F#m Bm
Shine your light in the air
Bsus4 Bm F#sus4 G6 G Emadd9/B
Win - ter rose, win - ter rose,
Asus4 A F#m Bm
Shine your light every - where.

Instrumental | Asus4 A | G | F#m | F# |

| Bsus4 Bm | G | Asus4 A | G |

| F#m | F# | F#aug ||

||: Bsus4 Bm | F#sus4 | G6 G | Emadd9/B |

| Asus4 A | G F#m | Bm | Bm :||

Chorus 2

```
G/A       D              A
Love a - wake, toll the bell
          E7                 A6  A
Tell the world how glad you are ——
G/A       D          A
Love a - wake to the day
                 E7     D          A
When we can make our love a - wake.
```

Verse 2

```
A7                                D                     D C# D
   Lord knows we need it any time we can get it
A7                          A7#5        D
   But if we forget it every now and then,
A7                                D                     D C# D
   But if you don't feel it, later on you'll regret it
A7                       E7                 A    Asus4  A
   And if we let it   we could set it free, you and me.
```

Chorus 3 As Chorus 2

Coda

```
G                            C#m7b5
   Snowfalls in the winter
Em      G7/D        Cmaj7  A  D
Spring brings the rain
(D)                     A               Em        B7       Em    A
   But it's never too long before the summer comes again
   Em       B7      Bm  A
It always comes a  -  gain!
G/A       D
Love a - wake.
```

With A Little Luck

Words & Music by
Paul McCartney

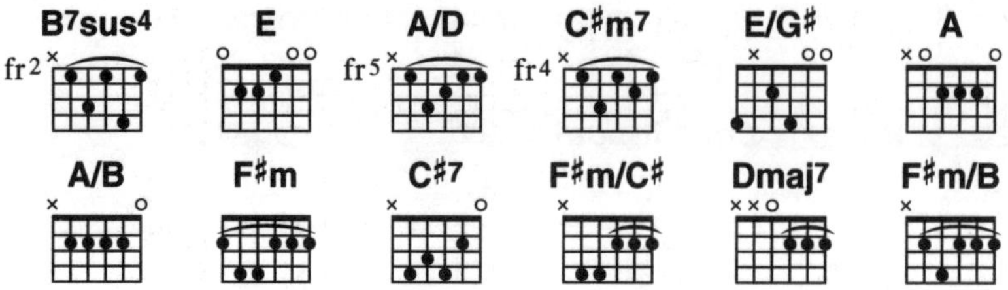

Intro | B7sus4 | B7sus4 | E | (E) |

| B7sus4 | A/D C#m7 | B7sus4 E

Verse 1

(E) E/G# A
With a little luck, we can help it out
A/B E
We can make this whole damn thing work out
E/G# A
With a little love, we can lay it down
A/B C#m7 | C#m7 |
Can't you feel the town exploding?

Bridge 1

F#m C#7 F#m C#7
There is no end to what we can do together (together, ooh ——)
F#m C#7 F#m/C# C#7
There is no end, there is no end (there is no end)
F#m C#7 Dmaj7
The willow turns his back on inclement weather
F#m/B B7sus4 E
And if he can do it, we can do it, just me and you.

Verse 2

```
(E)              E/G♯                    A
And a little luck, we can clear it up
                              A/B
We can bring it in for a landing
E                    E/G♯                    A
  With a little luck, we can turn it on
                          A/B                       C♯m7 | C♯m7 |
There can be no misunderstanding. ——
```

Bridge 2

```
F♯m                 C♯7                    F♯m         C♯7
  There is no end to what we can do together,  (together, ooh ——)
F♯m                 C♯7                F♯m/C♯            C♯7
  There is no end, there is no end, (there is no end)
F♯m                 C♯7                Dmaj7
  The willow turns his back on inclement weather
F♯m/B                  B7sus4       E
  We can do it, just me and you.
```

Verse 3

```
(E)              E/G♯                    A
With a little push, we could set it off
                         A/B
We can send it rocketing skywards
E                    E/G♯                A
  With a little love, we could shake it up
                              A/B                   C♯m7 | C♯m7 |
Don't you feel the comet exploding?
```

Outro

```
||:      E                          E/G♯
  With a little luck, with a little luck
      A                             A/B          :||
With a little luck, a little luck, a little luck
                                 E/G♯
With a little luck. with a little luck
A                            A/B
  We could shake it up,   oh, yeah. ——

                                                Play 3 times
| E       | E        | B7sus4   ||: A/D  C♯m7 | B7sus4  E  :||

| A/D   C♯m7 | (C♯m7) | (C♯m7) | B7sus4 | B7sus4 | E (fermata) ||
```

Winedark Open Sea

Words & Music by
Paul McCartney

Badd11 C♯m7 E A

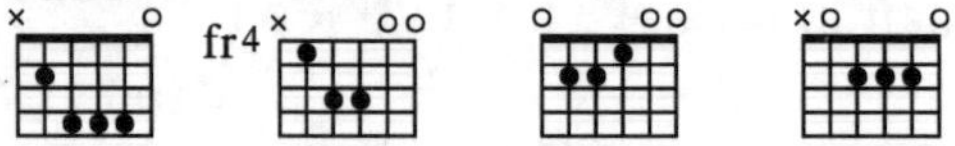

Verse 1

Badd11 C♯m7
Open up your heart
E A
If you want to set me free
E A
Full of love, your love.

Chorus 1

E A
Sailing on a winedark open sea,
E A
Sailing on a winedark open sea.

Verse 2

Badd11 C♯m7
Lighten up, my heart
E A
Leave it to the evening breeze
E A
Give me love, your love.

Chorus 2

E A
Sailing on a winedark open sea,
E A
Sailing on a winedark open sea.

Bridge 1

```
C#m7 Badd11   A
Oh my,    I feel love for you
                                 Badd11
Spreading through my body
      E
I re - member how
C#m7    Badd11  A
We can be so    loving
      E                          A
I feel love for you now,
      E                          A
I feel love for you right now.
```

Link 1

```
| E          | A          | E          | A          ||
      Ah!          Ah!          Ah!          Ah!
```

Verse 3

```
Badd11              C#m7
Loosen up, my heart
E                                  A
Let me have some time to be
E                   A
With a love, my____ love.
```

Chorus 3

```
E                             A
Sailing on a winedark open sea,
E                             A
Sailing on a winedark open sea.
```

Bridge 2 As Bridge 1

Link 2 As Link 1

Chorus 4

```
||:        E                             A
  (We're) sailing on a winedark open sea,
E                               A         :|| Play 4 times
Sailing on a winedark open sea.
```

Interlude

```
| E          | A         | E         | A  (fermata)  ||
(whispered)Ah!    Ah!       Ah!       Ah!
|: E         | A         | E         | A            :| Play 4 times
(whispered)Ah!    Ah!       Ah!       Ah!

             E                     A
Oh, I feel love for you now

          E                         A
I feel love for you right now

          E                 A
I feel love for you now

               E                     A
Baby, I feel love for you right now.
```

Outro

```
          E                         A
We're sailing on a winedark open sea

E                         A
Sailing on a winedark open sea.___

| E     | A     | E     | A     | E              | A (fermata)  ||
                                  Finish it now!
```

The World Tonight

Words & Music by
Paul McCartney

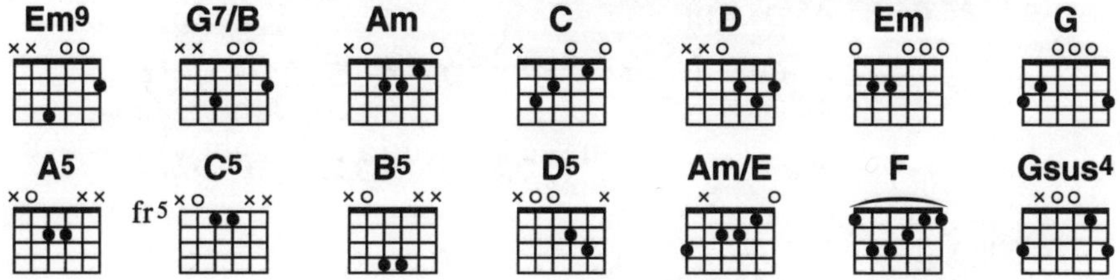

Chord names refer to implied harmony

Intro | Em9 | G7/B || Am | Am | Am | Am ||

Verse 1

Am
I saw you sitting at the centre of a circle
C D
Everybody, everybody wanted something from you
Am
I saw you sitting there.

Verse 2

Am
I saw you swaying to the rhythm of the music
C D
Caught you playing, caught you praying to the voice inside you
Am
I saw you swaying there.

Pre-Chorus 1

Em Am
I don't care what you wanna be
Em Am
I go back so far; I'm in front of me!
Em Am
It doesn't matter what they say
Em G
They're giving the game away , hey, hey.——

A5 riff

Chorus1

A5 C5 B5 A5 D5 Am
I can see the world tonight
A5 C5 B5 A5 D5 Am
Look into the future
A5 C5 B5 A5 D5 Am
See it in a different light
A5 C5 B5 A5 D5 Am/G Am | Am ||
I can see the world to - night

Verse 3

Am
I heard you listening to a secret conversation
C D
You were crying, you were trying not to let them hear you
Am
I heard you listening in.

Pre-Chorus 2

Em Am
Never mind what they wanna do
Em Am
You've got a right to your point of view
Em Am
It doesn't matter what they say
Em G
They're giving the game away, hey, hey.——

Chorus 2

As Chorus 1

Instrumental

F	G	F	Am
F	Gsus4	G	G	
|: Em9	G7/B	Em9	G7/B :|

Verse 4

Am
I saw you hiding from a flock of paparazzi
C D
You were hoping, you were hoping that the ground would swallow yo
Am
I saw you hiding there.

Pre-Chorus 3 As Pre - Chorus 2

Chorus 3 As Chorus 1

Outro

| A5riff Am | Am |

| A5riff Am | Am |
Look into the fu - ture

| A5riff Am | Am |
I can see the world to - night

| A5riff Am | Am |
See it in a different light

|: A5riff | Am :| *Repeat to fade*
I can see the world tonight

Write Away

Words & Music by
Paul McCartney & Eric Stewart

Fm7/C C Cm7 Dm7 E♭maj7

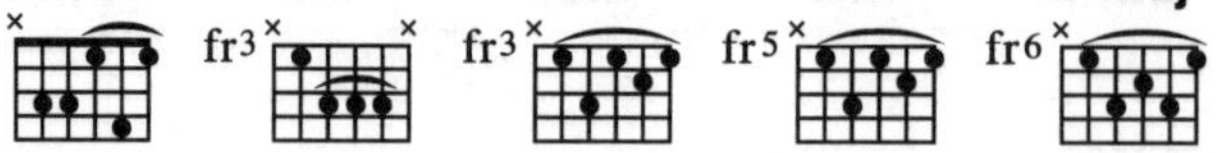

Intro

| N.C. (C+*8va*) | (C+*8va*) | (C+*8va*) | (C+*8va*) ‖
Hey yeah!

‖: Fm7/C | C | Fm7/C | C :‖
2° Ooh. —— yeah, yeah…

Chorus 1

Fm7/C C Fm7/C C
You need love, write a letter, you need love write a - way
Fm7/C C Fm7/C C
Get it down, you'll feel better, send it now, write a - way

Verse 1

Cm7 Dm7
Hey Cinderella, did you need that other fella?
E♭maj7 Dm7
On the wrong side of midnight your defences slipped away
Cm7 Dm7
You need attention, so I think it's worth a mention
E♭maj7
That if I can deliver
Dm7 C
Well, there wouldn't be no heavy price to pay.

Chorus 2

Fm7/C C Fm7/C C
You need love, write a letter, you need love, write a - way
Fm7/C C Fm7/C C
If you need to feel better, do it now, write a - way, yee - hee - hee!

Instrumental ‖: Fm7/C | C | Fm7/C | C :‖

Verse 2

Cm7 Dm7
Hey, Marguerita, I can think of nothing sweeter
E♭maj7 Dm7
But the taste of your nectar seems to lead the boys astray
Cm7 Dm7
Don't forget it, well you know you won't regret it
E♭maj7
Say, I've got the answer
Dm7 C
You were looking at it long before to - day,—— hee.——

Chorus 3

Fm7/C C Fm7/C C
You need love, so write a letter, you need love, write a - way
Fm7/C C Fm7/C C
Get it down, you'll feel better, send it now, write a - way
Fm7/C C
You need love, love, love write a letter
Fm7/C C
You need love, write a - way
Fm7/C C Fm7/C C
If you need to feel better, do it now, now, now, write a - way.——

You Gave Me The Answer

Words & Music by
Paul McCartney & Linda McCartney

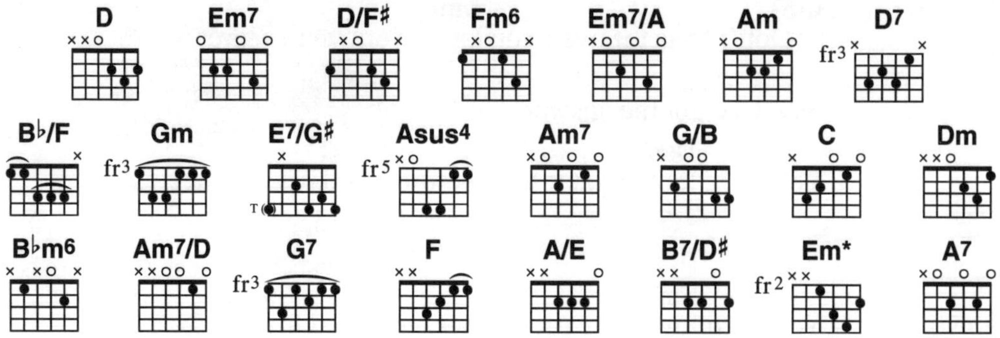

Intro (double tempo)

| D Em7 | D/F♯ G | Am G D/♯ Fm6 | Em7 Em7/A | D ‖
| Am G | D/F♯ Fm6 | Em7 Em7/A | Em7/A |

Verse 1

```
D                      Em7
   You gave me the answer
    D/F♯          G
To love eternal - ly
Am  G    D/F♯  Fm6 Em7
I   love you   and  you
    Em7/A      D
You seem to like me.
```

Verse 2

```
D                 Em7
   Wherever we wander
     D/F♯         G
The local folk a - gree
Am  G    D/F♯  Fm6 Em7
I   love you   and  you
    Em7/A      D
You seem to like me
```

Bridge 1

```
D7                          G
Heading back to old familiar places
Bb/F              D/F#            Gm
Places where the cobwebs blow a - way
             E7/G#             Asus4         Am   D7
I can for - get the airs and graces, ___ ooh ___
```

Instrumental

```
||: G     | Am7     | G/B     | C                        |
                           1° Shall we dance?
| Dm  C  N.C. | G/B  Bbm6  N.C. | Am7  Am7/D | G         :||
                                        1° This is fun!
| G7     | G7     | C     | C     |

| F      | A/E      | Dm         | B7/D#     |
               You should do this more often!
| Em*    | Em*      | Em  A7     | A7        ||
```

Verse 3

```
D                    Em7
   You'll never be crowned by
    D/F#        G
The aristocra - cy
   Am                  G
To their delight, you'd merely invite
       D/F#     Fm6    Em Em7/A
Them in for a cup of tea
     A G    D/F# Fm6 Em7
And I love you and you,
     Em7/A
You seem to like

You seem to like

You seem to like
D      | Em7     | D        ||
Me.___           Oh.
```

You Want Her Too

Words & Music by
Paul McCartney & Declan MacManus

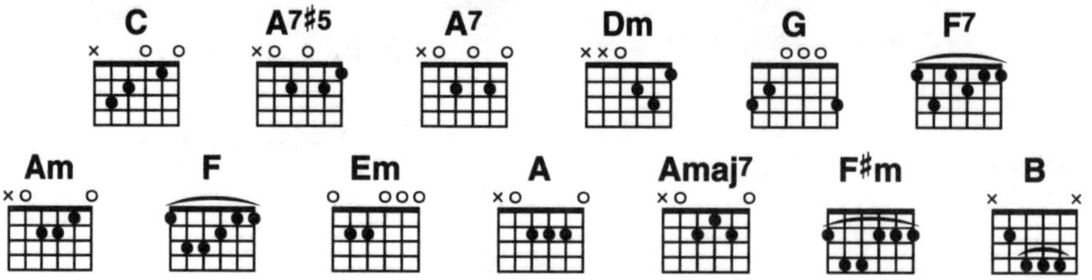

Intro | N.C. (Cadd9) | (C) | (Cmaj7) | (C6) ||

Verse 1

C A7♯5 A7 Dm
She makes me go so wrong
G
(Yeah, you kept me awake you know you did)
C A7♯5 A7 Dm
I've loved her, oh so long
G
(So why don't you come right out and say it, stupid?)

Chorus 1

F7 G
She makes me do things I don't want to do
F7 Am
I don't know why I should be telling you
F C N.C.
I know that you want her too.

Verse 2

A7♯5 A7 Dm
My intentions are quite sin - cere.
G
(That's not what you said the other night)
C A7♯5 A7 Dm
And all you can do is sneer
G
(So go ahead and kid your - self you're right).

Chorus 2

```
F7              C
   She makes me do things I don't want to do
F7            Am
   I don't know why I should be telling you
                 F                C  N.C.
I know that you want her too.
```

Bridge

```
                   Dm                   G
I've got a better chance than you do
Am               F               C
I know that you want her too
(C)                   Dm             G
You're such a hopeless ro - mantic
Em                                      A              Amaj7 | A   Amaj7 |
She told me you're so pre - dictable and nice
F#m                                        B
She only did you a favour once or twice
                       C  N.C.
Once or twice.
```

Verse 3

```
                      A7#5 A7 Dm
She makes me go    so  wrong
                                       G
(So why don't you lie back and enjoy it?)
C                                      A7#5 A7  Dm
Oh, my conscience is clear and strong
                                  G
(Yes she says I'm just the boy for it).
```

Chorus 3

```
F7              C
   She makes me do things I don't want to do
F7            Am
   I don't know why I should be telling you
                 F                C
I know that you want her too
Am               F               C
I know that you want her too
Am               F               C
I know that you want her too.
```

Your Loving Flame

Words & Music by
Paul McCartney

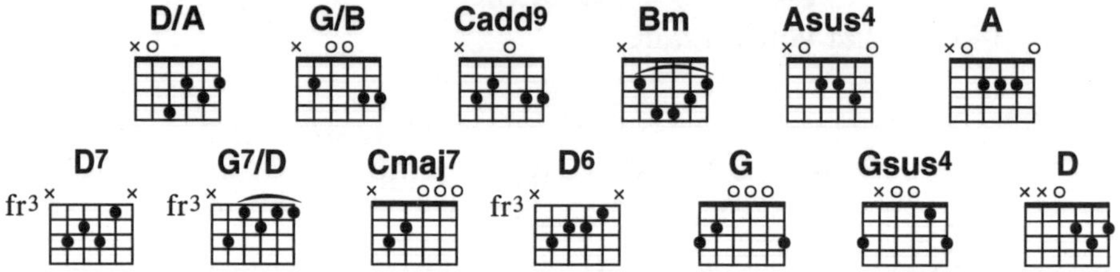

Capo 1st Fret

```
Intro      | D/A   G/B  | D/A   G/B  ||

           D/A          G/B D/A                      G/B
Verse 1      How can I___  hope to reach your love
           Cadd9                         Bm              Asus4  A
             Help to discover what it is your thinking of.___

           D/A                    G/B D/A                      G/B
Verse 2      Cause when we kiss,___  nothing feels the same
           Cadd9                        Bm             Asus4  A
             I can spend eternity in - side your lovin' flame.___

           D7         G7/D
Bridge 1   What am I to if I don't have you
           D7                       G7/D
           I'll be feeling blue just sitting here without you
           Cmaj7                                    D6      G     Gsus4 | G    ||
           You can be the one to chase my blues away, a - way.___

Solo       | D/A  G/B | D/A  G/B | Cadd9 | Bm    | Asus4   A ||

           D/A          G/B  D/A                       G/B
Verse 3      So tell me how,___  how to reach your love
           Cadd9                         Bm              Asus4  A
             Help to discover what it is your thinking of.___
```

Verse 4 As Verse 2

Bridge 2 As Bridge 1

Verse 5

```
D/A                       G/B D/A                    G/B
   'Cause when we kiss,___ nothing feels the same
Cadd9                          Bm            Asus4 A
   I could spend eternity inside your lovin flame___
```

Verse 6

```
D/A             G/B  D/A                     G/B
   So tell me how,___ how to reach your love
Cadd9                         Bm            Asus4    A
   Help to discover what it is your thinking of,___ ooh.___
```

Coda

```
D/A                 G/B D/A                   G/B
   And how can I,___ hope to reach your love
D/A                G/B          D
   Here forever in your loving flame.
```

Young Boy

Words & Music by
Paul McCartney

Intro

```
| C      | Am     | Em     | F  G  ||
```

Verse 1

```
C                          Am                    Em         F G
   He's just a young boy looking for a way to find love
C                 Am                       Em        F   G
   It isn't easy, nothing you can say will help him find love
F                    G
   He's got to do it for himself
Am                  Dm
   And it can take so long
C                          Am                    Em         F  G
   He's just a young boy looking for a way to find love.
```

Verse 2

```
C                          Am                        Em        F G
   He doesn't need a - nother helping hand from someone
C                              Am                        Em          F        G
   But don't you think he doesn't understand what he wants, some - one
F                          G
   Though independence means a lot
Am                     Dm
   He's still got to be strong
C                          Am                    Em         F  G
   He's just a young boy looking for a way to find love.
```

Bridge 1

```
Em   Am          F        G
Find love, a perfect combina - tion
Em   Am        F      G
Find love, what - ever you do
Em   Am    F            G
Find love, a cause for celebra - tion
F                   Dm
   And it might come looking
                  Gsus4 D
Come looking for you.——
```

Solo

| C | Am | Em | F G |

| C | Am | Em | F G |

| F | G | Am | Dm | Dm ||

Bridge 2

```
Em   Am     F         G
Find love, in any situa - tion
Em   Am        F      G
Find love, what - ever you do
Em   Am    F            G
Find love, a cause for celebra - tion
F                   Dm
   Then it might come looking
                  Gsus4 G
Come looking for you.——
```

Verse 3 As Verse 1

Link (half tempo)

| C | Am | Em | F G |

| C | Am | Em | F G |

Outro

```
Em   Am    F                    G
Find love, a time for medita - tion
Em   Am    F                       G
Find love, a source of inspiration
Em   Am       F                        G
Find love, in - stead of confrontation
Em   Am
Find love
      F                          G  C          Am | F  G | C     ||
And love will come looking for you, ——     ooh.
```